WRITTEN AND UNWRITTEN

Although the 13 United States courts of appeals are the final word on 99 percent of all federal cases, there is no detailed account of how these courts operate. How do judges decide which decisions are binding precedents and which are not? Who decides whether appeals are argued orally? What administrative structures do these courts have? The answers to these and hundreds of other questions are largely unknown, not only to lawyers and legal academics but also to many within the judiciary itself. *Written and Unwritten* is the first book to provide an inside look at how these courts operate. An unprecedented contribution to the field of judicial administration, the book collects the differing local rules and internal procedures of each court of appeals. In-depth interviews of the chief judges of all 13 circuits and surveys of all clerks of court reveal previously undisclosed practices and customs.

Jon O. Newman is a senior United States Circuit Judge of the US Court of Appeals for the Second Circuit, now in his 52nd year as a federal judge. Newman, a former Chief Judge, is the 2016 recipient of the Devitt Award, the federal judiciary's highest honor. Newman is the author of more than 1,300 opinions, *Benched*, a memoir, scores of law review articles, and coauthor of *A Genealogical Chart of Greek Mythology* (with Harold Newman).

Marin K. Levy is Professor of Law at Duke University School of Law. Levy's work on the federal courts and judicial administration has been published in the *Yale Law Journal*, *University of Chicago Law Review*, *University of Pennsylvania Law Review*, and *California Law Review*, among other scholarly journals, and has been discussed in the *New York Times*, *Washington Post*, *Atlantic*, and other public outlets. Levy has also testified before Congress and the Presidential Commission on the Supreme Court of the United States and is a member of the American Law Institute.

Written and Unwritten

THE RULES, INTERNAL PROCEDURES, AND CUSTOMS OF THE UNITED STATES COURTS OF APPEALS

JON O. NEWMAN
U.S. Court of Appeals for the Second Circuit

MARIN K. LEVY
Duke University School of Law

CAMBRIDGE
UNIVERSITY PRESS

CAMBRIDGE
UNIVERSITY PRESS

Shaftesbury Road, Cambridge CB2 8EA, United Kingdom

One Liberty Plaza, 20th Floor, New York, NY 10006, USA

477 Williamstown Road, Port Melbourne, VIC 3207, Australia

314–321, 3rd Floor, Plot 3, Splendor Forum, Jasola District Centre, New Delhi – 110025, India

103 Penang Road, #05–06/07, Visioncrest Commercial, Singapore 238467

Cambridge University Press is part of Cambridge University Press & Assessment, a department of the University of Cambridge.

We share the University's mission to contribute to society through the pursuit of education, learning and research at the highest international levels of excellence.

www.cambridge.org
Information on this title: www.cambridge.org/9781009426183

DOI: 10.1017/9781009426169

First published 2024

A catalogue record for this publication is available from the British Library

A Cataloging-in-Publication data record for this book is available from the Library of Congress

ISBN 978-1-009-42618-3 Hardback
ISBN 978-1-009-42619-0 Paperback

Judge Newman salutes the personnel of the clerk's office of all the federal courts of appeals. With great skill they keep the appellate process functioning.

To JAC and KS – I could not have asked for better "parents in law." Abrazos. – MKL

Contents

Tables

Foreword

Jon O. Newman, a great chief judge of the Second Circuit, and Professor Marin K. Levy have produced a book that fills a void, that will produce better appellate rules and practices, and which will greatly improve the federal system of justice. Through hard work, they have compiled and organized the different rules, practices, customs, both written and unwritten, that the federal courts of appeals use and follow as their judges carry out their jobs. The book means that lawyers can more readily find out how to present their cases in different circuits. It means that the judges of different circuits can far more easily learn how their counterparts elsewhere in the federal system organize the judicial appellate task. And it means knowledge will bring about improvement as judges in each circuit learn how others handle similar problems. The results: a judicial system that works better for those whom it serves.

We all, judges and lawyers and members of the general public, owe the authors a debt of gratitude. So, I say in this foreword, to Judge Newman and Professor Levy, on behalf of all of us, thank you very much.

Stephen Breyer
Associate Justice (Ret.)
Of the Supreme Court of the United States
September 20, 2022

Preface

Although all U.S. courts of appeals are engaged in essentially the same task – deciding appeals – it is remarkable that they differ, sometimes significantly, in many of their internal operations and in the topics on which they have chosen to prescribe procedures. We report these differences in this book, not to favor or criticize any particular practice but to bring these differences to the attention of judges, lawyers, scholars, and all others interested in the often neglected field of federal court administration, and in the hope that awareness of the differences might prompt some courts of appeals to consider whether what is done in other circuits might be worth considering for their circuit.

We are extremely grateful to the current and former circuit chief judges we interviewed; they were very helpful and very generous with their time. Equally helpful were the clerks of court who responded to our detailed questionnaire, endured follow-up inquiries, and reviewed and improved earlier drafts; they too deserve our thanks.

The responsibility for any inaccuracies is ours.

1

2

3

4

5

6

7

Courthouses on the Cover

1. First Circuit Court of Appeals, John Joseph Moakley U.S. Courthouse, Boston, MA
2. Eighth Circuit Court of Appeals, Thomas F. Eagleton U.S. Courthouse, St. Louis, MO
3. Ninth Circuit Court of Appeals, James R. Browning U.S. Courthouse, San Francisco, CA
4. Fifth Circuit Court of Appeals, John Minor Wisdom U.S. Courthouse, New Orleans, LA
5. Fourth Circuit Court of Appeals, Lewis F. Powell, Jr. U.S. Courthouse, Richmond, VA
6. Second Circuit Court of Appeals, Thurgood Marshall U.S. Courthouse, New York, NY
7. Seventh Circuit Court of Appeals, Everett McKinley Dirksen U.S. Courthouse, Chicago, IL

Introduction

"Judicial administration never stops. There is always a better way of doing something."
– Former Ninth Circuit Chief Judge J. Clifford Wallace

Although the Supreme Court can make the final decision in all federal court cases, the Nation's 13 courts of appeals have the final say in 99.7 percent of those cases. In the 12-month period ending September 30, 2022, the High Court agreed to review only 128[1] of the 46,362[2] cases decided by the courts of appeals of the 11 numbered circuits,[3] the D.C. Circuit, and the Federal Circuit. Despite the importance of these appellate courts, in the more than 130 years since the Evarts Act established the modern courts of appeals in 1891,[4] there has never been a comprehensive examination of their internal operations and practices – until now.[5]

1 Administrative Office of the U.S. Courts (AO), "Statistics & Reports" tab, "Data Tables" link, Table B-2 (September 30, 2022). The Supreme Court also reviews a few cases that come from state supreme courts or, very rarely, directly from federal district courts.

2 The 11 numbered courts of appeals and the Court of Appeals for the D.C. Circuit decided 44,902 cases, *id.*, Table B-1 (September 30, 2022), and the U.S. Court of Appeals for the Federal Circuit decided 1,460 cases, *id.*, Table B-8 (September 30, 2022).

3 The numbered circuits (1–11) together with the D.C. Circuit are often referred to as the "regional" circuits. We do not call these circuits "regional" because it seems odd to consider the District of Columbia a "region" along with the 11 other circuits, each of which comprises at least three states.

4 Act of March 3, 1891, ch. 517, 51st Cong., 2d Sess., § 2, 26 Stat. 826. The old circuit courts, established by the First Judiciary Act in 1789, Act of Sept. 24, 1789, ch. 20, 1st Cong., 1st Sess., § 4, 1 Stat. 73, 74, had appellate jurisdiction of some decisions of the district courts, *id.* § 22, 1 Stat. at 84, which were established in 1789, *id.* § 3, 1 Stat. at 73. The circuit courts were abolished in 1911. Act of Mar. 3. 1911, ch. 231, 61st Cong., 3d Sess., § 289, 36 Stat. 1087, 1167.

5 In 2011, the Federal Judicial Center prepared a monograph on the case management procedures of the courts of appeals. *See* L. Hooper, D. Miletich, and A. Levy, *Case Management Procedures in the Federal Courts of Appeals* (Federal Judicial Center 2011). In 2017, Judge Harry Edwards supplemented a lecture he had delivered on judicial collegiality with responses to a

How do each of the federal courts of appeals operate? How do they set their oral argument calendars, how often do they hear appeals, and how many appeals do they hear each day? How do they decide which opinions will be precedential, and who will write them? How do they treat judges who have elected to "take senior status," that is, entitled to work part-time? Do they permit visiting judges from other courts to join their panels, and, if so, who selects them? What internal-governance committees do they have, and who creates and staffs them? What are the responsibilities of the key administrators: the chief circuit judge, the circuit executive, and the clerk of court?

This book answers these and hundreds of other questions.

Of course, much has been written about these courts' history, structure, and jurisdiction, and many volumes and hundreds of articles about their decisions, but there is no detailed account of their internal operations and practices. One clerk of court has said, "The amount of information about each other that we don't know far exceeds what we do know."[6] Another has said, "Even after 38 years here, some matters are still unrevealed mysteries to me."

The information in this book is drawn primarily from three sources: (1) the written provisions of each circuit (local rules, internal operating procedures, general or administrative orders, and addenda), (2) interviews with those who were chief circuit judge at the time of the interview of all 13 circuits, and seven former chief circuit judges, and (3) responses to a questionnaire sent to the clerk of court of all 13 circuits.

Throughout this book, court practices are cited to the applicable local rule, internal operating procedure (IOP), or General Order (Gen. Ord.), or reported, without citation, based on interviews with chief circuit judges, which were agreed not to be recorded or attributed to named judges, and on responses to a questionnaire sent to the clerks of court.

We have not reported all differences in internal procedures; some variations are of minor significance. And, as to some topics, we have not reported the practice in every circuit because the responses in either the chief judge interview or the chief clerk questionnaire did not furnish sufficient information (perhaps owing to the imprecision of our question). As a result, *our report of what one or more circuits do concerning a particular topic should not be understood to mean that other circuits do not have a practice or procedure on that topic*. Where we believe that the practice of a circuit is unique, we have identified it as such.

questionnaire he had sent to circuit chief judges, inquiring about a few internal court operations. Harry T. Edwards, *Collegial Decision Making in the US Courts of Appeals*, lecture presented at All Souls College, Oxford University (July 2017) ("Edwards Questionnaire"). The responses to the Edwards Questionnaire did not identify circuits.

6 *See* Marin K. Levy, *The Mechanics of Federal Appeals: Uniformity and Case Management in the Circuit Courts*, 61 DUKE L. J. 315, 385 (2011).

For topics on which we can report the practice of all the circuits, we describe them in separate paragraphs, introduced with bold face identifications, for example, "**First Circuit**." For other topics, we usually group the practices of the relevant circuits, with an introductory identifying phrase, for example, "In the First Circuit, …"

Some of the differences in internal practices are attributable, at least in part, to the circuits' differences in geography, number of judges, and volume of cases. Congress determines the assignment of states within each circuit,[7] and the numbers of active, that is, full-time, judges allotted to each court of appeals.[8]

The number of judges on each court of appeals varies depending on the size of the circuit and the volume of appeals.

The volume of appeals is a function of the jurisdiction that Congress has given to the federal courts, the volume of cases decided by the district courts, and the rate of appeal from decisions of district courts to the courts of appeals. The jurisdiction of the courts of appeals in the 11 numbered circuits is uniform, but is slightly greater in the D.C. Circuit, and entirely different in the Federal Circuit. As would be expected, the volume of cases decided by the district courts within each circuit varies among the circuits because of the difference in the number of states within the circuits and the number of district courts within the circuits. For example, the Second Circuit comprises three states, and the Ninth Circuit comprises nine states; the First Circuit comprises five district courts and the Eighth Circuit comprises ten district courts. Less expected, and reported infrequently if at all, is the difference in the rate of appeal from district courts to courts of appeals in some circuits. For example, in 2022, the appeal rate in civil cases in the Third Circuit was 8 percent and in the Eleventh Circuit was 4 percent, but in the Sixth Circuit was 15 percent and in the Eighth Circuit was 19 percent.[9]

Another difference affecting the volume of cases in the courts of appeals results from differences in the number of petitions filed in those courts to review agency decisions. One notable example is the large number of

7 28 U.S.C. § 41.

8 *Id.* § 44.

9 These percentages are derived by dividing the number of appeals in civil cases filed in the courts of appeals in the 12-month period ending September 30, 2022 by the number of civil cases terminated in the district courts of the relevant circuits in the same 12-month period. (The AO reports some statistics only for the 12-month period ending September 30.) In 2022, the number of civil appeals from district courts commenced in the court of appeals for the Third Circuit was 1,472 and in the Eleventh Circuit was 2,719, AO, "Statistics & Reports" tab, "Data Tables" link, Table B-3A (September 30, 2022), and the number of civil cases terminated after court action in the district courts in the Third Circuit in that same 12-month period

petitions filed in the Second, Fifth, and Ninth Circuits to review decisions of the Board of Immigration Appeals filed by immigrants within those circuits seeking asylum.

Table I.1 shows the number of states, total population from the most recent census, number of district courts, and number of authorized judgeships and sitting senior judges of each court of appeals as of December 31, 2022.

TABLE I.1 *States, district courts, and judges data*

Circuit	States, districts, and territories covered[10]	Total population[11]	District courts[12]	Authorized judgeships[13]	Senior judges serving[14]
1st	MA, ME, NH, PR, RI	14,153,058	5	6	5
2nd	CT, NY, VT	24,450,270	6	13	15
3rd	DE, NJ, PA, VI	23,368,728	6	14	9
4th	MD, NC, SC, VA, WV	32,160,146	9	15	4
5th	LA, MS, TX	36,764,541	9	17	8
6th	KY, MI, OH, TN	33,293,455	9	16	13
7th	IL, IN, WI	25,491,754	7	11	6
8th	AR, IA, MO, MN, ND, NE, SD	21,690,565	10	11	3

was 17,676, and in the Eleventh Circuit was 76,519, *id.*, Table C-4A (September 30, 2022). Dividing 1,472 by 17,676 yields an 8 percent appeal rate for the Third Circuit; dividing 2,719 by 76,519 yields a 4 percent appeal rate for the Eleventh Circuit.

In 2022, the number of civil appeals from district courts commenced in the court of appeals for the Sixth Circuit was 1,848, and for the Eighth Circuit was 1,464, *id.*, Table B-3A (September 30, 2022), and the number of civil cases terminated after court action in the district courts of the Sixth Circuit in that year was 12,286, and in the Eighth Circuit was 7,906, *id.*, Table C-4A (September 30, 2022). Dividing 1,848 by 12,286 yields a 15 percent appeal rate for the Sixth Circuit; dividing 1,464 by 7,906 yields a 19 percent appeal rate for the Eighth Circuit.

Of course, not all the civil cases commenced in a court of appeals of a circuit in 2022 are the same cases terminated in the district courts of that circuit in the same year; a few were likely terminated toward the end of 2021. However, because the time for filing a notice of appeal from a district court's judgment in a civil case is 30 days, Fed. R. App. P. 4(a)(1)(A) (60 days if the United States or a United States agency or officer is a party, *id.*, 4(a)(1)(B)), most district court judgments in civil cases that are appealed arrive at a court of appeals in the same year that the judgments were filed. Furthermore, to whatever extent cases terminated in district courts in one year are not the same cases commenced in courts of appeals in that year, that discrepancy should not affect the calculated variations in appeal rates.

10 28 U.S.C. § 41.

11 U.S. Census Bureau, 2020 Census.

12 AO, "Statistics & Reports" tab, "Data Tables" link, Table C-1 (December 31, 2022).

13 *Id.*, "Statistics & Reports" tab, "Data Tables" link, "Federal Courts Management Statistics" publication, "U. S. Courts of Appeals–Federal Courts Management Statistics–Profiles" link (December 31, 2022).

14 *Id.*

TABLE I.1 *(continued)*

Circuit	States, districts, and territories covered	Total population	District courts	Authorized judgeships	Senior judges serving
9th	AL, AZ, CA, GU, HI, ID, MP, MT, NV, OR, WA	67,050,034	15	29	23
10th	CO, KS, OK, NM, UT, WY	18,636,936	8	12	7
11th	AL, FL, GA	37,274,374	9	12	10
D.C.	District of Columbia	689,545	1	11	8
Fed.	N/A	N/A	N/A	12	7

TABLE I.2 *Filings and terminations*

Circuit	Filings	Terminations on the merits
1st	1,031	743
2nd	3,965	2,035
3rd	2,567	1,693
4th	3,827	2,898
5th	5,782	4,559
6th	3,225	2,392
7th	2,362	1,337
8th	2,621	2,190
9th	8,268	5,932
10th	1,647	1,019
11th	4,583	2,559
D.C.	991	605

Table I.2 shows the number of filings and terminations on the merits of each circuit for the 12-month period ending December 31, 2022.[15]

Finally, a note on capital letters and numbers. We do not capitalize "judge," "clerk," or other official positions when not linked to a named person, or "court" or "circuit" when not linked to a particular court or circuit, except in chapter and section headings. We use Arabic numbers above ten, except when beginning sentences or quoting a statute or rule, or when comparing numbers in order to make the reported differences readily apparent.

[15] AO, "Statistics & Reports" tab, "Data Table" link, Tables B-1, B-8 (December 31, 2022). The AO's table does not include data for the Federal Circuit. The table that does include data for the Federal Circuit, B-8, unfortunately does not provide a direct comparison as it reports only "terminations," which includes terminations on procedural grounds.

1

The Chief Judge of a Circuit

Although this book is about the many differences among the courts of appeals, this chapter on the role of the chief circuit judge concerns a topic on which there are very few differences. Specifically, this chapter considers the office of the chief circuit judge, including such topics as eligibility to become a chief judge, selection of the chief judge, and the term of the chief judge. It also details the role of the chief judge, including how current and several recent chief judges have carried out their responsibilities. Some aspects of a chief judge's role are elaborated in subsequent chapters on specific topics, including Chapter 2 on the administrative structure of the courts and Chapter 11 on promoting the expeditious disposition of appeals.

1.1 QUALIFICATIONS TO BECOME CHIEF JUDGE

Prior to 1948, the circuit judge with the most seniority was the chief administrative officer of the circuit. That judge was referred to as the "senior circuit judge," the title used in the 1922 statute that required the Chief Justice of the United States to summon to an annual conference "the senior circuit judge of each circuit."[1] The title, "chief judge of the circuit," was introduced in 1948 when Congress made extensive amendments to the Judicial Code.[2]

In 1948, the only qualification for becoming a chief judge was seniority over the other circuit judges of the circuit.[3] In 1951, Congress added the

[1] Act of Sept. 14, 1922, ch. 306, 67th Cong., 2nd Sess., § 3, 42 Stat. 837, 839.

[2] Act of June 25, 1948, ch. 646, 80th Cong., 2nd Sess., § 45, 62 Stat. 869, 871.

[3] *Id.* § 45. Seniority is determined by the date of a judge's commission, the official document memorializing the judge's appointment by the President and confirmation by the Senate. It bears the signature of the President and the Attorney General and the seal of the United States. *See Marbury v. Madison*, 5 U.S. (1 Cranch) 137, 138 (1803) ("A commission is not necessary to the appointment of an officer by the executive – Semb. A commission is only *evidence* of an appointment.") (emphasis in original). If the commissions of two judges are signed on the same date, the older judge has seniority. 28 U.S.C. § 45(b).

qualification that the chief judge of a circuit must be a circuit judge in regular active service.[4] In 1958, Congress imposed the additional qualifications that the chief judge must be under the age of 70 and must have served as a circuit judge for at least one year.[5] In 1982, Congress lowered the maximum age for becoming a chief judge from 69 to 64 and added the qualification that the chief judge must not have served as chief judge previously.[6]

Thus, to become a chief judge today, a circuit judge must be the most senior active judge who is not over the age of 64, who has served at least one year as a circuit judge, and who has not served previously as the chief judge.[7] If no circuit judge meets the statutory qualifications, the youngest circuit judge in regular active service who is 65 or older and has served as a circuit judge for at least one year acts as the chief judge.[8] If no judge 65 or older has served as a circuit judge for at least one year, the circuit judge in regular active service who is senior in commission and has not served previously as chief judge acts as chief judge.[9]

We note that the age limitation for becoming a chief judge sometimes results in circuit judges becoming chief judges when circuit judges in their late 60s and early 70s with considerably more judicial experience are ineligible. Several chief judges we interviewed expressed the view that the eligibility age limitation should be raised. We suggest that it be raised to 68, enabling a 68-year-old circuit judge, otherwise eligible, to become chief judge and serve the currently prescribed maximum seven-year term until age 75. If the term were reduced to five years (a possibility we consider later in this chapter), the eligibility age limit should be raised to 70, enabling a 70-year-old circuit judge, otherwise eligible, to become chief judge and serve a five-year term until age 75.

The age limitation affects the extent of chief judges' prior service as federal judges before becoming chief judge. Table 1.1 shows the number of years that the incumbent chief judges we interviewed in 2020 had served as a circuit judge prior to becoming chief judge.

In the event that a chief judge is "temporarily unable to perform his duties," those duties are performed by the active judge "who is next in precedence."[10]

4 Act of Oct. 31, 1951, ch. 655, 82d Cong., 1st Sess., § 35 (amending 28 U.S.C. § 45(a)), 65 Stat. 710, 723.

5 Act of Aug. 6, 1958, Pub. L. 85-593, § 1, 72 Stat. 497. The 1958 Act also provided that if all the circuit judges in regular active service are 70 or older, the youngest shall act as chief judge until a circuit judge has been appointed who is under the age of 70 and has served for at least one year. *Id.*

6 Federal Courts Improvement Act of 1982, Pub. L. No. 97-164, § 201(a)(1)(A), (C), 96 Stat. 25, 51 (codified at 28 U.S.C. § 45(a)(1)).

7 28 U.S.C. § 45(a)(1).

8 *Id.* 45(a)(2)(A).

9 *Id.* 45(a)(2)(B).

10 28 U.S.C. § 45(d). Precedence is determined by the date of a judge's commission, the formal document appointing the judge.

TABLE 1.1 *Prior Circuit Court Service before Chief Judgeship*

Circuit	Name	Prior years as a circuit judge
1st	Jeffrey Howard	13
2nd	Robert A. Katzmann	14
3rd	D. Brooks Smith	14
4th	Roger Gregory	15
5th	Priscilla Owen	14
6th	R. Guy Cole, Jr.	19
7th	Diane Wood	18
8th	Lavenski Smith	15
9th	Sidney Thomas	18
10th	Timothy Tymkovich	12
11th	William H. Pryor Jr.	16
D.C.	Sri Srinivasan	7
Fed.	Sharon Prost	13

In addition to illness or other temporary disability, the need for a temporary replacement can arise when a misconduct complaint is filed against a chief judge and an investigating committee is appointed.[11]

1.2 SELECTION OF THE CHIEF JUDGE

The statutory requirement that a new chief judge is the circuit judge senior to the other active judges (among other qualifications) obviously makes seniority the primary method for selecting circuit chief judges.[12] Seniority is also used to select the chief judges of U.S. district courts, subject to the same qualifications applicable to the selection of circuit chief judges,[13] and most

[11] Rules for Judicial-Conduct and Judicial-Disability Proceedings 25(e), (f).

[12] There is one historical exception. The first chief judge of the Court of Appeals for the Federal Circuit, created in 1982, *see* Federal Courts Improvement Act of 1982, Pub. L. No. 97-164, §§ 101, 165, 96 Stat. 25, 50, was selected by seniority but with a slight adjustment. Because that court was formed by combining the judges of the appellate division of the U.S. Court of Claims and the judges of the U.S. Court of Customs and Patent Appeals, *id.*, the first chief judge of the new court was the chief judge of either of the two predecessor courts depending on which one had served longer as chief judge, *id.*, § 166; 28 U.S.C. § 45, Historical and Statutory Notes, Appointment of Chief Judge of Court of Appeals for the Federal Circuit. That judge turned out to be Howard Markey, who had been chief judge of the U.S. Court of Claims. The chief judge who did not become the first chief judge of the Federal Circuit was deemed senior in commission, while in regular active service, to all the judges of the Court of Appeals for the Federal Circuit except the chief judge of the Federal Circuit, *id.*, but this provision had no effect on the selection of the second chief judge of the Federal Circuit. Thereafter, seniority, with the age qualifications applicable to chief judges of all courts of appeals, determined the selection of successor chief judges, *id.*

[13] 28 U.S.C. § 136(a)(1).

Article I courts,[14] but is not used to select chief judges of all federal courts. The most familiar example in the federal judiciary of appointment of a court's presiding officer selected without regard to seniority is the President's appointment of the Chief Justice of the United States, who functions as the chief judge of the Supreme Court.[15] The chief judge of the U.S. Tax Court is elected by the judges of that court.[16] Otherwise, selection by seniority applies in all federal courts.[17]

All the current and former chief judges we interviewed approved of seniority as the method for selecting a chief circuit judge. Many noted that they found the method to be imperfect, as someone perhaps not well-suited to the office could end up occupying it. But the consensus was that seniority is preferable to the alternatives of election[18] or appointment (perhaps by the President or the Chief Justice) and had some clear benefits. Among the virtues identified were assuring that a chief circuit judge usually has considerable experience on the court of appeals and providing early identification of a successor chief judge, which facilitates the successor's becoming familiar with the duties of the office.

On rare occasions, a circuit judge eligible to become chief judge has resigned from the judiciary to take a position in the private sector or has remained a circuit judge but declined the position. Several judges suggested that an additional virtue of the seniority selection method is that, because the position is "voluntary," a judge need not become chief judge.

14 *See, e.g.*, 10 U.S.C. § 943(a) (Court of Appeals for the Armed Forces); 38 U.S.C. § 7253(d) (Court of Appeals for Veterans Claims).

15 There is no explicit constitutional or statutory provision authorizing the President to appoint the Chief Justice of the United States. The Constitution authorizes the President, with the advice and consent of the Senate, to appoint "judges [*sic*] of the Supreme Court," U.S. Const., art. II, § 2, cl. 2, and assumes the existence of a Chief Justice by providing that "the Chief Justice shall preside" at an impeachment trial of the President, *id.* art I, § 3, cl. 6. Congress provided that the Supreme Court shall consist of "a Chief Justice and five associate justices." Act of Sept. 24, 1789, ch. 20, 1st Cong., § 1, 1 Stat. 73.

16 26 U.S.C. § 7444(b) (chief judge designated by the Tax Court at least biennially).

17 In the state courts, chief judges are either appointed by the Governor, *see, e.g.*, N.Y. Const., art. 6, § 4(c) (Governor appoints chief judges of Appellate Divisions), sometimes from a list assembled by a judicial nominating commission, *see, e.g.*, N.Y. Jud. L. art. 3-A, § 62 (Commission on Judicial Nominations); elected by voters, *see, e.g.*, N.Y. Const., art. 6, § 6(c) (justices of Supreme Courts (trial courts) elected); appointed by the Chief Justice of the state's Supreme Court, *see, e.g.*, Colo. Const., art. 6, § 5(4) (Chief Justice of Supreme Court appoints chief judges of 22 judicial districts); or in the case of Colorado's Supreme Court, selected by the justices of that court, *see* Colo. Const. art. 6, § 5(2).

18 In 1995, a suggestion was made to the Long-Range Planning Committee that a chief circuit judge should be elected by members of a court of appeals from the three most senior active judges of the court, but the proposal attracted no interest.

1.3 TERM OF THE CHIEF JUDGE

Before 1982, there was no limit on the number of years a chief judge could serve, nor had there previously been a limit on the number of years a circuit judge could serve as the senior circuit judge. In the Second Circuit, Learned Hand served as senior circuit judge (retitled chief judge) for 12 years, and J. Edward Lumbard also served as chief judge for 12 years. In 1982, a seven-year term was established,[19] with the slight additional limitation that a chief judge must stop serving as chief judge at age 70 (unless no other circuit judge is eligible to assume the office).[20] Thus, a circuit judge who becomes chief judge at age 64 would have to relinquish the office slightly before the end of the seven-year term.

Some chief judges we interviewed thought that the term should be shortened somewhat, perhaps to five years, but most thought seven years was appropriate.

Sometimes, a chief judge relinquishes the office before the end of the seven-year term. A chief judge wishing to relinquish the office before the term ends notifies the Chief Justice of the United States.[21] The usual reason is to afford an opportunity to become chief judge to a successor who would be 65 or older, and hence ineligible to become chief judge, when the current chief judge's full term would have ended.[22] Another reason, generally thought improper by those interviewed, is to block the judge second in line from becoming chief judge because that judge will be too old to be eligible to become chief judge when the judge first in line completes a full term.

1.4 ROLE OF THE CHIEF JUDGE

The responsibilities of a chief circuit judge are many and varied.[23] Internally, the chief judge presides at every oral argument before a panel that includes the chief judge, including all en banc panels,[24] and usually makes the opinion assignments when in the majority (*see* Chapter 8).[25] The chief judge influences how the court's sitting calendar is set (*see* Chapter 3).

19 Federal Courts Improvement Act of 1982, Pub. L. No. 97-164, § 201, 96 Stat. 25, 52 (codified at 28 U.S.C. § 45(a)(3)(A)).

20 *Id.* (codified at 28 U.S.C. § 45(a)(3)(C)).

21 28 U.S.C. § 45(c).

22 *Id.* § 45(a)(1)(A).

23 *See* Marin K. Levy & Jon O. Newman, *The Office of Chief Circuit Judge*, 169 U. PENN. L. REV. 2423 (2021).

24 *See* 28 U.S.C. § 45(b) ("The chief judge shall have precedence and preside at any session of the court which he attends.").

25 *See id.* Indeed, in the Fourth Circuit, the chief judge officially decides who will author each opinion even when the chief judge is *not* on the panel (though this is done after the chief judge receives recommendations about opinion assignments from each lead panel judge).

The chief judge has a significant role in inviting judges of other courts to sit on the court of appeals and authorizing circuit and district judges of the circuit to sit on other courts. The chief judge may request the Chief Justice of the United States to designate a circuit judge from another circuit to sit with the chief judge's circuit,[26] and may assign any circuit judge within the circuit to hold a district court within the circuit.[27] The chief judge may also assign a district judge within the circuit to sit with the court of appeals[28] or to hold any district court within the circuit.[29]

The chief judge manages several court administrative units – including the clerk's office and the staff attorney's office – and oversees the circuit's budget (*see* Chapter 2).[30] The chief judge receives complaints of misconduct against judges in the circuit,[31] and conducts a preliminary review of each complaint (*see* Chapter 14).[32] Chief judges make decisions about their court's own governance structure, including which judges are to be assigned to which committees (*see* Chapter 2), and lead their circuit's judicial council[33] and judicial conference (*see* Chapter 14).[34] Externally, the chief judge serves as the court's representative to the U.S. Judicial Conference, the national policymaking body for the federal courts.[35] Outside of official duties, the chief judge may initiate projects,[36] which are carried out in the name of their court.[37] Each of these topics will be considered in greater detail in subsequent chapters, though a few of the most important responsibilities are discussed here.

One of the primary duties of the chief judge is to oversee the creation of the oral argument calendar, though some chief judges play a more direct role

[26] *See* 28 U.S.C. § 291(a).

[27] *Id.* 28 U.S.C. § 291(b).

[28] *Id.* 28 U.S.C. § 292(a).

[29] *Id.* 28 U.S.C. § 292(b).

[30] FED. JUD. CTR., RESOURCE GUIDE FOR CHIEF CIRCUIT JUDGES' DESKBOOK 7 (2019).

[31] *See* 28 U.S.C. § 351(c) (Upon receipt of a complaint against a judge, "the clerk shall promptly transmit the complaint to the chief judge of the circuit…."). These are usually complaints against district judges within the circuit; complaints against circuit judges are generally referred by the Chief Justice to the chief judge of another circuit.

[32] *See id.* § 352(a).

[33] *See id.* § 332.

[34] *See id.* § 333.

[35] *See id.* § 331.

[36] For example, then-Chief Judge Robert A. Katzmann developed "Justice for All – Courts and the Community," a Civic Education Initiative of the Federal Courts of the Second Circuit, https://justiceforall.ca2.uscourts.gov.

[37] Even this list is not exhaustive. For example, a chief judge may also be in charge of such matters as emergency preparedness and appointment of *pro bono* counsel. They will also need to certify the eligibility for pay increases of senior judges and determine whether and where to hold a court retreat.

in setting the calendar than others, in part due to the practices of their circuit. Specifically, the chief judges of several circuits reported that they have a hand in deciding, based upon the caseload, how many days each active judge will hear appeals each year and how many appeals will be heard each day. But in one circuit, the chief judge noted that he sends possible calendar options to his court's Case Management Committee for its approval, and in another, the chief judge reported that there is a designated judge called a "proctor" who helps considerably with this task.

A related way in which chief judges play a role in setting the calendar concerns whether judges from other courts will be invited to sit by designation or "visit" – and then whom to invite. In some circuits, under some chief judges, the decision about whether to have visiting judges at all has been largely left to the chief judge. For example, a former chief judge for the Seventh Circuit made the decision to stop inviting judges from outside of the circuit to visit and sit by designation. But not all circuits viewed the question of whether there should be visitors as one that was solely the prerogative of the chief judge. Indeed, the chief judge of one court noted that the decision to limit the use of visiting judges was one that was put to a vote by all judges of his court. Regarding the question of who would be invited if visitors were to be used, several of the chief judges interviewed reported that this was a question for the chief judge to decide.

After helping to set the calendar, another significant responsibility of the chief judge is to ensure the prompt filing of opinions or "move the business of the court." While there was widespread agreement among those interviewed that this aspect of the job is significant, there was some variation when it came to how the chief judges accomplished that job. Some of the variation stemmed from the fact that some circuits have in place internal policies to monitor outstanding opinions (*see* Chapter 11). For example, in the D.C. Circuit, if a judge has more than two uncirculated opinions, that judge may not sit when the new term of court begins in September.

The majority of chief judges, however, rely, at least in part, on their court's generating a report that lists the cases in which the judge assigned to write the opinion has not circulated a draft. There were differences across circuits in the particulars of the reports – for example, one judge said that his court prepares a list of cases under submission for 60 days, another said that his court prepares lists of cases under submission for 60 days and 90 days, and another noted that his court has a 75-day list. But the key point is that in many circuits, some such list is circulated to the other members of the court and sometimes discussed at a court meeting. The underlying mechanism, is, as one judge put it, "social pressure."

Separately, there is the matter of how a chief judge responds if the internal policies or the circulation of a report prove insufficient. Here, again, there is variation. In several circuits, a judge who is known to have a backlog will be assigned fewer opinions to author. Specifically, under a former chief judge of the Ninth Circuit, a delinquent judge could not author an en banc opinion. A chief judge of another circuit said that if he sits with a judge who is currently behind on his or her caseload, the chief judge will not assign that judge any opinions from that sitting week. And a few other chief judges mentioned the possibility of reassigning opinions – either at the behest of the chief judge or on offer from another judge – if a given judge has fallen behind. Several chief judges also noted the possibility – though rarely used – of providing "calendar relief" to judges who are behind on their workload. Such an option would amount to giving the delinquent judge some number of days off the argument calendar to help the judge become current.

A chief judge plays an important role in the administration of the Judicial Conduct and Disability Act of 1980.[38] The Act permits any person to file a complaint alleging misconduct or disability against a judge. The complaint is first considered by the chief judge of the judge's circuit.[39] Most complaints alleging misconduct are dismissed because they relate to the merits of a case; such complaints are excluded from the coverage of the Act.[40] A chief judge may conclude the proceedings if "appropriate corrective action has been taken."[41] A complainant or a judge aggrieved by an order of a chief judge may seek review by the circuit's judicial council.[42] If a complaint has sufficient merit to survive dismissal, the chief judge appoints an investigating committee consisting of the chief judge and an equal number of circuit and district judges.[43] The committee's report is sent to the judicial council.[44] (The role of the council with respect to misconduct complaints is considered in Chapter 14.)

A chief judge has a role with respect to personnel matters within the court of appeals. Appeals from adverse decisions made within the court's employee disciplinary procedure are taken for decision by the chief judge.

Chief judges consider fostering collegiality among members of their courts to be one of their most important roles. How a chief judge fosters collegiality depends upon a number of factors, including characteristics of the judge's circuit – for example, if the judges are all in the same courthouse or have chambers across several states, if the court is composed of 10 judges or 50. Appreciating these key differences between circuits, many of the judges we interviewed spoke

38 28 U.S.C. §§ 351–364.

39 *Id.* § 351(a). The complaint may allege that a judge "has engaged in conduct prejudicial to the effective and expeditious administration of the business of the courts" or "is unable to discharge all the duties of office by reason of mental or physical disability." *Id.*

40 *Id.* § 352(b)(1)(A)(ii).

41 *Id.* § 352(b)(2).

42 *Id.* § 352(c).

43 *Id.* § 353(a)(1).

44 *Id.* § 353(c).

of social events that they organize to foster collegiality, including court dinners, lunches, and retreats. By providing ways for the judges to interact socially, including sometimes with spouses, the general view was the judges would come together, as one chief judge put it, "as a court family." Several chief judges noted a particular need for such social functions when several new members join the court – all to stress the importance of collegiality to the new judges.

Apart from their internal court responsibilities, chief circuit judges have several outside-of-court obligations. First, chief judges oversee their own circuit's judicial council meetings each year (*see* Chapter 14), which can mean setting the agenda and leading the meetings themselves. Second, chief judges attend meetings of the U.S. Judicial Conference. Several judges interviewed here stressed that their Judicial Conference responsibilities depended upon their committee assignments, with a particular workload increase associated with being appointed to the Conference's Executive Committee. Third, chief judges may attend bar association meetings and other public events as a representative of their court, though there was variation on this score. Some chief judges engage in more of this public-facing work than others, in part because of geography (including whether a chief judge is of a circuit in which many of the bar associations are concentrated in the chief's city or if the associations are spread out across many cities and states). Some variation also stems from the personal preferences of the office-holder – some self-proclaimed introverts noted doing less of such work.

1.5 CASELOAD OF THE CHIEF JUDGE

In order to accommodate their chief judge work, most chief judges take a reduced caseload. Several take between two-thirds and three-quarters of the caseload of active judges on their court. A few judges might take an additional sitting day if a panel vacancy arises (e.g., because a judge becomes ill).

In the Ninth Circuit, the chief judge takes a reduced caseload[45] of about half of the standard caseload. However, because the chief judge sits on all en banc rehearings – unlike other active judges on that court who are selected randomly for 11-judge en banc panels (*see* Chapter 10) – and the Ninth Circuit can have as many as 25 en bancs per year, the chief judge's caseload approximates that of other active judges.

Finally, a few chief judges take the same number of sitting days as an active judge, but several take workload reductions in other ways. A few take a reduced role in considering motions, in screening cases for oral argument, or in deciding cases not put on the argument calendar.

[45] *See* 9th Cir. Gen. Ord. 3.2(b).

2

Administrative Structure

This chapter considers the administrative structure of the circuits and the courts of appeals, including the administrative roles of the judges and senior staff.

Like all organizations, the courts of appeals face a range of administrative tasks distinct from the basic role to decide appeals from decisions of 94 district courts and numerous administrative agencies. These administrative tasks of the courts of appeals concern such matters as budgets, personnel, buildings, supplies, and security.

Some aspects of circuit administration are determined nationally by statutes, by the Judicial Conference of the United States, and by the federal judiciary's administrative agency, the Administrative Office of the U.S. Courts (AO). The 27-member Judicial Conference is headed by the Chief Justice of the United States and includes (1) the chief judges of the 13 circuits, serving for the duration of their chief judgeship (*see* Chapter 1), (2) one district judge from each of the 11 numbered circuits and the D.C. Circuit,[1] selected by the circuit and district judges of these circuits at their circuit conferences (*see* Chapter 14) and serving for terms of three to five years,[2] and (3) the chief judge of the Court of International Trade.[3]

1 The Federal Circuit, which can hear appeals (within its specialized subject matter jurisdiction, *see* 28 U.S.C. § 1295) from every district court, has no district court representative on the Judicial Conference.

2 28 U.S.C. § 331. The district judge members of the Judicial Conference may be active or senior judges (a distinction considered in Chapter 13). The length of the term (between three and five years) of a district judge member of the Judicial Conference is determined by majority vote of the circuit and district judges of the judge's circuit. *Id.*

3 *Id.* The nine-member Court of International Trade is an Article III trial court, *id.* § 251, with jurisdiction over many matters arising under the Tariff Act of 1930 and many tariff and customs decisions of the Secretary of the Treasury and the Customs Service, *id.* § 1581.

Within this national administrative structure, the circuits vary in their circuit administrative structures. Heading these structures are the circuit chief judges (*see* Chapter 1 for a discussion of their duties). Circuit councils, composed of the chief judge and an equal number of other court of appeals judges and district court judges, determine some administrative matters affecting the circuit as a whole, including matters affecting the courts of appeals and the district courts within each circuit (*see* Chapter 14). Administrative matters affecting only the courts of appeals are determined by the judges of those courts serving on various committees and by the courts' management staff.

The courts of appeals vary in the judicial administrative structures that they have established. The largest circuit, the Ninth Circuit, with 29 active judges and 23 senior judges, has an executive committee, in addition to 25 committees of the court and the Circuit Council. In contrast, the smallest circuit, the First Circuit, with just six active judges and five senior judges, has no judicial management structure (other than court committees).

The Ninth Circuit's Executive Committee acts on all administrative matters for the court, with some exceptions such as determining the number of sittings, size of calendars, rules, and major personnel decisions (though the Committee reviews and makes recommendations on these matters).[4] The Executive Committee is composed of the chief judge, an active judge who is eligible to become chief judge during the term of the current chief judge (if there is more than one, the chief judge chooses the committee member), the three judges who head administrative units, a senior judge drawn by lot from among the senior judges willing to be considered, and three other active judges drawn by lot from those willing to be considered.[5] Judges drawn by lot serve three-year staggered terms.[6] The committee generally meets four to six times a year.[7]

One other circuit has an executive committee. In the Third Circuit, the executive committee consists of the chief judge and the two previous chief judges. In the Second Circuit, the chief judge and the next two judges in line to become chief judge function as an informal management committee.

In most of the circuits, the chief judge appoints committees of judges with responsibility for supervision of various administrative units such as the clerk's office, the staff attorney's office, the office of information technology, and the library. Of note, in the Second Circuit, one judge is the clerk's office "committee." In the Fifth Circuit, the chief judge selects a number of judges to

4 9th Cir. Gen. Ord. 10.1(b).

5 *Id.* Gen. Ord. 10.1(a).

6 *Id.*

7 *Id.* Gen. Ord. 10.1(c).

serve as "proctors," each responsible for supervising a different function of the court's operations. In the Ninth Circuit, there are no committees with responsibility for supervision of the administrative units; the chief judge and clerk work in tandem to supervise the overall operation of the court and go to the Executive Committee as needed.

All of the judges of each court of appeals meet together throughout the year. The frequency of these meetings varies. For example, in the Second Circuit, they are quarterly, in the Sixth Circuit, semiannually, in the Eleventh Circuit, three times a year.

Federal law permits any circuit with more than 15 active judges "to constitute itself into administrative units."[8] Although the Fifth, Sixth, and Ninth Circuits have more than 15 active judges,[9] only the Ninth Circuit has implemented this authority. The Ninth Circuit has established three administrative units: the Northern Unit, composed of the districts of Alaska, Idaho, Montana, Oregon, and Eastern and Western Washington; the Middle Unit, composed of the districts of Arizona, Northern and Eastern California, Hawaii, Nevada, Guam, and the Northern Mariana Islands; and the Southern Unit, composed of the districts of Central and Southern California.[10]

In the Ninth Circuit, an administrative judge of a unit is the most senior active judge in the administrative unit who is willing to serve.[11] An administrative judge has a variety of duties including maintaining contact with circuit judges within the unit and reporting on their needs,[12] being attentive to court of appeals support services and facilities within the unit (including reviewing space needs, facility improvements, and security),[13] and such other duties as requested by the chief judge or the court.[14]

As noted earlier, all circuits employ court administrators. The senior staff officer in most circuits is the circuit executive, authorized by statute to be appointed by the circuit council,[15] but in practice usually appointed by the chief judge. Senior officers, authorized by statute to be appointed by the court of appeals, are the clerk,[16] the senior staff attorney,[17] and the

8 28 U.S.C. § 41, Historical and Statutory Notes, Appeals Court Administrative Units; Act of Oct. 20, 1978, Pub. L. 95-486, § 6, 92 Stat. 1629, 1633.

9 28 U.S.C. § 44.

10 9th Cir. Gen. Ord. 1.11.

11 *Id.* Gen. Ord. 1.5(a).

12 *Id.* Gen. Ord. 11.1(8).

13 *Id.* Gen. Ord. 11.1(4).

14 *Id.* Gen. Ord. 11.1(15).

15 28 U.S.C. § 332(e).

16 *Id.* § 711(a).

17 *Id.* § 715(a).

librarian.[18] The circuit executive, authorized to appoint necessary employees,[19] typically appoints the heads of various circuit offices such as information technology, administrative services, budget, human resources, and space and facilities.

The circuit executive's duties typically include assisting the chief judge with all of the court's external activities, that is, those not concerned with the adjudication of cases. These activities include assisting the chief judge with preparation for the semiannual meetings of the U.S. Judicial Conference and the work of its various committees, and relationships with the community and state and local bar associations. The circuit executive also has non-case-related internal responsibilities concerning such matters as the internal allotment of money for court operations after the circuit's budget has been determined by the AO.[20]

By statute, the court of appeals for the Federal Circuit is authorized to appoint either a circuit executive or a clerk, but not both, or may appoint a combined circuit executive/clerk,[21] as the court currently does.

The clerk of court supervises several case managers whose primary task is docketing (noting on the court's records) the content of the large number of documents filed by litigants each day on paper and electronically. The docket for a single appeal might include more than 100 entries, and there might be thousands of appeals pending in a court of appeals at any one time. The case managers also endeavor to assist lawyers and especially parties without counsel in complying with the often detailed requirements for filing an appeal and processing it through the appellate process.

The staff attorney's office (called "Legal Division" or "Office of Legal Affairs" in some circuits and "Office of General Counsel" in the Federal Circuit) has several lawyers, often recent law school graduates, who review motions and other matters, recommend dispositions, and sometimes draft orders. The librarian, assisted by a staff, manages the library of the court of appeals and supervises several branch libraries serving district courts throughout the circuit. Similarly, the director of the office of information technology, assisted by a staff, provides services for the hundreds of computers and other electronic devices of the court of appeals and the district courts of the circuit.

Some circuits have staff officers in addition to these standard positions. The Ninth Circuit in 1994 created the position of appellate commissioner,

[18] *Id.* § 713(a).

[19] *Id.* § 332(f)(3).

[20] In the Ninth Circuit, all the court units operate with a single budget and a chief financial officer, and the circuit executive and clerk have joint authority over it.

[21] 28 U.S.C. § 332(h)(5).

appointed by the court, who is authorized to rule on and make recommendations on a variety of non-dispositive matters, such as an application for appointed counsel under the Criminal Justice Act, and to serve as a special master; the court considers the position analogous to a magistrate judge in a district court.[22] In the D.C. Circuit, there is a special assistant to the chief judge.[23] The Federal Circuit is authorized to appoint a "senior technical assistant."[24]

As can be seen, although all courts of appeals have similar administrative tasks, there is variation in how they are structured to perform those tasks. Moreover, the judges themselves assume major responsibilities for the administrative work of each circuit and court of appeals. For many judges, these tasks are not at all what they expected would occupy a fair amount of their time, although a few came to their court with valuable administrative experience and skills acquired in law firms, government offices, and law schools. Fortunately, judges, ably assisted by extremely competent staff, keep the administrative machinery of the circuits and the courts of appeals running smoothly.

[22] 9th Cir. R. Court Structure and Procedures (C)(2); *id.* Gen. Ord. 1.8.

[23] D.C. Cir. website, "Site Map" link, "Resources & Contacts" heading, "Special Assistant to the ChiefJudge," www.cadc.uscourts.gov/internet/home.nsf/Content/VL+-+Human+Resources+-+Special+Assistant+to+the+Chief+Judge.

[24] 28 U.S.C. § 715(c).

3

Calendars, Panels, and Assignment of Cases

This chapter considers the courts of appeals' practices concerning court calendars, composition of three-judge panels, and assignment of cases. We note at the outset that some of the descriptions here refer to the "random" assignment of judges or cases to panels. We recognize that such assignments are never perfectly random because of various constraints – for example, some judges are unavailable for sitting assignments for certain days or weeks.[1] Throughout this chapter, we use "random" or "randomly" to mean within such constraints.

3.1 COURT CALENDARS

The circuits vary in the number of weeks in a year when appeals are argued. Some of the circuits, including the Second, Third, Ninth, Eleventh, and D.C. Circuits, have at least one panel hearing oral arguments during most weeks of the year; the other circuits hear arguments in fewer weeks, but usually have more than one panel hearing arguments during the same week.

First Circuit: A calendar of three-judge panels is prepared for the court year from September to August. From January through June and from October through December, the court usually sits for one week starting on the first Monday of each month. In either July or August, the court sits for one week. In September, the court sits for three days starting on the Wednesday after Labor Day and for five days in the following week. In November and March, the court sits for two weeks, one week in Boston and one week in Puerto Rico.

Once the appellee's brief is filed, the case is placed in a pool with other cases ready for oral argument assignment, unless the case is within one of the

[1] See Marin K. Levy, *Panel Assignment in the Federal Courts of Appeals*, 103 Cornell L. Rev. 65 (2017).

four exceptions noted by the court.[2] The cases in the pool are then randomly assigned to one of the days of the next sitting before the panel of judges scheduled to sit on that day.

Second Circuit: The chief judge prepares a calendar of panels for the court year usually beginning in mid-August. For 2021–22, one and occasionally two panels heard arguments in 42 weeks, every week (usually five days) except for two weeks in December, one week in April, and from the last week of June through the first two weeks of August.

Third Circuit: Panels are designated for the calendar year along with proposed sitting weeks.[3] The court traditionally does not hear arguments in August. Sittings are scheduled for all remaining months. For October 1, 2020 through September 20, 2021, the court was scheduled to sit 33 times, with the understanding that there might be additional sittings to cover emergency merits dispositions and/or death penalty cases.

Fourth Circuit: The court has a formal term that runs from September through May, and there are six argument weeks in each term.[4] The court also schedules, on average, two special sessions per term at law schools around the circuit. The court is not in session the remaining weeks but will grant expedited oral argument, as needed, outside a regularly scheduled session.

Fifth Circuit: The court hears argument at least one week of every month of the year. Typically, between three to six panels sit for four days during the oral argument week. In an average year, the court holds oral argument for 12 weeks (and in addition holds special hearings and hears appeals en banc).

As for how the calendar is created, the clerk prepares a proposed court schedule for the court year (July 1 to June 30), which is approved by the "scheduling

[2] 1st Cir. IOP VII(D). These exceptions are where the case is (1) a "sequel to, or offshoot of, a case previously decided by the court"; (2) where the case was "presented to the duty panel in the regular course of duties"; (3) where a case was assigned to a panel but the case must now be rescheduled on account of scheduling changes or changes in the "procedural handling of the case"; and (4) where the case has been assigned to a panel but then a judge must recuse or becomes unavailable and so the case must be transferred to a different panel or a replacement judge must be found.

[3] 3d Cir. IOP 3.1 says that "composition of a panel is determined at the time cases are assigned to a panel," but the clerk explained that three-judge panels are designated for the calendar year along with proposed sitting weeks, and the cases are randomly assigned to a panel eight weeks before the sitting date. According to the clerk, then, the composition of the panels is set at the time of assignment.

[4] The Fourth Circuit's local rule notes the possibility of additional weeks: "The Court sits in Richmond, Virginia, to hear cases during six to eight separate argument weeks scheduled between September and June." 4th Cir. R. 34(c).

proctor" (the court's phrase) and the chief judge.[5] Then, the scheduling proctor and the clerk create panels for the year,[6] using a computer program that provides four options that minimize recurring pairings of the same judges, and the chief judge selects a preferred option.

Sixth Circuit: The court hears argument in 14 weeks during the calendar year, over one- to two-week periods, which provide judges at least five weeks between sittings, and active judges are generally scheduled to sit four days during one of the two weeks.[7] Sittings for a single case are added for death penalty cases, emergencies, and cases remanded from the Supreme Court. At least six active judges are assigned at random to one of the two weeks; the rest of the court's active judges are assigned to the other sitting week.[8]

Seventh Circuit: The court hears arguments in 30 weeks of the year. The court is in recess in June, July, and August, although it does have two "Short Argument Day" cases in each of those months, and will also hear emergency arguments as needed. Judges are assigned to panels with an algorithm that assures that every judge sit the same number of times with every other judge over a two-year period.

Eighth Circuit: The court normally sits only in the second full week of each month from September through June.[9] The clerk's office prepares and publishes an oral argument calendar approximately one month before a court session.[10] The clerk's office uses software to form the panels and randomly assign cases.[11] At least three non-argument panels (also called screening panels) are in operation at all times.[12]

Ninth Circuit: The court sits every month for at least two weeks, though often more. Overall, the Ninth Circuit averages between 400 and 450 sitting "days." The court sits for en bancs quarterly in addition to regular sittings, averaging 20 en banc sittings per year.

Cases involving the same legal issue may either be advanced for argument or deferred to be heard at the same time.[13] About 14 weeks before argument, parties are notified of the month being considered for argument, and about

[5] 5th Cir. IOP Screening (Court Year Schedule).
[6] *Id.* IOP Judge Assignments (Panel Selection Procedure).
[7] 6th Cir. IOP 34(a)(1).
[8] *Id.*
[9] 8th Cir. IOP I(D)(1).
[10] *Id.*
[11] *Id.*
[12] *Id.* IOP I(D)(2).
[13] 9th Cir. R. 34-4, Cir. Adv. Comm. N. (1).

ten weeks before argument are notified of the time and place of the argument.[14] (Parties are encouraged to contact the clerk if a notice of the date for oral argument or submission on the briefs has not been received within 15 months after completion of briefing.)[15]

Tenth Circuit: The court hears arguments on a regularly scheduled basis for a total of five weeks per year – one week in January, March, May, September, and November. An additional three to five special sessions take place during the year.

Eleventh Circuit: The circuit executive, in collaboration with the clerk's office, prepares a proposed court schedule for an entire year, which is then approved by the scheduling committee of the court, consisting of active judges.[16] The court has 27 argument weeks per year, excluding en banc and specially scheduled hearings, and more than one panel may sit in a week.

The assignment of judges to panels and the assignment of cases to panels are separated "[t]o insure complete objectivity."[17] The circuit executive and the scheduling committee take into account a fixed number of weeks for each active judge and the available sittings for the court's senior judges and judges sitting by designation.[18] After this is done, names of active judges for the sessions of court are drawn by lot from a matrix for the entire year.[19] The clerk is not given the names of panel members for a session until the court calendar of appeals has been prepared and approved.[20]

D.C. Circuit: The court hears arguments in about 35 weeks from September to mid-May. However, emergency arguments may be scheduled in the summer. In forming panels, the clerk attempts to pair each active judge with every other active judge an equal number of sitting days during the term.[21]

Federal Circuit: The court typically hears argument the first full week of every month, for a total of 12 weeks, plus occasional other times. The chief judge provides the clerk's office with a list of judges who are available for each day of an argument session.[22] The clerk's office then runs a computer program

14 *Id.* Gen. Ord. 3.4.
15 *Id.* 25-2, Cir. Adv. Comm. N. (2).
16 11th Cir. R. 34-4, IOP 2(a).
17 *Id.* R. 34-4, IOP 2(b).
18 *Id.*
19 *Id.*
20 *Id.*
21 D.C. Cir. Handbook of Practice and Internal Procedures Part X, The Court's Calendar (B).
22 Fed. Cir. IOP 3(1).

that randomly generates three-judge panels for each month, subject to the judges' availability.[23]

3.2 COMPOSITION OF PANELS

A federal statute requires panels of not more than three judges to hear appeals, unless an appeal is reheard en banc (*see* Chapter 10),[24] except that the Federal Circuit may have panels of more than three judges if its rules permit.[25] By local rule, the Federal Circuit provides that panels consist of an odd number of at least three judges.[26]

A federal statute also requires that a majority of a panel be judges of the circuit, unless such judges cannot sit because recused or disqualified, or unless the chief judge certifies that there is an emergency.[27] A majority of a panel constitutes a quorum.[28]

The way in which panel composition is achieved varies from circuit to circuit but is generally meant to approximate randomness, within some constraints (e.g., taking into account the availability of the judges).[29]

3.3 UNAVAILABILITY OF A PANEL MEMBER

All the circuits have provisions concerning the unavailability of a judge assigned to a panel.

First Circuit: If a judge assigned to a panel becomes temporarily unavailable before oral argument and there is sufficient time, the chief judge asks a non-recused judge to join the panel. If the judge has died or retired, the remaining two judges can either decide the case or request the random selection of a third judge from the remaining non-recused active judges.

Second Circuit: After a matter has been assigned to a three-judge panel, if a judge ceases to participate, the two remaining judges, if they agree, may decide the matter or request the clerk to randomly select a third judge.[30]

23 *Id.*
24 28 U.S.C. § 46(c).
25 *Id.*
26 Fed. Cir. R. 47.2(a).
27 28 U.S.C. § 46(b).
28 *Id.* § 46(d).
29 Levy, *Panel Assignment in the Federal Courts of Appeal*, *supra* note 1.
30 2d Cir. IOP(E)(b). The IOP permits two judges of a panel "which has heard argument or taken under submission an appeal" to decide the appeal if a third judge is unable to proceed, but the court has ruled that it applies when a third judge declines to participate immediately prior to oral argument. *See Murray v. National Broadcasting Co.*, 35 F.3d 45, 47 (2d Cir. 1994).

Third Circuit: If a judge assigned to a panel becomes unavailable for any reason, the chief judge will decide whether to name a substitute.[31] In general, if a panel member becomes unavailable after the distribution of the briefs but before the disposition date, the chief judge will usually name a substitute.[32] If, however, a panel member becomes unavailable after the disposition date but before the opinion is filed with the clerk, the two remaining judges will inform the chief judge of the status of the case, including whether they agree on the disposition of the case, and the chief judge will decide whether to name a substitute judge (a case may be decided without a substitute if the remaining judges agree on the disposition).[33]

Fourth Circuit: If a judge assigned to a submission panel becomes unavailable, a replacement judge is randomly selected. If a judge assigned to an argument panel becomes unavailable, a senior judge is contacted to serve as a replacement; if no senior judge is available, a visiting judge is contacted to serve as a replacement, or the case is continued and a replacement judge is selected randomly.

Fifth Circuit: When the court's computer program creates administrative, emergency, and screening panels, it identifies a first and second "backup judge" to serve in the event a primary judge on the panel is recused, on respite, or unavailable for any other reason. When a panel member is unable to participate, the initiating judge can bring in a backup judge or enter a quorum ruling. The court always selects the first backup judge first and if that judge is unavailable, the second backup judge is selected.

The court maintains a backup log to identify a judge when one is needed to place a judge on an oral argument panel or when neither of the backup judges is available in one of the scenarios described earlier. The log lists all active judges (except the chief judge), and the court assigns a judge next on the list to one of the panels previously listed when both backup judges are unavailable, or to an oral argument panel when one of the three judges becomes unavailable. (For oral argument panels, this is most often necessary if a case returning to the court from the Supreme Court on remand is returned to the original oral argument panel, but a judge who served on that panel is no longer with the court.)

Sixth Circuit: When a third judge is needed to complete a panel (because an original panel member has become unavailable), the clerk draws a name

[31] 3d Cir. IOP 12.1.

[32] *Id.* 12.1(a).

[33] *Id.* 12.1(b).

from among the active and senior judges not already on the panel.[34] The judge will sit on the panel regardless of whether the judge is scheduled to sit during the same weeks as the other panel members.[35] The court's internal operating procedure (IOP) notes that the random drawing will be witnessed by the circuit executive.[36]

Seventh Circuit: If a judge becomes unavailable before argument, a third judge is randomly drawn; after argument, if both judges agree, they may decide the appeal. If there is disagreement, a third judge is randomly drawn, and the revised panel considers whether the appeal should be reargued.

Eighth Circuit: If a judge becomes unavailable after argument, the two remaining judges may dispose of the case if in agreement, but either judge may request a third judge.[37] If the two judges are not in agreement or if either of the two requests a third judge, the clerk will randomly designate another judge to join the panel.[38]

Ninth Circuit: When a judge is disqualified or recused before the case is submitted, the clerk tries to find a replacement by switching cases or judges with panels at the same location; if unsuccessful, the clerk randomly selects an active judge.[39] In rare instances, argument.[40] If a judge becomes unavailable after submission, the remaining two judges, if in agreement, may decide the appeal or request that the clerk draw a replacement judge.[41] If the two judges are not in agreement, the clerk shall draw a replacement judge.[42] If a replacement judge is requested, the clerk shall draw, by lot, a replacement judge from among active judges and senior judges willing to serve.[43]

Tenth Circuit: When a judge becomes unavailable, the clerk randomly selects a replacement judge.

Eleventh Circuit: If, prior to argument, a judge of an oral argument panel becomes unable to participate for reasons other than recusal or disqualification, the two remaining judges, whether or not judges of the Eleventh Circuit, may hear the argument and decide the appeal.[44] If the third judge is later able to

34 6th Cir. IOP 34(b)(2).
35 *Id.*
36 *Id.*
37 8th Cir. R. 47E.
38 *Id.*
39 9th Cir. Gen. Ord. 3.2(i).
40 *Id.*
41 *Id.* Gen. Ord. 3.2(h).
42 *Id.*
43 *Id.*
44 11th Cir. R. 34-2.

participate as a panel member, that judge may listen to the oral argument recording and participate in the decision.[45] If a judge becomes unable to participate on an oral argument panel because of recusal or disqualification, the two remaining judges, whether or not judges of the Eleventh Circuit, may hear argument and decide the appeal, return the appeal for reassignment to another panel, or request the chief judge or a delegate of the chief judge to designate a third judge.[46]

If, after submission, a panel member is not able to participate in the decision, the two remaining judges, whether or not judges of the court, may decide the appeal or request the chief judge or a delegate of the chief judge to designate a third judge.[47]

D.C. Circuit: When a judge becomes unavailable, the clerk's office draws a name randomly for a replacement judge.

Federal Circuit: If a judge becomes unavailable before argument or submission, the chief judge will select a substitute to serve as though originally a member of the panel.[48] If a judge of a panel that has heard oral argument or taken under submission any appeal, petition, or motion is unable to continue with consideration of the matter, the remaining judges will determine the matter if they are in agreement and no remaining judge requests the designation of a third judge.[49] If the remaining judges are not in agreement or if any remaining judge requests the designation of a third judge, the chief judge will secure another judge to sit with the panel.[50]

3.4 ASSIGNMENT OF CASES TO CALENDARS

First Circuit: A local rule states that cases are selected on a first-in-first-out basis, according to the completion of briefing,[51] but fully briefed cases are also placed in a pool and randomly drawn for assignment to panels. Approximately six weeks before the hearing, the clerk contacts counsel regarding the assignment of the case to a specific day and to request the name of the counsel who will argue.[52]

Second Circuit: Cases are selected on a first-in-first-out basis, according to the completion of briefing.

45 *Id.*
46 *Id.*
47 *Id.*
48 Fed. Cir. IOP 5(3).
49 *Id.* R. 47.11.
50 *Id.*
51 1st Cir. R. 34.1(b)(1).
52 *Id.* 34.1(c).

Third Circuit: Cases are selected from a pool of fully briefed cases, averaging 50 cases, and randomly assigned to a three-judge panel,[53] eight weeks before the sitting date.

Fourth Circuit: Briefs are reviewed by counsel to the clerk as they are filed. Counsel to the clerk either places the case on a calendar or "screens" it to the office of staff counsel (OSC) for possible submission on the briefs. Screened cases are reviewed by staff attorneys in OSC, who either submit the case to a randomly selected submission panel or return it to the clerk's office for placement on an argument calendar. Members of submission panels either unanimously agree upon a submitted disposition or return the case to the clerk's office for an oral argument calendar. The clerk merges the list of cases ready for argument each month with a list of three-judge panels generated randomly.[54] An effort is made to assign oral argument cases to judges with previous involvement in a case through a motions panel or a prior appeal.[55] In general, the same panel is used for a subsequent appeal in the same case.

An appeal may be held in abeyance pending disposition of matters before the court or other courts that "may affect the ultimate resolution of an appeal."[56]

Fifth Circuit: The clerk prepares calendars of cases,[57] endeavoring to ensure that different panels have an equal number of different types of cases (civil versus criminal).[58] If the court will have five panels sitting during a court session, the clerk selects cases from the next 100 cases ready to be argued and assigns 20 to each of the five panels without knowing the identity of the judges on these panels. For a case that is deemed to have "significant public interest," a special panel is drawn by lot.

Sixth Circuit: The clerk prepares the calendar for a session before the composition of panels is determined.[59] The clerk balances the calendars by dividing the cases as evenly as possible among the panels according to three case types: civil, criminal, and "other."[60] The number of cases sent to the panels for each session depends on the number of cases ready for decision; each panel for the session receives the same number of cases.

[53] 3d Cir. IOP 1.1.
[54] 4th Cir. IOP 34.1.
[55] *Id.*
[56] *Id.* R. 12(d).
[57] 5th Cir. IOP Preparation and Publishing Calendars (General).
[58] *Id.* IOP Preparation and Publishing Calendars (Calendaring by Case Type).
[59] 6th Cir. IOP 34(a)(b)(2).
[60] *Id.* IOP 34(a)(b)(3).

Seventh Circuit: Cases are randomly assigned to panels.

Eighth Circuit: The clerk's office assigns cases to hearing panels using a computer program that randomly assigns cases. Cases screened for submission without argument are sent to the staff attorneys for preparation of a memo and a proposed opinion, which are sent to a screening panel of three judges who serve for three months. These panels either accept the proposed opinion, revise it, or set the case for argument before them or a randomly selected panel.

Ninth Circuit: Cases are selected for calendaring according to the order in which notices of appeal, petitions, or applications for enforcement were filed;[61] exceptions are made, and priority is given, to direct criminal appeals, capital cases, civil appeals having priority by statute, and non-custody petitions for review of a Board of Immigration Appeals (BIA) order, which are calendared in the order in which the principal briefing is completed.[62] Once selected for calendaring, cases are assigned to panels using a computer application that takes into account the number of panel sitting days, known recusals, and the location and month of oral argument.[63] The chief judge, in consultation with the clerk or a motions or screening panel, may determine that a case should be assigned to a panel of three judges of the court (and not visiting judges sitting by designation) if the decision is likely to set circuit precedent for a large number of cases or is a case of exceptional importance.[64]

Tenth Circuit: The clerk's office uses a computer program that randomly generates three-judge panels and assigns cases to them.

Eleventh Circuit: Cases are calendared for hearing on a first-in-first-out basis.[65] Absent special priority, those appeals that are oldest in point of time of availability of briefs are calendared first for hearing, insofar as practicable with other requirements of the docket.[66] The clerk attempts to balance cases among panels so that each panel has an equitable number of different types of cases.[67]

D.C. Circuit: The clerk's office uses a computer program that randomly assigns cases. Normally the three cases per panel per day include an agency case, a civil case, and a criminal case, but sometimes there are not enough criminal cases.

[61] 9th Cir. Gen. Ord. 3.3(c).
[62] *Id.*; *id.* R. 34-3.
[63] *Id.* Gen. Ord. 3.3(d).
[64] *Id.* Gen. Ord. 3.3(h).
[65] 11th Cir. R. 34-4, IOP 3(c).
[66] *Id.*
[67] *Id.* IOP 3(b).

Federal Circuit: A computer program randomly assigns the calendar-ready cases in order of completion of merits briefing,[68] and assigns cases to provide judges with a cross-section of cases within the Federal Circuit's specialized jurisdiction.[69]

3.5 PANEL RETAINING A CASE

Some circuits have provisions authorizing a panel considering a preliminary issue to have the merits appeal assigned to it.

In the First Circuit, a panel that expands a certificate of appealability by adding an additional claim will usually adjudicate the merits of the appeal.[70]

In the Second, Fourth, Sixth, and Eighth Circuits, a panel hearing a motion may have the merits of the appeal assigned to it.

In the Fifth Circuit, a panel hearing an appeal may designate itself the permanent panel for all subsequent appeals.

In the Sixth Circuit, a panel can remand and "retain" jurisdiction, although the chief judge may order the case assigned to another panel.[71]

In the Eleventh Circuit, a motions panel ordinarily does not have a related merits appeal assigned to it.

In the D.C. Circuit, the "special panel," composed of active judges who serve on a rotating basis throughout the year, which serves as the motions panel, may retain an appeal where "super" expedition is required and decide the case expeditiously.

In the Federal Circuit. a motions panel that grants a motion to expedite an appeal may decide, by majority vote, to consider the merits of the appeal.[72]

3.6 SUBSEQUENT APPEALS

If a case returns after a remand, the circuits, except the D.C. Circuit, generally assign the subsequent appeal to the same panel or a panel with at least one judge that heard the original appeal. There are some slight variations in the circuits' practices.

[68] Fed. Cir. IOP 3(1).

[69] 28 U.S.C. § 46(b); Fed. Cir R. 47.2(b).

[70] *See Bui v. DiPaolo*, 170 F.3d 232, 238 (1st Cir. 1999).

[71] 6th Cir. IOP 34(b)(3). The word retain is in quotation marks in the text because unless a mandate is issued, the district court does not properly reacquire jurisdiction.

[72] Fed. Cir. IOP 2(11).

First Circuit: A case that is a "sequel to, or offshoot of" a case previously decided by the court is assigned to "a particular panel or to a panel including a particular judge."[73]

Second Circuit: If a case is remanded for a limited purpose, such as to find a fact or explain a criminal sentence, under the court's *Jacobson* procedure,[74] the case returns to the same panel. If the case returns after a remand for broader purposes, such as an order for a new trial, the case is assigned to a panel with at least one judge from the prior panel, with a preference for the judge who wrote the majority opinion. A panel remanding a case can direct that it will hear any subsequent appeal.

Third Circuit: A panel can direct that a subsequent appeal in the same case be assigned to it. If the same panel can no longer sit owing to death or change in status of a panel member, the case will be assigned to the remaining available panel members.

Fourth Circuit: In general, a case that is remanded after argument will be argued before the same panel on a second appeal. A case that is submitted after argument will be submitted to the same panel on a second appeal.

Fifth Circuit: In either a full or partial remand, a panel could direct the clerk to return the appeal to that panel. The court has no policy requiring a member of the original panel to be on a case when it returns on appeal.

Sixth Circuit: In the event of a subsequent appeal, the original panel determines whether it or a new panel, selected at random, will hear the case.[75]

Seventh Circuit: A successive appeal in a case that the court has previously heard is assigned to the same panel; if the subsequent appeal involves the same issues, the original panel will keep the case, but if it raises different issues, the original panel decides whether to retain the case.[76]

Eighth Circuit: Panels that remand the case typically serve as the panel on return from remand. But if the panel cannot be easily reassembled, the subsequent appeal is assigned to a panel that includes the judge who wrote the opinion in the original appeal, any other available members of the original panel, and a randomly selected judge or judges.

Ninth Circuit: A case returning with the same parties and issues is known as a "Comeback Case."[77] Cases remanded from the Supreme Court are referred to the panel that previously heard them.[78] An en banc court decides whether

[73] 1st Cir. IOP VII(D).
[74] *United States v. Jacobson*, 15 F.3d 19 (2d Cir. 1994).
[75] 6th Cir. IOP 34(b)(1).
[76] 7th Cir. OP 6.
[77] 9th Cir. Gen. Ord. 1.12.
[78] *Id.* Gen. Ord. 3.6(a).

to retain a new appeal taken after a remand from that court or refer it to the three-judge panel.[79] When a new appeal is taken following a three-judge panel's remand, the clerk notifies the panel, which is encouraged to accept the new appeal if it involves interpretation of the prior decision (except when it is impossible to reconstitute the prior panel).[80] The votes of two judges of the prior panel suffice for retention; if the third judge on the prior panel is unavailable, the clerk shall draw a replacement, using a list of active judges randomly drawn by lot.[81]

Tenth Circuit: When a new appeal is taken following a three-judge panel's remand, the clerk notifies the panel, which is encouraged to accept the new appeal if it involves interpretation of the prior decision.

Eleventh Circuit: The principal retention of a remanded case occurs with death penalty cases.[82]

D.C. Circuit: There is no prohibition on a panel directing that a subsequent appeal be assigned to it, but this rarely occurs. Under ordinary circumstances, no effort is made to assign a subsequent appeal to a judge who sat on an earlier appeal.

Federal Circuit: When an appeal is docketed in a case that was previously remanded by this court, or when an appeal concerning attorney fees is docketed after any appeal on the underlying merits is decided, the clerk's office attempts to assign the appeal to the previous panel, to a panel including at least two members of the previous panel (if one of those members was the writing judge), or to a panel that contains the writing judge (if such a panel is otherwise constituted and available on a subsequent argument calendar).[83] A case that is remanded by the Supreme Court is ordinarily referred to the panel or to the en banc court that previously decided the matter.[84]

79 *Id.* 3.6(b).
80 *Id.* 3.6(d).
81 *Id.*
82 11th Cir. R. 22-4.
83 Fed. Cir. IOP 3(1).
84 *Id.*

4

Motions

This chapter considers the practices of the courts of appeals concerning procedures for calendaring and adjudicating most motions. Requests for some forms of relief – to expedite an appeal or for a rehearing en banc – are considered in chapters dealing with those topics: *see* Chapter 5 (expedited appeals) and Chapter 10 (rehearings en banc).

Rule 27(c) of the Federal Rules of Appellate Procedure (FRAP) authorizes one judge to act on any motion, except a motion to dismiss or determine an appeal.[1] FRAP provides that the court may, by rule or by order in a particular case, authorize the clerk to act on specified types of motions for a procedural order.[2] The courts of appeals vary in the ways they supplement this general authority concerning the handling of motions. Authority to rule on some motions has been delegated to staff, some motions are ruled on by one judge, and some by three judges.

First Circuit: The clerk is authorized to rule on certain routine matters,[3] such as motions for enlargement of time for counsel to file a document, to consolidate related cases, to correct captions, and to withdraw as counsel.[4]

Three-judge motions are sent to a monthly motions panel, called a "duty panel," made up of three randomly assigned active judges. If the motion is eligible for decision by one judge, the first judge listed on the duty panel decides the motion.

A provision, unique among the circuits, provides that motions will not necessarily be allowed even though assented to.[5]

1 Fed. R. App. P. 27(c).
2 *Id.* 27(b).
3 1st Cir. R. 27.0(d); *id.* IOP V(C).
4 *Id.* IOP V(C).
5 *Id.* R. 27.0(a).

Other provisions of note are that motions to extend time to file briefs or to file briefs in excess of applicable length limits are discouraged, and any such motion must be filed well before the expiration of the time limit.[6] Motions to file an oversized opening brief must be filed at least ten days before the due date; for an oversized reply brief, at least seven days before the due date.[7]

Second Circuit: The clerk is authorized to decide routine, unopposed procedural motions.[8] This authority, for some motions, has been delegated to the court's administrative attorneys.

One-judge motions are sent to the junior active judge on each day's panel, who serves as the "applications" judge. If two members of the panel are senior judges, the presiding judge is the applications judge. For matters that might require a prompt decision, such as a motion for a stay of a district court's judgment pending appeal, the applications judge can grant temporary relief. Then, depending on the urgency of the matter, the judge can refer the motion to the first panel already scheduled to hear appeals that will accept the motion, the three-judge panel hearing counseled motions on a Tuesday, the panel already scheduled to hear the appeal, or the panel that will be scheduled to hear the appeal.

For three-judge motions, the Second Circuit, unlike other circuits, does not use a motions panel when a merits panel is sitting. Three-judge motions are considered by each of the regular panels hearing cases each day, with the motions allocated to particular days by subject matter. Motions for leave to file a successive habeas corpus petition[9] are heard on Monday, counseled motions on Tuesday, *pro se* motions on Wednesday and Thursday, and *Anders*[10] motions on Friday. This system is feasible because this court has a panel sitting most weeks; for summer or holiday recess weeks, active judges sign up, a year in advance, for one week of duty determining single-judge motions, and three motions panels.

If a counsel's request for argument on a motion is granted, the regular panel hears the motion on a Tuesday ahead of the day's argued cases,[11] with five minutes normally allotted to each side. Oral argument on an emergency motion can be heard as quickly as the morning after a ruling by a district court.

6 1st Cir. Rulebook, Notice to Litigants 5.
7 *Id.* R. 32.4.
8 2d Cir. R. 27.1(c).
9 *See* 28 U.S.C. § 2244(a)(3)(A).
10 *Anders v. California*, 386 U.S. 738 (1967) (authorizing defense counsel, after determining that a criminal appeal raises no nonfrivolous issue, to move to have the appeal dismissed).
11 2d Cir. IOP 27.1.

The court has substantially reduced the number of motions to extend the time to file briefs by permitting parties to select their own briefing deadlines within an outer limit of 91 days after receipt of the transcript,[12] instead of the FRAP limits of 40 days for the appellant and 30 days for the appellee.[13] If the parties fail to select a briefing deadline, the clerk's office imposes the normal FRAP deadlines.[14] To achieve consistency in rulings on motions for extension of time beyond the 91-day limit, the court sends all such motions to one of the three judges serving on an extensions committee. Briefing time limits are tolled by the filing of a dispositive motion, a motion to proceed *in forma pauperis*, or a stipulation to dismiss.[15]

The Second Circuit has administrative attorneys in the clerk's office who review all motions filed with the court and assure that they are routed properly within the court. They also process one-judge motions and the initial stages of emergency motions, providing brief explanations to the applications judge on duty. Staff attorneys process three-judge motions seeking relief such as proceeding *in forma pauperis*, appointment of counsel, granting a certificate of appealability (COA), and leave to file a successive petition for habeas corpus; route the motions to panels for the appropriate day of a sitting week; and prepare memos and proposed orders.

Motions to file an oversized brief are generally disfavored, but, if made, must be filed at least 14 days before the due date,[16] and state the requested length.[17]

Third Circuit: The clerk may be authorized to rule on any motion other than those that are case-dispositive or required by statute or rule to be decided by judges.[18] The clerk and the senior staff attorney are authorized to grant, but not deny, an unopposed motion to proceed *in forma pauperis*.[19]

One-judge motions are sent to the junior active judge of a standing motions panel (SMP), which is appointed by the chief judge.[20] One judge may grant various nondispositive motions,[21] including motions to stay an appeal, intervene, or seal or unseal documents.[22]

12 *Id.* R. 31.2(a)(1)(A), (B).
13 Fed. R. App. P. 31(a)(1).
14 2d Cir. R. 31.2(a)(1)(A), (B).
15 *Id.* R. 31.2(a)(3).
16 *Id.* R. 27.1(e)(2), (3).
17 *Id.* R. 27.1(e)(2).
18 3d Cir. IOP. 10.4.
19 *Id.* Standing Orders, Granting In Forma Pauperis Motions (January 22, 1987).
20 *Id.* IOP 10.1.
21 *Id.* IOP 10.5.1.
22 *Id.* IOP 10.5.2(a), (f), (h).

Three-judge motions are sent to an SMP, which considers all such motions not sent to a merits panel,[23] determines its own procedures for conferences and disposition,[24] and determines whether to hear oral argument.[25] If an SMP votes to deny a motion seeking to dismiss an appeal for lack of jurisdiction or untimeliness, the motion is referred to the merits panel.[26] Motions related to a case assigned to a merits panel are generally ruled on by the panel presider if they are administrative.[27]

An SMP rules on motions to exceed page or word limitations for briefs.[28]

Because a stay of a mandate is ordinarily not a requirement for filing a petition to the Supreme Court for a writ of certiorari (requesting review), the court's practice is not to grant a motion for such a stay.[29]

Fourth Circuit: The clerk is authorized to enter orders on unopposed procedural motions and motions that relate to the preparation and printing of briefs and the appendix "or are such as are ordinarily granted as of course and without notice or hearing."[30] A party adversely affected by a clerk's ruling may request review by the court.[31]

The Fourth Circuit has a "strong presumption" that all but routine procedural matters will be disposed of by panels.[32] In a case where a request for a single judge action is made to the clerk and action by a panel is not feasible, the clerk will assign the matter to a judge selected at random.[33] In cases where a single judge, selected at random, has found it necessary to take some temporary action, the clerk will then fill out the panel with two randomly selected additional judges.[34]

In exceptional cases in which counsel has made an application to one judge (and then notified the clerk's office), and the judge has found it necessary to take some temporary action, the clerk will assign the matter to a three-judge panel selected at random, which may or may not include the single judge who acted in the case.[35]

[23] *Id.* IOP 10.1.
[24] *Id.* IOP 10.3.1.
[25] *Id.* IOP 10.3.4.
[26] *Id.* IOP 10.3.5.
[27] *Id.* IOP 10.7.1.
[28] 3d Cir. Standings Orders, Motions to Exceed the Page or Word Limitations (January 9, 2012).
[29] *Id.* IOP 10.8.2.
[30] 4th Cir. R. 27(b).
[31] *Id.*
[32] *Id.* R. 27(e).
[33] *Id.*
[34] *Id.*
[35] *Id.*

Fifth Circuit: The clerk is authorized to act on procedural motions seeking 20 forms of relief, including motions to stay the mandate pending a petition for certiorari in civil cases, consolidation of appeals, file an amicus brief, proceed *in forma pauperis*, appoint counsel, and obtain a free transcript.[36] Such rulings by the clerk may be reviewed by one judge.[37]

The clerk is also authorized to act on, or refer to the court, a timely motion for an extension of time to file a petition for rehearing or rehearing en banc, for a period not longer than 14 days or 30 days if the applicant is a prisoner proceeding *pro se*.[38]

A motion to reinstate an appeal dismissed by the clerk must be made as soon as "reasonably possible" and not later than 45 days after dismissal.[39]

One judge is authorized to act on procedural motions including intervention in agency proceedings, applications for a COA, extension of time prescribed by FRAP or by local rules, except to enlarge time for filing a notice of appeal, and issue various stays.[40]

Three-judge motions are submitted to motions panels,[41] drawn randomly from the active judges.[42]

Motions or matters requiring judges' consideration are assigned in rotation to all active judges on a "routing log."[43] The clerk creates an assignment log at the beginning of a court year that lists judges in random order. Throughout the court year, the clerk assigns matters to the judges using this order (assuming no recusal issues) as matters are filed.

The clerk assembles the necessary materials and submits them to the next judge in that random rotation. That judge serves as the "initiating judge" for the panel.[44] The initiating judge may act on the matter if court rules permit a single judge to do so.[45] For actions requiring panel concurrence, the initiating judge reviews the matter and forwards a proposed action to the other panel members for consideration or approval.

The clerk maintains a separate log for assigning emergency motions. The procedure for creating this log, and assigning matters, is the same, except due

36 5th Cir. R. 27.1.5, .9, .14, .17, .18, .19.

37 *Id.* R. 27.1.

38 *Id.* IOP General Standards for Ruling on Motions (Post-Decision Motions).

39 *Id.* IOP General Standards for Ruling on Motions (Reinstatement of Cases Dismissed by the Clerk).

40 *Id.* R. 27.2.2, .3, .4, .6.

41 *Id.* IOP General Standards for Ruling on Motions (Motions Panels).

42 *Id.*

43 *Id.* IOP Distribution (To Judges).

44 *Id.*

45 *Id.*

to time constraints in emergencies, the clerk forwards all materials to each panel member at the same time.[46]

Once the clerk assigns a case to a merits panel, the clerk submits motions to the hearing panel rather than the motions panel. The senior active judge on the panel is considered the initiating judge for all merit panels.[47]

Sixth Circuit: The clerk is authorized to act on various motions including procedural motions and seven other matters.[48]

The Sixth Circuit does not designate a judge as a duty judge or an applications judge. One-judge motions are submitted weekly in rotation to judges serving on quarterly non-argument panels. Those panels are randomly assembled from active and senior judges and visiting judges designated to sit with the court.[49] A panel reviewing a single judge's decision will not include that judge.[50]

Three-judge motions in cases not yet assigned to a merits panel are sent to the quarterly non-argument panels.[51] Once a case is assigned to the oral argument calendar, motions are assigned to the merits panel.[52]

The court will not consider a motion to affirm a judgment.[53]

A motion to stay issuance of a mandate must be filed within seven days after the time to file a petition for rehearing expires or after an order on a petition for rehearing.[54] Motions to extend briefing deadlines are not favored.[55]

Seventh Circuit: Court staff is authorized to rule on motions for 20 types of relief, which are identified as routine.[56] If there is a question whether to grant or deny a routine motion, the designated staff member consults with the motions judge, unless the case has been assigned for argument or submission or has been argued or submitted, in which case the staff member consults with the presiding judge.[57] For 17 types of motions, which are identified as nonroutine, court staff present the matter to a motions judge or a motions panel.[58] Included are motions to stay or recall a mandate, appoint counsel, or issue a COA (if one has

46 *Id.* IOP Distribution (Emergency Motions).

47 *Id.* IOP Distribution (Motions After Assignment to Calendar).

48 6th Cir. R. 45(a)(1)–(8). These other matters range from motions involving production or filing of the appendix or briefs on appeal to orders granting remands and limited remands where the motion includes a notice under Fed. R. App. P. 12.1(a).

49 *Id.* IOP 27(a)(1).

50 *Id.* R. 27(a)(3).

51 *Id.* IOP 27(a)(1).

52 *Id.* IOP 27(a)(2).

53 *Id.* R. 27(e).

54 *Id.* R. 41(b).

55 *Id.* IOP 26(a).

56 7th Cir. OP 1(c)(2), (7).

57 *Id.* OP 1(c)(2).

58 *Id.* OP 1(c)(3), (7).

been denied by the district court).[59] After the staff member is advised of the decision on the motion, the staff member prepares an order, and, if the order states detailed reasons, presents the order to a motions judge or a motions panel for approval.[60] The clerk is authorized to reject repetitious motions to reconsider.[61]

One judge is authorized to rule on most motions for other relief, but at least two judges act on requests for bail, district court denials of a COA, and district court denials of leave to proceed *in forma pauperis*.[62] And three judges act to dismiss or otherwise finally determine an appeal or other proceeding, unless the dismissal is by stipulation or is for procedural reasons.[63] Three judges also act to deny a motion to expedite an appeal when the denial may result in the mooting of the appeal, though a smaller number of judges than provided in all of these procedures may decide any motion "in the interest of expediting a decision or for other good cause."[64] Responsibility for handling motions is rotated among the active judges on a weekly basis.[65]

One judge or a motions panel acts on emergency motions for nine types of relief, including a motion to stay an injunction or for leave to appeal an interlocutory order under 28 U.S.C. § 1292(b).[66]

Motions to extend time for briefs are not favored, and should be filed at least seven days before the brief is due.[67] Furthermore, the court lists three grounds that may merit consideration, including engagement in other litigation, the complexity of the matter under appeal, and extreme hardship to counsel unless an extension is granted.[68]

A motion for leave to file a successive habeas corpus petition pursuant to 28 U.S.C. § 2244(b)(3)(A) is sent to the panel that heard the prior appeal.[69] When a motions panel decides that a motion should be set for oral argument or expedited, it may recommend to the chief judge that the merits appeal be assigned to that panel.[70]

Eighth Circuit: The clerk is authorized to enter orders in 25 listed procedural matters including extension of time to file briefs,[71] and consolidation of

59 *Id.*
60 *Id.*
61 *Id.* OP (1)(c)(8).
62 *Id.* OP (1)(a)(1).
63 *Id.*
64 *Id.*
65 *Id.* OP (1)(b).
66 *Id.* OP (1)(c)(1).
67 *Id.* R. 26.
68 *Id.*
69 *Id.* OP 6(c).
70 *Id.* OP 6(d).
71 8th Cir. R. 27A(a)(2).

appeals.[72] One judge (subject to FRAP 27(c)) may order a temporary stay of any proceeding pending the determination of a stay application by a three-judge panel.[73] Any party adversely affected by an order previously noted may file a motion to reconsider, vacate, or modify the order within 14 days after its entry; the motion will be referred to a three-judge panel that includes all judges who previously acted on the matter.[74]

A panel of three judges, known as an "administrative panel,"[75] will act in all other matters,[76] including ten identified matters, such as a motion to proceed *in forma pauperis*, an application for a COA, a motion for appointment of counsel, a motion for a free transcript, an application for a stay pending appeal, and a motion to dismiss for lack of jurisdiction.[77]

The court has three administrative panels each month. The composition of the panels changes each month and is set by the chief judge; judges are randomly selected to serve on the panels. The three judges on a panel take turns serving as lead, second, and tie-breaker; the lead and second judges decide the motion and call on the tie-breaker in the event of disagreement.

Ninth Circuit: The Ninth Circuit has delegated the authority to decide a number of motions to deputized court staff. Specifically, most nondispositive procedural motions,[78] including 27 identified matters,[79] can be acted upon by a deputy clerk, staff attorney, the chief circuit mediator, and an appellate commissioner, appointed by the court.[80] The clerk is also authorized to rule on eight other identified matters,[81] including a *sua sponte* order to show cause why an attorney should not be disciplined.[82] The circuit mediators and the staff attorneys have the same authority to act on procedural motions as the clerk, and are further authorized to issue orders on eight other specified matters, including orders granting unopposed motions for attorney's fees and orders denying untimely petitions for permissive interlocutory appeals.[83] The appellate commissioner is also authorized to issue nondispositive orders in all

72 *Id.* R. 27A(a)(8).
73 *Id.* R. 27A(b).
74 *Id.* R. 27A(d).
75 *Id.* IOP(D)(3).
76 *Id.* R. 27A(c).
77 *Id.* IOP(D)(3).
78 9th Cir. Gen. Orders, App'x A.
79 *Id.* Gen. Orders, App'x A(1)–(15), (17)–(24), (26)–(29).
80 *Id.* R. 27-1, Cir. Adv. Comm. N. (1).
81 *Id.* Gen. Orders, App'x (A)(38)–(43), (46)–(47).
82 *Id.* (A)(39).
83 *Id.* (A)(50)–(57).

appeals except those that would reverse a decision by a district judge or where eight identified forms of relief are sought.[84]

The Ninth Circuit abrogated the general authority of one judge to rule on specific motions in 2014.[85] Where cases have been calendared for argument or submission, the panel may delegate to one judge on the panel authority to rule on procedural matters and a motion to grant or expand a COA pursuant to 28 U.S.C. § 2253(c).[86]

Two judges may rule on various matters including a request for a COA, leave to proceed *in forma pauperis* in civil cases, and injunctive relief pending appeal.[87] Requests for COAs are placed on a separate COA calendar,[88] which is presented to a two-judge COA panel that meets for one day during each sitting week.[89] Active judges are expected to serve on one COA panel a year.

Three judges serve on a motions panel,[90] which rules on substantive motions, including motions to dismiss, for summary affirmance, and for bail.[91] Judges are ordinarily assigned to the motions panel on a rotating basis by the clerk for a term of one month,[92] and sit at least three days per month.[93]

The Ninth Circuit has a special procedure for petitions for a writ of mandamus, prohibition, or other extraordinary relief.[94] A motions panel may deny such a petition if it believes the petition does not make a prima facie showing justifying issuance of the writ, but that denial "is not regarded as a decision on the merits."[95] Or the panel may call for an answer and send the petition to a new motions panel.[96] The new motions panel may grant or deny the petition or calendar it for oral argument.[97]

A motion for a COA may be filed within 35 days of the later of a district court's denial of a COA or the filing of a notice of appeal or amended notice of appeal.[98]

84 *Id.* R. 27-1, Cir. Adv. Comm. N. (1); *id.* Gen. Ord. 6.3(e).
85 *Id.* Gen. Ord. 6.3(f).
86 *Id.* 6.3(b).
87 *Id.* 6.3(g).
88 *Id.* 6.1(k).
89 *Id.* 6.2(b).
90 *Id.* R. 27-1, Cir. Adv. Comm. N. (3)(b).
91 *Id.* R. 27-1, Cir. Adv. Comm. N. (3)(a).
92 *Id.* R. 27-1, Cir. Adv. Comm. N. (3)(b).
93 *Id.* Gen. Ord. 6.2(d).
94 *Id.* R. 21-1.
95 *Id.* R. 21-1 to 21-4, Cir. Adv. Comm. N.
96 *Id.*
97 *Id.*
98 *Id.* R. 22-1(d).

Special requirements are prescribed for the content of emergency motions, including the date by which relief is needed.[99] A motion that requests relief by a certain date must specify the date in bold on the caption page.[100]

By rule, most motions do not stay the briefing schedule,[101] though in practice, the court will generally reset the schedule if needed upon resolving most motions. Parties are encouraged to notify the clerk if a motion has been pending for longer than four months.[102]

Tenth Circuit: The clerk is authorized to act on motions for 11 forms of relief, including to consolidate appeals and to substitute parties,[103] plus any other motion that the court may authorize the clerk to rule on.[104]

Prior to the assignment of an appeal to a merits panel, there is a standing two-judge panel, called a "clerk's panel," available to decide contested motions and motions that the clerk has not been delegated authority to decide. Judges may volunteer to serve on the clerk's panel, or if there are no volunteers, the chief judge appoints the members of the clerk's panel. There is no set term of service on the clerk's panel, and the current composition of the clerk's panel has remained the same for many years. Senior judges are eligible to serve on the clerk's panel, but they generally do not do so.

When a case has been assigned to a panel, one judge on the panel may issue any interlocutory order or act on any motion filed under FRAP 8, 9(b), 22(a), or 22(b).[105]

Eleventh Circuit: The clerk is authorized to act on various unopposed motions, subject to review by the court.[106] Additionally, the clerk is authorized, subject to review by the court, to act for the court on opposed procedural motions, to grant first requests for an extension of up to 30 days to file or correct a deficiency in the briefs and appendices in appeals not yet assigned or under submission, and to expedite briefing in a direct appeal of a criminal conviction and/or sentence when an incarcerated defendant's projected release is expected to occur prior to the conclusion of appellate proceedings.[107]

[99] *Id.* R. 27-3, 27-4.
[100] *Id.* R. 27-1(3).
[101] *Id.* R. 27-11.
[102] *Id.* R. 25-2, Cir. Adv. Comm. N. (1).
[103] 10th Cir. R. 27.5(A)(1)–(11).
[104] *Id.* R. (A)(12).
[105] *Id.* R. 27.7(A).
[106] 11th Cir. R. 27-1(c).
[107] *Id.*; *id.* R. 9-1.

One judge may act on various motions, including a motion for a COA,[108] to appeal *in forma pauperis*,[109] and to appoint counsel for an indigent appellant in a criminal case.[110]

Two-judge motions panels may act on motions as determined by the court.[111]

Judges are assigned to three-judge motions panels in October of each court year (and when a new judge joins the court).[112] The three judges use a sequential voting system whereby the first judge ("initiating judge") sends the motion papers to a second judge with a recommendation, and the second judge sends the motion papers to a third judge, and the third judge returns the file and an order to the clerk.[113]

A ruling on a motion or other interlocutory matter, whether entered by one judge or a panel, is not binding upon the panel to which the appeal is assigned on the merits, and the merits panel may alter, amend, or vacate it.[114]

In habeas corpus cases, if a party does not file a motion for a COA, the court will construe a timely notice of appeal as an application for a COA.[115]

A motion for panel rehearing must be filed within 21 days after judgment (except that a petition for rehearing in a civil appeal in which the United States or an officer or agency is a party, in which case it must be filed within 45 days after judgment), rather than as provided by FRAP 40(a)(1).[116]

D.C. Circuit: The clerk may dispose of routine procedural motions.[117]

A "special panel" of judges, assigned on a rotational basis, considers motions, cases recommended for disposition without oral argument, and emergency matters.[118] The special panel consists of three active judges who serve for about two months during the regular sitting term (September through May) and a term of two weeks during the summer months. The date when a special panel will consider a motion is not publicly disclosed.[119] Once a case is assigned to a merits panel, all motions relating to the case are submitted to the panel.[120]

108 *Id.* R. 27-1(d)(2).
109 *Id.* R. 27-1(d)(3).
110 *Id.* R. 27-1(d)(4).
111 *Id.* R. 27-1(e).
112 *Id.* R. 27 IOP 1.
113 *Id.*
114 *Id.* R. 27-1(g).
115 *Id.* R. 22-1(b).
116 *Id.* R. 40-3.
117 D.C. Cir. R. 27(e)(1); D.C. Cir. Handbook of Practice and Internal Procedures VII Motions Practice (C) Disposition by the Clerk.
118 *Id.* (D) Disposition by a Panel.
119 *Id.*
120 *Id.* (E) Disposition by a Merits Panel.

A motion for dispositive relief must be filed within 45 days of the docketing of the case, unless the court permits a later filing.[121] A motion to extend time to file motions or replies must be filed at least five days before the due date,[122] and if the court does not act on the motion by the end of the second business day before the filing deadline, the deadline is automatically extended until the court rules on the motion.[123]

Federal Circuit: The clerk is authorized to act on any procedural motion or unopposed nonprocedural motion, except those that require action by a judge or panel.[124]

The Federal Circuit has a monthly motions panel, with a lead judge designated by the chief judge of the circuit.[125] Emergency motions are presented to the lead judge, who then chooses whether to decide the motion alone or to obtain a decision by the motions panel.[126]

A party moving for a stay of agency action pending review who requests immediate action must, before filing, notify all parties that the motion will be filed and must use an expedited method of service.[127] A motion to extend time must be made seven days before the due date, but may, in extraordinary circumstances, be made after the due date.[128]

[121] *Id.* R. 27(g)(1).
[122] *Id.* R. 27(h)(1).
[123] *Id.* R. 27(h)(4).
[124] Fed. Cir. R. 27(h).
[125] *Id.* IOP 2(1).
[126] *Id.* IOP 4(b).
[127] *Id.* R. 18(c)(1).
[128] *Id.* R. 26(b)(1).

5

Expedited Appeals

This chapter considers the procedures that courts of appeals use for expediting the hearing of appeals and the consequences of granting expedited hearings. Appeals are expedited for various reasons. For example, if normal scheduling of filing briefs and hearing oral argument were maintained, a corporate merger might occur before an appeal from a ruling permitting the merger would be heard or a prisoner's sentence might expire before an appeal challenging the length of the sentence would be heard.

All circuits have some provisions for expediting appeals, but their provisions are not always clear as to the exact consequences of granting a motion to expedite. Typically, a shortened briefing schedule is established, and sometimes an early argument date is set. Not infrequently, however, after a motion to expedite is granted, it is left to the clerk to determine the consequences. Advancing the argument date can mean either that after full briefing on the shortened briefing schedule is completed, the appeal is added to a calendar of already scheduled cases, or is only moved to the head of the line of all fully briefed appeals and placed on the next calendar to be prepared; the difference between these techniques can be several weeks.

First Circuit: When there is a motion to expedite (which should be made shortly after the case is docketed),[1] a duty judge or duty panel will approve, if appropriate, an order to expedite a case and set an expedited briefing schedule and sometimes set a date for oral argument. If no argument date is set, the case will be scheduled for the next sitting, ahead of other fully briefed cases.

The court can also *sua sponte* set an expedited schedule in certain cases, and this is done automatically in cases where it is required by statute – for example, recalcitrant witness cases.[2]

[1] 1st Cir. IOP VII(B).
[2] *Id.*

Second Circuit: One judge or a three-judge panel can order that an appeal be expedited.

If a motion to expedite an appeal has been granted, the appeal is assigned, after briefing under shortened time limits has been completed, to the first weekly calendar after already issued calendars (usually six weeks later). When a panel granting a motion to expedite wants to accord the appeal speedier expedition, the case is assigned, after briefing is completed, to the first panel with an existing calendar whose presider will accept the added case.

The Second Circuit has an expedited appeals calendar (XAC) to expedite all appeals from threshold dismissals of complaints for lack of jurisdiction or failure to state a valid claim.[3] Each side's briefing time is 35 days.[4] Either side can request exemption from the XAC.[5] Exemption is usually granted for plaintiffs because the XAC was established for their benefit. Appeals on the XAC are heard along with appeals on the court's regular calendar of argued cases.

Third Circuit: A party seeking to expedite a case must file a motion within 14 days after the notice of appeal or the occurrence that is the basis of the motion.[6] A motion to expedite must include a proposed briefing schedule. The motions panel will either accept the proposed schedule or designate a different schedule. The court can expedite for briefing or disposition or both. An expedited case is ordinarily assigned to the next available panel on the schedule unless a decision on the matter is required sooner. If a decision is required sooner, the case can be added to a panel which already has received the full complement of cases or a special panel may be convened.

Fourth Circuit: The court on its own motion or on a motion of the parties may expedite an appeal for briefing and oral argument.[7] If argument is not needed, the briefing schedule may be accelerated, and the case submitted to the office of staff counsel for accelerated review and submission to a panel. If argument is needed, an expedited oral argument can be scheduled outside a regularly scheduled session.

Fifth Circuit: The court may, on its own motion or for good cause on the motion of either party, advance any case for hearing, and prescribe an abbreviated briefing schedule.[8] In practice, a screening judge can expedite a case to oral argument by instructing the clerk to docket the matter on the next available calendar

[3] 2d Cir. R 31.2(b); *see also* Jon O. Newman, *The Second Circuit's Expedited Appeals Calendar for Threshold Dismissals*, 80 Brook. L. Rev. 429 (2015).

[4] 2d Cir. R. 31.2(b)(3).

[5] *Id.* R. 31.2(b)(2).

[6] 3d Cir. L.A.R. 4.1.

[7] 4th Cir. R. 12(c).

[8] 5th Cir. R. 34.5.

or on an already-published calendar. Absent special instructions, the case is sent to the next available oral argument calendar and randomly assigned. If time is of the essence, the clerk can contact a randomly selected scheduled panel to determine whether it can take the case as an extra or in lieu of an already scheduled case.

If the expedited case can be disposed of on the summary calendar, it will be immediately routed if briefing is complete. If briefing is not complete or the case will go to the oral argument calendar, the court directs an expedited schedule.

The court further sets out that a defendant who is incarcerated for one year or less pursuant to the sentence appealed may file a motion to expedite the appeal upon a showing of irreparable harm.[9]

Sixth Circuit: Some cases are expedited by local rule, internal operating procedure (IOP), or practice; others by the clerk on a party's motion. If the clerk declines to grant a motion to expedite, or expedites over a party's objection, a party may seek review by a single judge sitting on a quarterly motions panel.

If expedited, the clerk's order often expedites preparation of the transcript (usually by prohibiting extensions of time), either shortens briefing deadlines or prohibits extensions, and directs submission to a merits panel as soon as possible after the filing of the appellee's brief. The panel can schedule argument earlier than the next sitting or can take the case on the briefs and issue an earlier ruling.

The court directs the parties to file briefs on an expedited basis and then schedules an oral hearing or submission on the briefs as soon as possible in appeals by those found in contempt of grand jury proceedings and by recalcitrant witnesses confined for failure to comply with an order to testify or produce documents to a court or a grand jury.[10] Issuance of a routine briefing schedule and expedited argument or submission on the briefs is directed in appeals from an order denying or granting preliminary or temporary injunctions, interlocutory appeals under 28 U.S.C. § 1292(b), direct criminal appeals, and appeals in cases filed pursuant to 28 U.S.C. §§ 2241, 2254, and 2255.[11]

Seventh Circuit: Although court staff is authorized to rule on motions to expedite,[12] such a motion usually goes to one of the active judges who rotate

9 *Id.* R. 47.10.2.

10 6th Cir. IOP 28(c).

11 *Id.* That the IOP provides for a "routine briefing schedule" in cases concerning preliminary injunctions and all direct criminal appeals, as well as interlocutory appeals under 28 U.S.C. § 1292(b) and habeas corpus cases, is in seeming conflict with 6th Cir. R. 31(c)(2)(A), which says that briefs are filed on an expedited basis in cases concerning preliminary injunctions, direct criminal appeals where the sentence is 15 months or less, grand jury contempts, and recalcitrant witness appeals. The practice of the Sixth Circuit is to expedite briefing by shortening the filing times in recalcitrant witness and grand jury contempt appeals. In other matters specified in 6th Cir. 31(c)(2)(A), the court issues standard briefing times, but limits extensions, unless otherwise requested or directed. The latter matters are then expedited for submission.

12 7th Cir. OP 1(c)(2).

on a weekly basis as a motions judge. If expedited, the judges decide how quickly it will be scheduled. Because the court has no backlog of fully briefed cases, there is no distinction between being scheduled before, or only after, such cases are calendared.

Three judges act to deny a motion to expedite an appeal when denial may result in mooting the appeal.[13]

Eighth Circuit: A motion to expedite can be granted by the clerk or by an administrative panel. The clerk generally limits orders to expediting briefing. If an expedited hearing is requested, the matter is referred to an administrative panel or a future hearing panel, usually a panel sitting in the following month. If the matter is referred to a hearing panel and they agree to expedite it, they will generally retain the appeal and add it to their coming calendar.

If the motion comes at docketing and there are open calendars not yet filled, the clerk can grant the motion and add the appeal to a future calendar. That would result in a random assignment to a hearing panel. If the motion is opposed, the matter would go to a three-judge motions panel. They might or might not keep the case for argument if it is expedited.

Ninth Circuit: Appeals can be expedited by the clerk, an appellate commissioner, or a motions or screening panel.[14] The expedited appeal will then be assigned through a randomized calendaring system to the next available panel in the appropriate administrative unit (*see* Chapter 2) when the panels sitting for that calendar have not yet been assigned their cases.[15]

Appeals are expedited for good cause,[16] which includes cases with a guideline sentence or date of release from confinement that is not longer than 12 months from a notice of appeal.[17] For cases involving a confined recalcitrant witness, the record must be filed as soon as possible after filing a notice of appeal, and an expedited briefing schedule will be set.[18]

The clerk, the appellate commissioner, or a motions or screening panel may also determine that a case is an "urgent case" required to be heard within a specified time; urgent cases are randomly assigned to an existing calendar of cases of a panel sitting in the month in which the case must be heard.[19] Examples are cases that might become moot absent a prompt decision.[20]

[13] *Id.* (1)(a)(1).
[14] 9th Cir. Gen. Ord., App'x A(21).
[15] *Id.* Gen. Ord. 3.3(f).
[16] *Id.* R. 27-12.
[17] *Id.*
[18] *Id.* R. 3-5, Cir. Adv. Comm. N.
[19] *Id.* Gen. Ord. 3.3(g). This panel assignment is to be made regardless of geographic location, excluding Honolulu and Anchorage (unless the urgent case originates from that location).
[20] *Id.*

Absent extraordinary circumstances, the assigned panel is expected to accept the additional case.[21]

Tenth Circuit: Appeals are almost always expedited at the request of one or more of the parties. Prior to the assignment of an appeal to a merits panel, only briefing will be expedited, either by the clerk (if unopposed) or by the clerk's panel (if opposed). Requests to expedite oral argument and/or the issuance of a decision are referred to the merits panel. The clerk works with the chief judge to determine whether a matter should be assigned to a scheduled merits panel earlier than usual or by a randomly selected "off calendar" panel.

Review of a district court's release order is generally expedited.[22]

Eleventh Circuit: The court may, on its own motion or for good cause shown on the motion of a party, advance an appeal for hearing and prescribe an abbreviated briefing schedule.[23] An appeal may be expedited by one judge (subject to review by the court, meaning a panel),[24] or by the court.[25] Unless otherwise specified, the clerk sets a briefing schedule and an early argument date.[26]

The clerk is authorized to expedite briefing in a criminal case when the inmate's projected release date is expected to occur before the determination of the appeal.[27]

D.C. Circuit: Generally appeals are expedited only on motions of the parties. The "special panel" determines whether expedition is warranted and may also order expedited briefing and argument. In cases where "super" expedition is required, the special panel may retain the appeal and decide the case expeditiously.

An appeal from a pretrial release or detention order must be expedited.[28] Not later than ten days after the transcript is filed, the appellant must file its memorandum of law,[29] the appellee may file a responsive memorandum within ten days of the appellant's memorandum,[30] and the appellant may file a reply memorandum within seven days.[31] Upon filing a notice of appeal in habeas corpus and sentencing appeals, the appellant must immediately notify

21 *Id.*
22 10th Cir. R. 9.1(A).
23 11th Cir. R. 34-4.
24 *Id.* R. 27-1(d)(9).
25 *Id.* R. 27-1 IOP 3, R. 34-4(f).
26 *Id.*
27 *Id.* R. 31-4.
28 D.C. Cir. R. 9(a).
29 *Id.* R. 9(a)(1).
30 *Id.* R. 9(a)(2).
31 *Id.* R. 9(a)(3).

the clerks of the court of appeals and the district court, and the circuit clerk will issue an expedited briefing schedule.[32]

Separately, the court maintains a stand-by pool of cases ready for argument if a scheduled appeal needs to be replaced. To enter the stand-by pool, the parties must agree to an expedited briefing schedule.[33] Such an appeal will not be scheduled earlier than in 45 days.[34]

Federal Circuit: Decisions to expedite are set forth in orders placed on the docket. The consequences are often case-specific, depending on whether the parties or a panel has a specific month and/or dates in mind as to when argument would be scheduled. If a motions panel decides to expedite an appeal, it may constitute itself as the merits panel.[35] If a motions judge decides to expedite proceedings where the motions panel is not reconstituting itself to decide the merits (and thus will not themselves be hearing argument), the judge's order sometimes schedules oral argument for a particular month or a particular date and sometimes directs that the case come ahead of other cases for calendaring.

[32] *Id.* R. 47.2.

[33] D.C. Cir. Handbook of Practice and Internal Procedures, X Court Calendar, E(4) Scheduling in Particular Cases, Stipulated Stand-by Pool.

[34] *Id.*

[35] Fed. Cir. IOP 3(1).

6

Briefs of Parties and Amici Curiae

This chapter considers the courts of appeals' requirement for briefs, including separate requirements for briefs of amici curiae.

6.1 BRIEFS OF PARTIES

Federal Rules of Appellate Procedure (FRAP) 28–32 contain several detailed provisions concerning appellate briefs. FRAP 31(a)(1) sets time limits. Rule 28 specifies the content of parties' briefs, and Rule 29 adds requirements for the briefs of amici curiae. Rule 30 specifies the content of appendices. Rule 32 specifies length, form, and typeface requirements.

Almost all the circuits have local rules or internal operating procedures (IOPs) supplementing the FRAP provisions. They cover several different aspects of the requirements for briefs.[1]

6.1.1 *Time for Filing Parties' Briefs*

According to FRAP 31(a)(1), the appellant must file its brief within 40 days after the record is filed, the appellee must file its brief within 30 days after the appellant's brief is served, and the appellant may file a reply brief within 21 days after the appellee's brief is served (but at least seven days before oral argument unless the court allows a later filing).

[1] 1st Cir. R. 28.0, 28.1, 31.0, 32.0, 32.2, 32.4; 2d Cir. R. 28.1, 31.1, 31.2, 32.1; 3d Cir. L.A.R. 28.1-.4, 30.1, 30.3, 31.1-.4, 32.1, 32.2; 4th Cir. R. 28(a)–(f), 30(a)–(d), 31(a)–(d), 32(a)–(c); 5th Cir. R. 28.1-.7, IOP Miscellaneous Brief Information, R. 30, 31, IOP following R. 31, R. 32; 6th Cir. R. 28, IOP 28, R. 30, 32; 7th Cir. R. 28, 28.1, 30, 31, 32; 8th Cir. R. 28A, 30A, 32A; 9th Cir. R. 28-1-6, 28.1-1, 29-1-3, 30-1-3, 31-1-2, 32, 32-1-3; 10th Cir. R. 28, 28.1-.3, 29, 30.1-.3, 31.1-.5, 32(A)–(B); 11th Cir. R. 28-1-5, IOP 1-7, R. 28.1-1-2, IOP 1-2, R. 29-1-4, 30-1-3, 31-1-5, IOP Briefing Schedule, R. 32-1-4; D.C. Cir. R. 28(a)–(f), 28.1(c)–(f), 30(a)–(e), 31(a)–(b), 32(a)–(g); Fed. Cir. R. 28, 28.1, 30, 31, 32.

The Second Circuit has adopted the most extensive variation from FRAP time limits for filing briefs. The court permits counsel for each side to select a brief deadline within a 91-day interval.[2] The appellant's interval starts after the later of the receipt of the final trial court transcripts, a notice that a transcript will not be ordered, or the filing of the record in appeals from agency decisions (the "ready date").[3] The appellant must notify the court of its brief filing deadline within 14 days of the ready date,[4] and the appellee must notify the court of its brief deadline within 14 days of receiving the appellant's brief.[5] If the appellant fails to give timely notice of its filing date, the court sets a 40-day schedule;[6] if the appellee fails to give timely notice of its filing date, the court sets a 30-day schedule.[7] The order setting the due date for the appellant's brief states that the appeal is automatically dismissed if the brief is not timely filed. The appellee's scheduling order states that upon failing to timely file the brief, the appellee will be required to make a motion for permission to argue the appeal. These extended deadlines and automatic dismissal and forfeiture language were adopted to reduce the time the staff and judges expend on motions to extend the FRAP time limits. These motions were usually granted and are now less frequently made.

It is arguable that the Second Circuit's time limit provisions exceed the court's authority. Rule 31(a)(2) of FRAP provides that a court of appeals that routinely considers cases on the merits promptly after cases are filed may *shorten* the time to file briefs. The US Judicial Conference's Advisory Committee on Appellate Rules has explained that this provision was added to recognize the fact that the FRAP time limits are well within the time that must ordinarily elapse in most circuits before an appeal can be reached for consideration.[8] The Committee's note cautions that in those circuits, the time limits should not be disturbed.[9] However, Rule 26(b) of FRAP provides that the time prescribed by the national rules to perform any act (except filing a notice of appeal) may be extended for good cause, and the judges of the Second Circuit apparently believed that reducing the need for motions to extend brief deadlines, which consumed clerk's office time to docket and were routinely granted, was sufficient good cause.

[2] 2d Cir. R. 31.2(a)(1)(A), (B).
[3] *Id.* R. 31.2(a)(1)(A).
[4] *Id.*
[5] *Id.* R. 31.2(a)(1)(B).
[6] *Id.* R. 31.2(a)(1)(A).
[7] *Id.* R. 31.2(a)(1)(B).
[8] Fed R. App. P. 31, Notes of Advisory Committee on Rules–1970 Amendment.
[9] *Id.*

Some circuits have slight variations from FRAP briefing time limits. For example, in the Fourth Circuit, the court issues a briefing order, setting the time for filing briefs;[10] in criminal cases, the appellant's brief is due within 35 days after the briefing order is filed, the appellee's brief is due within 21 days after service of the appellants' brief, and the appellant's reply brief is due within ten days after service of the appellee's brief.[11]

In the Ninth Circuit, for appeals involving preliminary injunctions, the appellant's brief is due within 28 days after docketing a notice of appeal, the appellee's brief is due within 28 days after service of the appellant's brief, and the appellant's reply brief is due within 21 days after service of the appellee's brief.[12] When a briefing schedule has been set by an order of the court, the additional three-day allowance for service by mail, authorized by FRAP 26(c), does not apply.[13] If a brief is not filed on time, the clerk may dismiss the appeal.[14] If a *pro se* appellant or *pro bono* counsel fails to file a timely opening brief in a civil case, the clerk shall dismiss the appeal no sooner than 14 days after the brief was due.[15]

In the Eleventh Circuit, in criminal cases, if an appellant's brief is not filed by the due date, the clerk issues a notice that the appeal will be dismissed 14 days hence unless the default has been remedied.[16] In civil cases, if the brief is not filed by the due date an appeal shall be treated as dismissed for failure to prosecute on the first business day following the due date.[17]

In the Federal Circuit, the appellant's initial brief must be filed within 60 days after docketing,[18] and an appellee or cross-appellant must file its brief within 40 days after appellant's brief is served.[19]

6.1.2 *Extension of Time for Filing Briefs*

Parties often request additional time for filing their briefs, and the circuits vary in their approach to such requests. Some have bright line rules (although vary in their additional time allotments), and others have standards for granting extensions.

10 4th Cir. R. 31(b).
11 *Id.* R. 31(a).
12 9th Cir. R. 3-3(b).
13 *Id.* R. 31-2.1(a).
14 *Id.* R. 42-1.
15 *Id.* Gen. Order 2.3(a).
16 11th Cir. R. 42-1(b).
17 *Id.* R. 42-2(c).
18 Fed. Cir. R. 31(a)(1)(A), (B).
19 *Id.* R. 31(a)(2).

In the Second Circuit, to achieve uniformity in extending briefing time limits, a committee has been designated to act on all motions to extend briefing time limits. Each judge on the committee rules on one-third of extension motions.

In the Fourth Circuit, a motion to extend the time for filing a brief must be filed "well in advance" of the due date.[20]

In the Fifth Circuit, a request to extend the time for filing a brief must be filed at least seven days before the due date, absent exceptional circumstances.[21] Extension of time limits will normally not exceed 40 days in criminal cases and 30 days in civil cases.[22] Extensions of up to 30 days are called "level 1 extensions," which the clerk may either act on or refer to the court.[23] Extensions of more than 30 days are called "level 2 extensions," which the clerk may either act on or refer to the court, but will be granted "only under the most extraordinary circumstances."[24] Extensions are not automatic even if unopposed.[25]

In the Sixth Circuit, the fact that the opposing party does not oppose an extension request is explicitly not dispositive.[26]

In the Ninth Circuit, a party that has not previously obtained an extension of time may obtain a single "streamlined extension" not to exceed 30 days.[27] All other extensions may be granted only on motion and must be filed at least seven days before the current deadline.[28]

In the Eleventh Circuit, a first request to extend the time to file a brief by 30 days or less may be made by telephone (or in writing) and may be granted by the clerk.[29] A first request to extend the time more than 30 days must be filed at least seven days before the due date.[30] A second request is disfavored and rarely granted.[31]

In the Federal Circuit, a one-time per-document extension of five days to resolve confidentiality issues is automatically granted.[32]

20 4th Cir. R. 31(c).
21 5th Cir. R. 31.4.1(a).
22 *Id.* IOP following R. 31.
23 *Id.* R. 31.4.3.1.
24 *Id.* R. 31.4.3.2.
25 *Id.* R. 31.4.1.
26 6th Cir. R. 26(a)(1).
27 9th Cir. R. 31-2.2(a).
28 *Id.* R. 31-2.2(b).
29 11th Cir. R. 31-2(a).
30 *Id.* R. 31-2(c).
31 *Id.* R. 31-2(d).
32 Fed. Cir. R. 26(b)(4).

6.1.3 *Content and Form of Briefs*

FRAP 28 specifies what the parties' briefs must contain. These requirements for the appellant's brief include a statement of the issues presented for review;[33] a concise statement of the case setting out the facts relevant to the issues submitted for review;[34] and the argument, which must contain appellant's contentions and a concise statement of the applicable standard of review for each issue.[35] FRAP 32 provides word limits for the entire brief;[36] some circuits permit more generous limits.

In the First Circuit, an appellant's brief must also include the text of the decision appealed from.[37] A motion to file an oversized opening brief must be made at least ten days before the brief is due and must specify the additional length; for an oversized reply brief, seven days.[38]

In the Second Circuit, the principal briefs may each contain up to 14,000 words.[39] A reply brief may contain up to 7,000 words.[40] For cross-appeals, appellant's principal brief and response-and-reply brief may each contain up to 14,000 words, the appellee's principal-and-response brief may contain up to 16,500 words, and the appellee's reply brief may contain up to 7,000 words.[41] A *pro se* party's brief must disclose if the brief was drafted in whole or substantial part by an attorney.[42]

In the Fifth Circuit, unless specifically directed by court order, a party represented by counsel may not file a *pro se* brief.[43]

In the Seventh Circuit, principal briefs may contain 14,000 words and reply briefs may contain 7,000 words,[44] limits slightly longer than the 13,000- and 6,500-word limits of FRAP 32(a)(7)(A). Also, briefs are exempt from the 14-point font size requirement of FRAP 32(a)(5)(A) but must be in at least 12-point type.[45]

33 Fed. R. App. P. 28(a)(5).
34 *Id.* 28(a)(6).
35 *Id.* 28(a)(8)(A); *id.* 28(a)(8)(B).
36 *Id.* 32(a)(7)(B).
37 1st Cir. R. 28.0(a)(1).
38 *Id.* R. 32.4.
39 2d Cir. R. 32.1(a)(4)(A).
40 *Id.* R. 32.1(a)(4)(B).
41 *Id.* R. 28.1.1.
42 *Id.* R. 32.2.
43 5th Cir. R. 28.6.
44 7th Cir. R. 32(c).
45 *Id.* R. 32(b).

In the Ninth Circuit, parties may not incorporate by reference briefs submitted to the court or to a district court in a prior appeal.[46] Briefs must contain on the last page of an initial brief any known related cases pending in the court,[47] and cases are "related" if they arise out of the same or consolidated cases in the district court or agency or raise the same or similar issues or involve the same transaction,[48] unless the list would be lengthy and counsel in good faith believes that the listing would not assist the court.[49] Pertinent texts of statutes and regulations must be set forth verbatim, and, if included in an addendum to the brief, must be separated by a distinctively colored page.[50] The opening and answering briefs filed by appellant and appellee may not exceed 14,000 words.[51] In cross-appeals, an appellee's principal and response briefs may not exceed 16,500 words.[52] FRAP 28(j) letters – that is, letters citing supplemental authorities – may not exceed 350 words.[53]

In the Eleventh Circuit, a paper appendix to a brief must have staggered tabs extending beyond the right edge of pages, with each tab number corresponding to the docket number of the document in the district court.[54] For electronic appendices, separator pages showing the appropriate tab numbers should be used.[55]

In the D.C. Circuit, all briefs containing abbreviations, including acronyms, must provide a glossary defining such abbreviations unless they are in common usage.[56]

In the Federal Circuit, principal briefs in patent cases must include the language of one or more exemplary patent claims illustrative of the issue(s) on the inside of the front cover (or directly following the front cover if reproducing the language requires more space).[57]

6.1.4 *Issues Not Briefed*

In the Ninth Circuit, if a panel determines it will decide a case on the basis of a significant point not raised in the briefs, it "shall give serious consideration" to requesting additional briefing.[58]

46 9th Cir. R. 28-1(b).
47 *Id.* R. 28-2.6.
48 *Id.* R. 28-2.6(a)–(c).
49 *Id.* R. 28-2.6, Cir. Adv. Comm. N.
50 *Id.* R. 28-2.7.
51 *Id.* R. 32-1(a).
52 *Id.* R. 28.1-1(c).
53 *Id.* R. 28-6.
54 11th Cir. R. 30, IOP 1.
55 *Id.*
56 D.C. Cir. R. 28(a)(3).
57 Fed. Cir. R. 32(a)(3).
58 9th Cir. Gen. Order 4.2.

6.1.5 *Informal Briefs*

The Fourth Circuit permits informal briefs, listing issues, supporting facts, and arguments in *pro se* cases and in appeals from denial of a certificate of appealability in habeas corpus cases.[59]

The Ninth Circuit permits *pro se* litigants to file informal form briefs provided by the clerk that need not comply with the technical requirements of FRAP.[60]

The Federal Circuit permits *pro se* litigants to file an informal brief on a form provided by the clerk.[61]

6.1.6 *Loaning Sample Briefs*

In the Fifth Circuit, the clerk may loan sample briefs to counsel and non-incarcerated *pro se* litigants,[62] and sample briefs are posted on the circuit's website. In the Sixth Circuit, the clerk's office will not give out sample briefs, but such briefs may be inspected in the clerk's office.[63] In the Eleventh Circuit, the clerk will loan counsel sample briefs.[64]

6.2 BRIEFS OF AMICI CURIAE

FRAP 29 sets out requirements for the brief of an amicus curiae, including content and time to file. FRAP 29(a)(2) permits courts of appeals to deny leave to file an amicus curiae brief that would result in a judge's disqualification. All circuits, except the First Circuit, have a rule concerning briefs of an amicus curiae; most either confirm the FRAP 29 requirements or add only slight refinements.[65]

The most significant supplemental provision is the rule of the Second, Fourth, Eighth, and D.C. Circuits generally prohibiting the filing of an amicus brief if it would result in the recusal of a member of the panel assigned to hear the appeal.[66] The Fifth Circuit applies this prohibition to amicus briefs

[59] 4th Cir. R. 34(b).
[60] 9th Cir. R. 28-1(c).
[61] Fed. Cir. R. 32(c).
[62] 5th Cir. IOP Miscellaneous Brief Information (B).
[63] 6th Cir. IOP 28(b).
[64] 11th Cir R. 32 IOP(3)(c).
[65] 2d Cir. R. 29.1; 3d Cir. L.A.R. 27.5, 29.1; 4th Cir. R. 26.1(b), 29(a); 5th Cir. R. 29, 31.2; 6th Cir. R. 29; 7th Cir. R. 29; 8th Cir. R. 29A; 9th Cir. R. 29-1-3; 10th Cir. R. 29; 11th Cir. R. 29-1-4; D.C. Cir. R. 29; Fed. Cir. R. 29 & Prac. N.
[66] 2d Cir. R. 29.1(a); 4th Cir. R. 29(a); 8th Cir. R. 29A(a); D.C. Cir. R. 29(b), 35(f) (en banc court).

sought to be filed *after* a panel opinion has been issued (presumably in support of a petition for panel or en banc rehearing).[67]

There is also variation when it comes to who may rule on a motion for leave to file an amicus brief. In the Fifth Circuit, the clerk may rule on such a motion,[68] though in practice the clerk normally defers motions to file amicus briefs to the court. In the Third Circuit, one judge may rule on a motion for leave to file an amicus brief.[69] (But an amicus will not argue in cases en banc unless at least four members of the en banc court vote otherwise.)[70] And in some others, a motion for leave to file an amicus brief is a three-judge motion – including in the Ninth Circuit, if the brief is submitted without consent.

In the Fifth Circuit, an amicus brief must be filed within seven days after filing of the brief whose position the amicus will support.[71]

In the Ninth Circuit, potential amici are encouraged to file joint briefs and not to repeat arguments of parties.[72] In the D.C. Circuit, amici curiae on the same side must join in a single brief "to the extent practicable,"[73] and an amicus curiae brief in response to, or in support of, a petition for rehearing en banc will not be received unless invited by the court.[74]

67 5th Cir. R. 29.4.
68 *Id.* R. 27.1.14.
69 3d Cir. L.A.R. 27.5.
70 *Id.* IOP 2.2.
71 5th Cir. R. 29.1.
72 9th Cir. R. 29-1, Cir. Adv. Comm. N.
73 D.C. Cir. R. 29(d).
74 *Id.* R. 35(f).

7

Oral Argument

This chapter considers the courts of appeals' practices concerning oral argument, including who makes the decision to permit oral argument; criteria for permitting oral argument; streaming, recording, and televising oral argument; where arguments are held; when counsel learn the identity of a panel; and how long counsel may argue. Practices for en banc oral arguments are considered in Chapter 10.

7.1 PERMITTING ORAL ARGUMENT

Federal Rule of Appellate Procedure (FRAP) 34(A)(2) provides that oral argument is allowed in every case unless a panel has unanimously decided it is "unnecessary" for any of three specified reasons considered in Section 7.2.

All circuits have some procedure to determine whether an appeal should be argued orally. That procedure can involve default policies – that certain kinds of cases are unlikely to receive oral argument – and can rely on input from staff attorneys, members of the clerk's office, and judges in the first instance. The ultimate decision is made by either a screening panel or the panel to which the merits appeal is assigned. The percentage of appeals argued orally varies significantly among the circuits. Table 7.1 indicates the percent of appeals terminated on the merits that were orally argued in 2022:

TABLE 7.1 *Percentage of appeals argued*

Circuit	Percentage argued[1]
1st	29%
2nd	30%
3rd	12%
4th	11%
5th	20%
6th	13%
7th	35%
8th	14%
9th	22%
10th	27%
11th	15%
D.C.	35%

The national average for that year was 20 percent.[2]

First Circuit: The senior staff attorney reviews the briefs to screen cases for oral argument; a panel of three judges then, after consultation with the staff attorney, determines whether oral argument is warranted.[3] Cases that are not selected for oral argument are randomly assigned to a merits panel, and any one judge of that merits panel can request oral argument and the case will be heard at oral argument by that merits panel.

Second Circuit: Each party, within 14 days of the filing of the appellee's brief, must file an oral argument statement.[4] Counsel notify the court whether (1) they request oral argument, (2) they request oral argument only if at least one other party requests it, or (3) they do not want oral argument.[5] Counsel are advised to notify the court at the time oral argument is requested of unavailable dates.[6]

Each panel to which an appeal is assigned may decide, in accordance with FRAP 34(a)(2), that the appeal does not merit oral argument.[7] The court generally permits nonincarcerated *pro se* parties to argue their appeals.

One category of cases not presumptively argued comprises petitions to review decisions of the Board of Immigration Appeals, which are placed on

1 Administrative Office of the U.S. Courts (AO), "Statistics & Reports" tab, "Data Tables" link, Table B-1 (December 31, 2022). The "percentage argued" was calculated by dividing the total number of cases terminated on the merits after oral argument by the total number of cases terminated on the merits. Again, this table does not include data for the Federal Circuit.
2 *Id.*
3 1st Cir. IOP VII(A) Screening and Calendaring.
4 2d Cir. R. 34.1(a).
5 *Id.* website, "Rules" link, "Forms and Instructions" link, "Oral Argument" heading, Oral Argument Statement.
6 *Id.*
7 *Id.* R. 34.1(b).

the court's non-argument calendar (NAC).[8] Another category of cases often not argued concerns prisoners, proceeding *pro se*, who challenge convictions in habeas corpus proceedings or file claims under 42 U.S.C. § 1983 challenging prison conditions. The court considers the merits of these cases in order to adjudicate motions for appointed counsel or a free transcript and denies the motion if it concludes that the appeal is frivolous, followed by dismissal of the appeal without briefing or oral argument.

Third Circuit: Each panel determines whether to have oral argument after reviewing the briefs.[9] One judge may require oral argument.[10] There is oral argument in an en banc case if it is requested by at least one judge of the en banc court.[11]

Fourth Circuit: Briefs are reviewed by counsel to the clerk as they are filed, and as counsel either places the case on the calendar or "screens" it to the office of staff counsel (OSC) for possible submission on the briefs. Screened cases are reviewed by staff attorneys in the OSC, who either submit the case to a random submission panel or return it to the clerk's office for calendaring. Members of the submission panel either unanimously agree upon a submitted disposition or return the case to the clerk's office for calendaring.[12]

Fifth Circuit: Cases are screened for oral argument by the judges with assistance from the staff attorney.[13] When the last brief is filed, a case is generally sent to the staff attorney for prescreening classification.[14] If the staff attorney concludes that oral argument is not warranted, the case is sent to one of the court's judges, selected in rotation[15] If that judge agrees that oral argument is not warranted, the briefs and a proposed opinion are sent to the two other judges on a screening panel.[16] All three judges must agree that oral argument is not warranted for oral argument not to take place.[17] If any panel member determines that oral argument is necessary, that member may refer the appeal for oral argument.

If the staff attorney concludes that oral argument is warranted, the case is sent to an active judge for screening.[18] If that judge agrees that oral argument is warranted, the case is placed on the next appropriate calendar.[19] If that

8 *Id.* R. 34.2.
9 3d Cir. IOP 2.1 Determination in Panel Cases.
10 *Id.*
11 *Id.* IOP 2.2 Determination in Cases En banc. Ordinarily an amicus will not argue unless at least four members of the en banc court vote otherwise. *Id.*
12 4th Cir. R. 34(a), IOP 34.1.
13 5th Cir. IOP Oral Argument (Screening (A)).
14 *Id.*
15 *Id.*
16 *Id.*
17 *Id.*
18 *Id.* IOP Oral Argument (Screening (B)).
19 *Id.*

judge disagrees, that judge's screening panel disposes of the case under the court's summary calendar procedure.[20] The summary calendar is the calendar for all nonargued cases.[21]

Sixth Circuit: Panels determine which of the cases assigned to them will receive oral argument and which do not require oral argument.[22]

Seventh Circuit: Unique among the circuits, the circuit executive screens cases for oral argument. When a motion panel decides that a motion should be set for oral argument, it may recommend to the chief judge that the matter be assigned for argument and decision to the same panel.[23]

Eighth Circuit: The court screens cases for oral argument. By internal operating procedure (IOP), the chief judge may appoint the clerk, a senior staff attorney, or a panel of judges to screen cases awaiting disposition.[24] In practice, the clerk screens all criminal appeals; the chief deputy clerk screens civil appeals from Arkansas, Missouri, Iowa, and Nebraska; and the deputy clerk in charge of the St. Paul office screens cases from North Dakota, South Dakota, and Minnesota.

Screened cases are placed in categories of (1) disposition without oral argument, (2) abbreviated argument, or (3) full argument.[25] The panel scheduled to hear an appeal may alter time allocations for oral argument or reclassify the case as suitable for disposition without oral argument.[26]

One judge of a non-argument panel may move a case to an argument calendar.[27] *Pro se* cases are screened for submission without oral argument, but the panel to which the case is assigned for disposition on the merits may determine that oral argument is necessary.[28]

Ninth Circuit: At any time prior to completion of briefing in a civil appeal or petition for review, a panel may, upon motion of a party and after giving the parties an opportunity to show cause, summarily dispose of an appeal without oral argument if clear error, an intervening decision, or recent legislation requires such action, or if it is manifest that the appeal involves issues so insubstantial as not to justify further proceedings.[29]

[20] *Id.*
[21] *Id.* R. 34.2.
[22] 6th Cir. IOP 34(a)(4).
[23] 7th Cir. OP 6(d).
[24] 8th Cir. R. 34A(a).
[25] *Id.* 34A(b).
[26] *Id.* 34A(c).
[27] *Id.* IOP I(D)(2) (Nonargument (Screening) Panels).
[28] *Id.* IOP III(J) (Calendaring).
[29] 9th Cir. R. 3-6(a).

All fully briefed cases are sent to staff attorneys who review each case for complexity and designate it as a "screening case" or an argument case. If the latter, they also assign it a weight (again based on complexity) and give 24 points worth of cases for each day of argument to equalize the workload. As part of this process, the staff attorney also drafts a description of the issues raised in each case and notes whether these same issues appear in other cases. Panels and staff use this information to avoid conflicts among panels and to batch cases raising similar issues before the same panel.

If a case is designated as a screening case, it will be worked up by a staff attorney. If the case is deemed suitable for an oral presentation, a staff attorney will prepare a proposed memorandum disposition,[30] and present it to a panel of three judges,[31] who sit at least three days per month.[32] Any one judge on a screening panel can "kick" a case to an argument panel. The case may be submitted on the briefs or argued. If one judge wants argument, it will be argued. In addition, "written" screening panels are used for some cases that are too factually complex for oral screening yet are not really argument cases. Written screening panels are made up of three judges,[33] who volunteer for such duty and serve for one year.[34]

Tenth Circuit: The front cover of each party's brief must state whether oral argument is requested.[35] The reasons why argument is necessary must follow the brief's conclusions.[36]

Individual judges screen civil (including habeas) cases for oral argument. Capital habeas cases are routed to the oral argument calendar as a matter of course, if a certificate of appealability is granted. Criminal appeals are routed to the oral argument calendar by the clerk or chief deputy clerk, per criteria established by the court. Senior judges may (but are not required to) participate in screening.

Eleventh Circuit: After briefing is complete, an appeal is sent to the staff attorney's office for classification.[37] If the staff attorney thinks that the appeal does not warrant oral argument, the appeal is returned to the clerk for routing to one of the court's judges, selected in rotation.[38] (In appeals involving

30 *Id.* Gen. Ord. 6.5(b)(1).
31 *Id.* Gen. Ord. 6.1(i).
32 *Id.* Gen. Ord. 6.2(d).
33 *Id.* Gen. Ord. 6.1(j).
34 *Id.* Gen. Ord. 6.2(c).
35 10th Cir. R. 28.2(C).
36 *Id.*
37 11th Cir. R. 34, IOP 1.
38 *Id.*

multiple parties, the staff attorney may recommend that the appeals of some parties be decided without oral argument and the appeals of the other parties be scheduled for argument.)[39] If the judge to whom an appeal is directed agrees that the appeal does not warrant oral argument, that judge forwards the briefs, together with a proposed opinion, to the two other judges who are part of a non-argument panel.[40] If a single member of the panel thinks that oral argument is warranted, the case will be calendared.[41]

In other appeals, when oral argument is requested by a party and the staff attorney thinks that oral argument should be heard, the staff attorney may recommend that the appeal be assigned to the oral argument calendar, subject to the review of the oral argument panel.[42] In general, when an appeal is assigned to an oral argument panel, the oral argument panel, may – if all of the judges are in agreement – determine that the appeal will be decided by the panel without oral argument, or transfer the appeal to the non-argument calendar.[43]

D.C. Circuit: The Staff Attorneys Office does a preliminary screening of cases for oral argument, erring on the side of sending the case on for oral argument. Once the case is assigned to a merits panel, any judge on the assigned panel may suggest or recommend that the case be decided only on the briefs.

If the court concludes that oral argument is not needed, the case may be disposed of without oral argument after notice is given to the parties.[44] A motion to reconsider dispensing with oral argument may be made within ten days of such notice, though such motions are disfavored.[45]

Federal Circuit: The court typically holds argument in counseled cases, but the determination of whether to hold argument in any case is left to the discretion of the merits panel. Under the court's IOPs, it is the court's policy to allow oral argument in counseled cases unless (1) the appeal is frivolous; (2) the dispositive issue or set of issues have recently been authoritatively decided; or (3) the facts and legal arguments are presented adequately in the briefs and record, and the decisional process would not be aided significantly by oral argument. Argument is rarely allowed in cases where the appellant or petitioner is unrepresented and appearing *pro se*. In a case that initially has been designated for no oral argument, oral argument will be held on request of one member of a panel.[46]

39 *Id.*
40 *Id.*
41 *Id.*
42 *Id.*
43 *Id.* Cir. R. 34-3(f).
44 D.C. R. 34(j)(1).
45 *Id.* R. 34(j)(2).
46 Fed. Cir. IOP 7(1).

7.2 CRITERIA FOR ORAL ARGUMENT

FRAP 34(a)(2) provides the following criteria for *not* having oral argument:

> (A) The appeal is frivolous; or
> (B) The dispositive issue or issues have been authoritatively decided; or
> (C) The facts and legal arguments are adequately presented in the briefs and record, and the decisional process would not be significantly aided by oral argument.[47]

A few circuits have additional criteria for permitting oral argument. The Third Circuit notes that:

> [e]xperience discloses that judges usually vote for oral argument when:
> (a) [t]he appeal presents a substantial and novel legal issue; (b) [t]he resolution of an issue presented by the appeal will be of institutional or precedential value; (c) [a] judge has questions to ask counsel to clarify an important legal, factual, or procedural point; (d) [d]ecision, legislation, or an event subsequent to the filing of the last brief may significantly bear on the case; (e) [a]n important public interest may be affected.[48]

In the Federal Circuit, an IOP generally incorporates the FRAP 34(a)(2) criteria.[49]

7.3 PRIORITY FOR SCHEDULING ORAL ARGUMENT

In the Seventh Circuit, priority for scheduling oral argument is given to: (1) appeals from an order of confinement after refusal of an immunized witness to testify before the grand jury,[50] (2) criminal appeals, (3) appeals from orders refusing or imposing conditions of release, which will be heard without the necessity of briefs, (4) appeals involving issues of public importance, (5) habeas corpus and 28 U.S.C. § 2255 appeals, (6) appeals from the granting, denying, or modifying of injunctions, (7) petitions for writs of mandamus and prohibition and other extraordinary writs, (8) other actions if good cause is shown ("good cause" is shown if a right under the Constitution or a federal

47 Fed. R. App. P. 34(a)(2).

48 3d Cir. IOP 2.4.2. But it is noted that "[t]he foregoing criteria shall not be construed to limit any judge's discretion in voting for oral argument."

49 Fed. Cir. IOP 7. The wording of the IOP differs just slightly from Fed. R. App. P. 34(a)(2), including the addition of the word "recently" in the phrase, "[t]he dispositive issue or set of issues recently has been authoritatively decided." *Id.*

50 These appeals must be decided within 30 days. 28 U.S.C. § 1826(b).

statute would be maintained in a factual context that indicates that a request for expedited consideration has merit).[51]

In the Ninth Circuit, priority for scheduling oral argument is given to cases involving habeas corpus petitions,[52] temporary or permanent injunctions,[53] denial of medical care or cruel and unusual punishment to incarcerated persons,[54] incarceration of recalcitrant witnesses,[55] and appeals entitled to priority on the basis of good cause under 28 U.S.C. § 1657.[56]

7.4 SITTING DAYS PER YEAR, CASES HEARD PER DAY, AND ARGUMENT TIMES

The circuits vary considerably in the number of days each active judge hears cases, but only slightly in the number of cases heard each week and the time allotted for oral arguments, as shown in Table 7.2.[57]

TABLE 7.2 *Sitting days per year, cases per day, and argument times*

Circuit	Sitting days per judge per year	Cases per day per panel[58]	Normal designated argument minutes per side[59]
1st	up to 30	up to 6	maximum 15
2nd	30–37	3–5[60]	10 or 15
3rd	24	2–3[61]	15

[51] 7th Cir. R. 34(b)(1) (quoting 28 U.S.C. § 1657(a)).

[52] 9th Cir. R. 34-3(2).

[53] *Id.* R. 34-3(3).

[54] *Id.* R.34-3(4).

[55] *Id.* R. 34-3(1). In an appeal involving incarceration of a recalcitrant witness, the appellant must notify the clerk's office by telephone within 24 hours of filing a notice of appeal, *id.* R. 3-5., and the appeal is decided within 30 days after filing the notice of appeal, *id.* R. 3-5, Cir. Adv. Comm. N.

[56] *Id.* R.34-3(5).

[57] 1st Cir. 34.0(c)(1); *id.* IOP VIII((B); 3d Cir. IOP 2.1; 4th Cir. R. 34(c), (d); 5th Cir. R. 34.11; *id.* IOP Preparation and Publishing Calendars (Number of Cases Assigned); 6th Cir. 34(f)(1); 7th Cir. R. 34(b)(1); 8th Cir. IOP III(K); Fed. Cir. IOP 7(1).

[58] Some circuits have more than one panel sitting on an argument day. Additionally, some circuits have one or two cases that are submitted on the briefs calendared for an argument day. For example, the total of six for the Federal Circuit includes up to four argued cases and up to two cases submitted on the briefs.

[59] Panel presiders sometimes permit oral argument to continue beyond the allotted time.

[60] There are usually three to five argued cases and two to three submitted cases per day.

[61] This range is derived from the fact that an average of seven cases are argued per sitting out of 20 to 25 altogether, and a sitting averages three days of oral argument.

TABLE 7.2 *(continued)*

Circuit	Sitting days per judge per year	Cases per day per panel	Normal designated argument minutes per side
4th	24–25[62]	4[63]	20[64]
5th	30	normally 5	20[65]
6th	28	varies	15[66]
7th	28–30	6–9	10–20
8th	34–42	5 or 6	10, 15, 20, or 30[67]
9th	minimum of 32	up to 8	10–20
10th	14 or 15	6	15[68]
11th	20	up to 5	15
D.C.	22–33	3	10–15
Fed.	40	6	15, maximum 30[69]

In the First Circuit, the senior staff attorney suggests argument time, but the panel presider ultimately sets the time. In the Second Circuit, the panel presider sets argument time. In the Third Circuit, the panel sets the time. In the Fourth Circuit, the time is prescribed by local rule,[70] though the presiding judge may allow additional time at oral argument. In the Fifth Circuit, argument times are determined by court policy and changes to the standard times are made only when the panel agrees unanimously. In the Seventh Circuit, the circuit executive sets time initially, but the panel presider ultimately decides. In the Eighth Circuit, the clerk, principal deputy, and deputy in charge of the St. Paul branch set argument times, which panels may adjust. In

62 These are oral argument days. Submitted cases are assigned randomly to panels throughout the year.

63 Four cases are calendared for argument each day, but the argument panel may unanimously agree to submit a calendared case on the briefs.

64 4th Cir. R. 34(d). Specifically, each side is normally allowed 20 minutes, even in consolidated cases, but the court may shorten or extend the time allotted. In social security disability cases, black lung cases, and labor cases where the primary issue is whether the agency's decision is supported by substantial evidence and in criminal cases where the primary issue involves the application of the sentencing guidelines, each side is limited to 15 minutes.

65 5th Cir. R. 34.11.

66 6th Cir. R. 34(f)(1). Specifically, each side has 15 minutes for oral argument unless the notice of oral argument provides otherwise. *Id.*

67 8th Cir. IOP III(K).

68 Though the standard for oral arguments is 15 minutes per side, each side receives 30 minutes in capital habeas cases.

69 Fed. Cir. IOP 7(1).

70 4th Cir. R. 34(d).

the D.C. Circuit, the clerk designates one member of the panel each day to set the time for oral arguments.[71] In the Federal Circuit, the time is prescribed by an IOP,[72] but the panel can change the time.

In the First and Fourth Circuits, an amber light indicates that five minutes remain in argument time;[73] in the Second, Fifth, and Eleventh Circuits, that two minutes remain.[74] In the Eighth Circuit, a yellow light indicates that five minutes or the time counsel has reserved for rebuttal remains.[75]

The circuits vary slightly in how far in advance the identity of panel members is disclosed, the days on which oral arguments are held, and the time oral arguments begin, as shown in Table 7.3.[76]

TABLE 7.3 *Disclosure of panel, argument days, and when arguments begin*

Circuit	Disclosure of panel	Argument days	Arguments begin
1st	Seven days before a session[77]	Mon.–Fri.	9:30
2nd	Thursday before sitting week	Mon.–Fri.	10[78]
3rd	Eighteen calendar days before first day of sitting	Mon.–Fri.[79]	set by panel[80]
4th	Morning of the argument	Tues.–Fri.	9:30 Tues.–Thurs., 8:30 on Fri.[81]
5th	Week before session[82]	Mon.–Thur.[83]	9 and 1

71 D.C. Cir. Handbook of Practice and Internal Procedures XI(C)(1) Oral Argument, Argument Time, Screening by the Panel.

72 Fed. Cir. IOP 7(1).

73 1st Cir. IOP VIII(C); 4th Cir. website, "Oral Argument" tab, "Courtroom Protocol for Counsel" link.

74 5th Cir. IOP Oral Argument (Lighting Signal Procedure); 11th Cir. R. 34-3, IOP 14(a) (yellow light).

75 8th Cir. IOP III(L)(6).

76 1st Cir. IOP VIII(B); 3d Cir. IOP 2.5(a); 4th Cir. R. 34(c); 5th Cir. IOP Preparation and Publishing Calendars (Number of Cases Assigned); 7th Cir. R. 34(b)(1); 9th Cir. Gen. Ord. 3.5; 11th Cir. R. 34-3, IOP 7.

77 1st Cir. IOP VIII(B).

78 Although the Second Circuit usually hears argument at 10 a.m., sometimes argument is scheduled for 2 p.m.

79 A panel averages three argument days, which are set by the panel.

80 This can be morning or afternoon.

81 4th Cir. R. 34(c). En banc rehearing arguments begin at 9 a.m. *Id.*

82 5th Cir. IOP Preparation and Publishing Calendars (Identity of Panels).

83 *Id.* IOP Preparation and Publishing Calendars (Number of Cases Assigned). The court normally sits Monday through Thursday; however, the court often schedules Tuesday through Friday sittings to account for holidays or special events that conflict with Monday proceedings.

TABLE 7.3 *(continued)*

Circuit	Disclosure of panel	Argument days	Arguments begin
6th	First business day of the week, two weeks before argument[84]	Tues.–Fri.	9 and 1
7th	The day of argument	Mon.–Fri.	9:30[85]
8th	Generally 30 days before hearing date	Mon.–Fri.[86]	9
9th	On the Monday of the week preceding the argument[87]	Mon.–Fri.	9,[88] 9:30, or 10
10th	7–10 days before argument	Mon.–Fri.	8:30 or 9
11th	2 weeks before argument[89]	Tues.–Fri.[90]	9
D.C.	30 days before argument[91]	Mon.–Fri.	9:30
Fed.	Morning of the argument	Mon.–Fri.	10

7.5 LOCATION OF ORAL ARGUMENT

A federal statute requires each court of appeals to hold regular sessions in specified cities.[92] Some courts of appeals hear almost all arguments in the circuit's major city, but others, especially those that cover many states, hear arguments in additional cities. While argument typically is held in federal courthouses, occasionally argument is held in law schools for the purpose of providing an educational opportunity for students.

First Circuit: Required by statute in Boston;[93] also Puerto Rico.

Second Circuit: Required by statute in New York City;[94] occasionally in Albany, Syracuse, New Haven, Hartford, and at law schools.

Third Circuit: Required by statute in Philadelphia;[95] also in Pittsburgh, Newark, St. Thomas, and St. Croix.

84 6th Cir. IOP 34(b)(4).
85 7th Cir. R. 34(b)(1).
86 On Mondays the court considers non-argument cases, generally sentencing appeals.
87 9th Cir. R. Court Structure and Procedures E(3); *id.* Gen. Ord. 3.5.
88 *Id.* R. Court Structure and Procedures E(7).
89 11th Cir. R. 34-3, IOP 7. This disclosure is the names of the judges for a week. When the clerk assigns cases to a specific day, the clerk advises counsel when the clerk's office may be contacted to learn the identify of panel members. *Id.*
90 *Id.* R. 34-4, IOP 3(d). A panel may decide to hear arguments Monday to Thursday.
91 D.C. Cir. Handbook of Practice and Internal Procedures, II, Preliminary Matters (8)(a).
92 28 U.S.C. § 48.
93 *Id.*
94 *Id.*
95 *Id.*

Fourth Circuit: Required by statute in Richmond and Asheville;[96] also at law schools within the circuit.[97]

Fifth Circuit: Required by statute in New Orleans, Fort Worth, Jackson;[98] also on occasion in other cities throughout the circuit including Austin, Houston, and San Antonio;[99] and in each of the states within the circuit, Louisiana, Mississippi, and Texas, at least once a year;[100] also at law schools.

Sixth Circuit: Required by statute in Cincinnati;[101] occasionally at law schools and other locations.

Seventh Circuit: Required by statute in Chicago.[102]

Eighth Circuit: Required by statute in St. Louis, Kansas City (MO), Omaha, and St. Paul.[103]

Ninth Circuit: Required by statute in San Francisco, Los Angeles (actually sitting in Pasadena), Portland, and Seattle;[104] also in Las Vegas, Honolulu, and Anchorage.[105]

Tenth Circuit: Required by statute in Denver, Wichita, and Oklahoma City;[106] also in Salt Lake City, Santa Fe, Roswell, Laramie, and several law schools.

Eleventh Circuit: Required by statute in Atlanta, Jacksonville, and Montgomery;[107] also in Miami, Tallahassee, and Tampa.

D.C. Circuit: Required by statute in the District of Columbia.[108]

Federal Circuit: Required by statute in the District of Columbia and "in any other place listed" in the statute "as the court by rule directs."[109] No local rule currently directs another place. That said, annually, the Federal Circuit hears cases outside of D.C., which has been a longstanding practice of the court, consistent with its national jurisdiction.

96 *Id.*
97 4th Cir. R. 34(c).
98 28 U.S.C. § 48.
99 5th Cir. website, "Attending Oral Arguments," www.ca5.uscourts.gov/oral-argument-information/attending-oral-arguments.
100 *Id.* R. 47.2.
101 28 U.S.C. § 48; 6th Cir R. 202(a).
102 28 U.S.C. § 48.
103 *Id.*; 8th Cir. website, "About the Court" tab, "Court Locations" link.
104 28 U.S.C. § 48.
105 9th Cir. R. Court Structure and Procedures E(4).
106 28 U.S.C. § 48.
107 *Id.*
108 *Id.*
109 *Id.*

7.6 LAW STUDENT PARTICIPATION

All circuits, except for two, have local rules permitting law student participation in oral arguments, although their terms vary slightly.[110] (The Fifth and Federal Circuits do not have such local rules, although Fifth Circuit policy is that panels have discretion to permit law student participation.)

7.7 ARGUING REMOTELY

Before the COVID-19 pandemic, some circuits permitted arguments either by telephone or video. During the pandemic, remote argument was routinely permitted and usually required. Today the circuits vary in their practices.

First Circuit: Prior to the pandemic, attorneys were not allowed to argue remotely absent emergency circumstances. (For example, during a hurricane in Puerto Rico, attorneys were allowed to call in via telephone and participate with audio only.) During the pandemic, the First Circuit held completely remote sittings where all the judges and all the attorneys were remote. Presently, if a sitting is held in the courthouse, the court does not allow attorneys to appear remotely.

Second Circuit: At an earlier time, lawyers were permitted to argue via video from courthouses equipped with appropriate facilities, but that practice ceased prior to 2007 when the court relocated to the Moynihan Courthouse at 500 Pearl Street in Manhattan. During the pandemic, arguments were held by Zoom video conferencing or teleconference at the discretion of each panel. Presently, a party who wishes to argue remotely must make a motion that establishes good cause. The presider determines the motion. Counsel or a *pro se* litigant who argues remotely must work with court staff in advance of argument to ensure that the technology functions properly.

Third Circuit: Before the pandemic, lawyers were permitted to argue from remote locations after filing a formal request. During the pandemic, the court at first conducted oral arguments by telephone only but then moved to Zoom.

Fourth Circuit: Before the pandemic, lawyers had on rare occasion participated remotely in oral arguments. During the pandemic, arguments were conducted remotely – at first teleconference arguments, then video arguments. Today, the clerk's office sends counsel a "calendaring notice" approximately six weeks prior to argument, advising counsel of the date and location of oral

[110] 1st Cir. R. 46.0(f); 2d Cir. R. 46.1(e); 3d Cir. L.A.R. 46.3; 4th Cir. R. 46(a); 6th Cir. R. 46(d); 7th Cir. R. 34(h); 8th Cir. R. 46B; 9th Cir. R. 46-4; 10th Cir. R. 46.7; 11th Cir. R. 46-11; D.C. Cir. R. 46(g).

argument, including whether the argument will be heard remotely. For cases scheduled to be argued in person, parties may file a motion for leave to argue remotely for good cause shown.

Fifth Circuit: Before the pandemic, with very rare exception, the court did not permit video or remote argument by counsel. During the pandemic, most panels conducted argument via Zoom. Post-pandemic, remote participation is at the discretion of the oral argument panel. It is generally not favored, except in the case of an emergency, such as attorney illness or travel complications.

Sixth Circuit: Before the pandemic, argument by telephone occurred occasionally. During the pandemic, arguments were conducted remotely with all participants using Zoom (though some judges did not appear by video but phoned into the Zoom platform). Today, the court may conduct oral argument by teleconference. In practice, the decision about whether to conduct an oral argument by teleconference or to permit counsel to participate rests with the presiding judge, who usually consults with the other panel members. Counsel may file a motion outlining the necessity for remote participation, but the court occasionally will order a remote argument *sua sponte*.

Seventh Circuit: Before the pandemic, oral arguments were permitted by telephone and video. During the pandemic, the court conducted both telephonic and video arguments. Today, the assigned panel may permit counsel to present oral argument telephonically or by a video-communications platform approved by the court. No later than 14 days before the argument date and after conferring with opposing counsel, a party may file a motion to present oral argument remotely. The motion shall state the reason for the request, whether the request is opposed, and identify which counsel wish to appear remotely.

Eighth Circuit: Before the pandemic, arguments were very occasionally permitted by telephone (owing to personal or weather emergencies). During the pandemic, arguments were conducted via video using Microsoft Teams. Today, parties are expected to appear in person for oral argument. Remote oral arguments are at the discretion of the court; parties may move for remote argument based on illness or sudden unavailability. Motions are not routinely granted.

Ninth Circuit: Before the pandemic, arguments were rarely conducted remotely, absent some sort of emergency of special circumstance. During the pandemic, all proceedings were conducted by video over Zoom. Beginning in January 2024, the court now requires a motion from any party who wishes to appear remotely. These motions will be granted upon a showing of hardship.

Tenth Circuit: Before the pandemic, arguments were rarely conducted remotely (by audio and video). During the pandemic, all proceedings were conducted first by telephone and then via video using Zoom. Today, requests to argue remotely must be made via motion. The court permits remote appearances when counsel shows that compelling circumstances make it impracticable to appear in person. Remote appearances continue to be rare, though they do occur more frequently than they did pre-pandemic.

Eleventh Circuit: During the pandemic, oral argument was held remotely through telephone conference call or by Zoom videoconference.[111] Today, panels are authorized to hear oral arguments by audio or video conferencing and parties may make a motion to appear remotely.

D.C. Circuit: Before the pandemic, remote argument was allowed in only the most extreme situations such as natural disasters that prevented travel. During the pandemic, arguments were first held by telephone and later by Zoom. Today, parties may file a notice with the clerk that they will participate remotely. The vast majority appear in person to present argument. Those who have participated remotely include attorneys who test positive for COVID before oral argument and attorneys arguing from locations far from D.C.

Federal Circuit: Before the pandemic, arguments were conducted via telephone on a case-by-case basis at the discretion of the panel. During the pandemic, appeals were argued remotely by telephone. Presently, the default for argument is in person, although counsel can move for leave to argue remotely in limited circumstances.

7.8 RECORDING AND POSTING ORAL ARGUMENTS

All courts of appeals post audio recordings of oral arguments on their court's website, although timing and other details vary.[112]

[111] 11th Cir. Amended Gen. Ord. 45.

[112] 1st Cir. website, "Opinion & Oral Arguments" tab, "Audio Recordings of Recent Oral Arguments" link; 2d Cir. website. "Archive of Audio Oral Arguments" link; 3d Cir. website, "Opinions & Oral Arguments" tab, "Oral Arguments Recordings Audio Only" link; 4th Cir. website, "Oral Argument" tab, "Listen to Oral Arguments" link; 5th Cir. website, "Oral Argument Information" tab, "Oral Argument Recordings" link; 6th Cir. website, "Opinions and Oral Argument" tab; 7th Cir. website, "Opinions and Oral Arguments" tab; 8th Cir. website, "Oral Arguments" link; 9th Cir. website, "Archived Audio and Video" link; 10th Cir. website, "Decisions/Oral Argument" tab; 11th Cir. website, "Opinions/Oral Arguments" tab; *id.* website, "Opinion/Oral Arguments" tab, "Oral Arguments" link, "Oral Argument Recordings" link; D.C. Cir. website, "Case Information" tab, "Oral Arguments" link; Fed. Cir. website, "Argument" tab, "Oral Argument Recordings" link.

First Circuit: The court makes audio recordings of oral arguments available at the conclusion of the day's arguments on their website.[113] Disk copies may be obtained for a fee.[114]

Second Circuit: Audio recordings of oral arguments are posted the day after the argument,[115] and disks can be purchased for a fee.

Third Circuit: The Third Circuit leaves posting of video recordings of oral arguments to the discretion of the panel,[116] after affording counsel an opportunity to object.[117] Audio recordings of oral arguments can be found on the court website, unless the panel directs otherwise.[118]

Fourth Circuit: Audio recordings of oral arguments are posted on the following business day.[119]

Fifth Circuit: Audio recordings of oral arguments are posted at the conclusion of the day's arguments,[120] and are available on a YouTube channel.[121]

Sixth Circuit: Audio recordings of oral argument are posted on the court's website, usually on the day of the arguments.[122]

Seventh Circuit: Video recording is permitted at the discretion of the panel, but the objection of one judge will normally be honored.[123] Audio recordings are posted each day after the arguments.[124]

Eighth Circuit: Audio recordings or oral arguments are posted as soon as practicable, usually the same day.[125] Arguments are also available as free podcasts from the iTunes store.[126]

Ninth Circuit: Audio and video recordings are generally posted by close of business on the day of argument, and no later than the following day.[127]

[113] 1st Cir. website, "Opinions and Oral Arguments" tab, "Sign Up for Opinions and Oral Arguments" link.

[114] *Id.* IOP VIII(D).

[115] 2d Cir. website, "Archive of Audio Oral Arguments" link, "View" or Year tab.

[116] 3d Cir. IOP 2.6.3.

[117] *Id.* IOP 2.6.2.

[118] *Id.* website, "Oral Argument Recordings," www.ca3.uscourts.gov/oral-argument-recordings; *id.* IOP 2.6.1 ("Posting of Oral Argument" on the Court's Website).

[119] 4th Cir. website, "Listen to Oral Arguments" link; *id.* IOP 34.3.

[120] 5th Cir. website, www.ca5.uscourts.gov/oral-argument-information/oral-argument-recordings.

[121] Official YouTube channel for the United States Court of Appeals for the Fifth Circuit, www.youtube.com/channel/UCzgzKXYsW9dC45Mqzu2yBxQ.

[122] 6th Cir. website, www.ca6.uscourts.gov/audio-files-completed-arguments.

[123] 7th Cir. OP 11(a)(3). Any video recording will show the judges and counsel at the podium but no others. *Id.* OP 11(a)(4).

[124] 7th Cir. website, http://media.ca7.uscourts.gov/oralArguments/oar.jsp.

[125] 8th Cir. IOP III (L)(5); 8th Cir. website www.ca8.uscourts.gov/oral-arguments.

[126] *Id.* IOP III (L)(5).

[127] 9th Cir. Local Rules, Court Structure and Procedures E(7); *id.* website www.ca9.uscourts.gov/media/.

Tenth Circuit: Audio recordings of oral arguments are posted to the Tenth Circuit website, unless the court directs otherwise, almost always the day of the hearing but always within 48 hours.[128]

Eleventh Circuit: Audio recordings of oral arguments are posted as soon as practicable,[129] and copies of the court's audio recordings of oral arguments are available for purchase on CD.[130]

D.C. Circuit: Audio recordings of oral arguments are posted by 2 p.m. on the day of the argument.[131]

Federal Circuit: Audio recordings are made available on the court's website.[132]

7.9 PHOTOGRAPHING AND BROADCASTING ORAL ARGUMENTS

In 1996, the U.S. Judicial Conference authorized each court of appeals to "decide for itself whether to permit the taking of photographs and radio and television coverage of appellate arguments."[133] Only the Second and Ninth Circuits currently permit such coverage.[134]

In the Second Circuit, guidelines govern "camera coverage," defined to mean using a still camera, sound recording equipment, or a television camera.[135] Camera coverage of all proceedings is permitted, except for criminal matters[136] and *pro se* cases.[137] Camera coverage is permitted by the news media, but if coverage is sought by more than one person or entity, a pool system must be used – one operator for still photographs and one for radio and television.[138] Additional camera coverage may be permitted by educational

[128] 10th Cir. R. 34.1(E)(1); *id.* website www.ca10.uscourts.gov/oralargument/search.

[129] 11th Cir. R. 34, IOP 17; *id.* website www.ca11.uscourts.gov/oral-argument-recordings-page.

[130] *Id.* R. 34, IOP 16.

[131] D.C. Cir. website, "Case Information" tab, "Oral Arguments" link, "Policy Regarding Live Audio Streaming of Arguments" link, www.cadc.uscourts.gov/internet/home.nsf/Content/Announcement+-+November+8%2C+2017+-+Policy+Regarding+Live+Audio+Streaming+of+Arguments.

[132] Fed. Cir. website, "Oral Argument" tab, "Listen to Oral Arguments" link, www.cafc.uscourts.gov/home/oral-argument/listen-to-oral-arguments/.

[133] Report of the Proceedings of the Judicial Conference of the United States 17 (March 12, 1996).

[134] 2d Cir. IOP App'x B; 9th Cir. website, "Cameras and Electronic Devices Policy" link.

[135] 2d Cir. IOP App'x B(1).

[136] Rule 53 of the Federal Rules of Criminal Procedure, applicable to all federal courts, Fed. R. Crim. P. 1, prohibits photographing and broadcasting judicial proceedings.

[137] 2d Cir. IOP App'x B(3).

[138] *Id.* IOP App'x B(4).

institutions.[139] Only one still camera and two television cameras are permitted in the courtroom; they must be at fixed locations, and they must be capable of silent operation or enclosed in a sound-muffling device.[140] A request for permission to provide camera coverage is made to the panel presider. Each panel retains discretion to prohibit coverage of any proceeding and will normally do so at the request of one panel member.[141]

The Ninth Circuit notes that it is "one of two federal appellate courts to regularly allow still and video cameras and audio recorders in the courtroom for purposes of reporting on the proceeding."[142] Its "Cameras and Electronic Devises Policy" includes that anyone may bring cameras into the courthouse, and photography or audio / video recording may be conducted with advance permission.[143]

In the First Circuit, cameras (and related electronic devices, including smart phones) are not allowed in the courtrooms.

In the Third Circuit, cameras and cell phones are not allowed in the courtrooms.

In the Fourth Circuit, electronic devices must not be used to take photographs or for audio or video recording. Devices that serve only as cameras or audio or video recorders are prohibited in the courthouse and annex absent express authorization by the court.

The Fifth Circuit prohibits cameras and sound recording devices without court approval.[144]

In the Sixth Circuit, photographs and video/audio recordings are not permitted, though counsel are permitted to use personally owned electronic devices in support of the proceedings before the court.

The Seventh Circuit prohibits, without court permission, the taking of photographs, radio or television broadcasting from the courtroom or any place on the 27th floor or adjacent judges' chambers or corridors or the 26th floor of the federal courthouse in Chicago.[145]

In the Eighth Circuit, camera and recording devices may not be used by counsel or spectators.

In the Tenth Circuit, all devices that can potentially be used for photography, recording, or broadcasting must be inactive or switched off

139 *Id.* IOP App'x B(5).
140 *Id.* IOP App'x B(8).
141 *Id.* IOP App'x B(7).
142 9th Cir. website, "Court Coverage Tutorial, General Information," www.ca9.uscourts.gov/news-media/media-education-1/.
143 *Id.* website, "Cameras and Electronic Devices Policy" link.
144 5th Cir. R. 34.7.
145 7th Cir. R. 55.

while in attendance at a court proceeding. No cameras (without other functionality) will be allowed inside the courthouse under any circumstances. Photography and recorded interviews are permitted only outside the courthouse.

In the Eleventh Circuit, the general policy is that visitors may not bring portable electronic devices, which include still and video cameras, into court facilities.

In the D.C. Circuit, devices can be brought into the courtroom, but using them to record or broadcast is prohibited.

In the Federal Circuit, electronic devices can enter the courtroom but may not be used while court is in session, with the exception of counsel during argument while seated at counsel table – although they may not record or transmit audio or video.

7.10 STREAMING ORAL ARGUMENTS

The Second, Third, Fourth, Sixth, Seventh, Ninth, Tenth, Eleventh, D.C., and Federal Circuits provide live streaming of oral arguments.[146]

[146] 2d Cir. website, "Livestream Audio of Oral Arguments" link; 3d Cir. website, "Opinions & Oral Argument" tab, "Oral Argument Audio Live Stream" link; 4th Cir. website, "Oral Argument" tab, "Remote Oral Arguments" link, "Audio Live Stream" instruction; 6th Cir. website, "Live Argument link," www.ca6.uscourts.gov/live-arguments; 7th Cir. website, "Opinions-Oral Arguments" tab, "Oral Arguments – Streaming Arguments (YouTube channel)" link; 9th Cir. website, "Live Video Streaming of Oral Arguments" link; 10th Cir. YouTube site, www.youtube.com/c/theuscourtofappealsforthe10thcircuit; 11th Cir. website, "Live Streaming of Oral Arguments" link, www.ca11.uscourts.gov/live-streaming-oral-arguments; D.C. Cir. website, "Case Information" tab, "Oral Arguments" link, "Policy Regarding Live Audio Streaming of Oral Arguments" link; Fed. Cir. website, "Listen to Oral Arguments" link, www.cafc.uscourts.gov/home/oral-argument/listen-to-oral-arguments/.

8

Precedential Opinions

This chapter starts with the important distinction between precedential and non-precedential opinions and then considers the courts of appeals' practices concerning precedential opinions. Non-precedential opinions are considered in Chapter 9.

8.1 PRECEDENTIAL VERSUS NON-PRECEDENTIAL OPINIONS

All courts of appeals make a basic distinction between opinions that are "precedential" and those that are "non-precedential." Precedential opinions are those that establish the law of the circuit and that subsequent panels are bound to follow. (Non-precedential opinions tend to be shorter dispositions that can be cited, per a Federal Rule of Appellate Procedure,[1] but do not establish any new law.)

In an earlier day, the distinction was reflected by the fact that precedential opinions were published by the West Publishing Company (West) and appeared in West's *Federal Reporter* series (current series cited "__ F. 4th __") – the hundreds of beige-colored books that have lined the shelves of judges and lawyers for decades. West did not originally publish non-precedential opinions. However, some non-precedential decisions were printed in other publications, usually loose-leaf volumes devoted to particular fields of law, such as *United States Patents Quarterly* or *Trade Regulation Reporter*. The absence of non-precedential opinions from West's *Federal Reporter* volumes gave rise to the practice of calling them "unpublished opinions," technically a misnomer, but a designation widely used throughout the judiciary, the legal profession, and the academy.

[1] Fed. R. App. P. 32.1.

The situation changed on September 1, 2001, when West began publishing a new series of law books called the Federal Appendix (cited "__ F. App'x __"), and included those non-precedential decisions that West thought merited publication in a standard national series, regardless of subject matter. West collected the text of those non-precedential decisions from courts' websites. If an appeal or petition for review is disposed of with the one word "affirmed" or "denied," West identifies the disposition in the Federal Reporter series with the case name followed by "(table)."[2]

Once West began to publish non-precedential opinions in the Federal Appendix series, it made no sense to continue calling the non-precedential opinions "unpublished." Nevertheless, the practice of calling them "unpublished" was so ingrained in federal courts that some kept the label,[3] and used it in local rules and internal operating procedures (IOPs) during the 20-year life of the Federal Appendix series.[4] Even some of the statistical tables compiled annually by the Administrative Office of the U.S. Courts (AO) still have categories of opinions labeled "unpublished" when reporting data for years in which the Federal Appendix published them.[5]

West discontinued the Federal Appendix series in 2021. Opinions of courts of appeals that are non-precedential are available online, located by a Westlaw citation.[6]

8.2 EFFECT OF PRECEDENTIAL OPINIONS ON SUBSEQUENT PANELS

The primary significance of the distinction between precedential and non-precedential opinions is that the courts of appeals regard only precedential opinions as binding on subsequent panels, unless abrogated by an en banc

2 This use of "table" in the Federal Reporter is not always understood. A Sixth Circuit IOP states, "Decisions not designated for publication are listed in table form in the Federal Reporter." 6th Cir. IOP 32.1(b)(3). In fact, unless such decisions say only "affirmed" or "denied," they were published in the Federal Appendix while that series existed.

3 *See, e.g.*, *Krupski v. Costa Crociere S.p.A.*, 560 U.S. 538, 546 (2010) (citing to the opinion of the court of appeals published in the Federal Appendix).

4 *See, e.g.*, 1st Cir R. 32.1.0(a) ("unpublished judicial opinion[s]").

5 *See, e.g.*, Administrative Office of the U.S. Courts (AO), "Statistics & Reports" tab, Data Tables, Table B-12 (listing for each circuit, within the broad category of "Written Opinion or Order," three subcategories labeled "Signed," "Reasoned, Unsigned," and "Unsigned, Without Comment," and subdividing each of these three subcategories into "Published" and "Unpublished."

6 However, Westlaw and other online databases do not collect all opinions of the courts of appeals because of some courts' incomplete reporting systems. *See* Merritt E. McAlister, *Missing Decision*, 169 U. PENN L. REV. 1101 (2021).

decision. In many of the circuits, this principle is expressed in a local rule.[7] In all but one circuit, the principle is expressed in caselaw.[8] The Seventh Circuit, however, has stated that "we are cognizant of the fact that we are not absolutely bound by [prior precedential decisions], and must give fair consideration to any *substantial* argument that a litigant makes for overruling a previous decision."[9]

8.3 DETERMINING WHETHER OPINIONS ARE PRECEDENTIAL

In the First, Second, Fifth, Sixth, and Ninth Circuits, any member of a panel may require an opinion to be published as a precedential opinion.[10] In the Third, Eighth, Eleventh, and Federal Circuits, a majority of the panel determines whether a decision should be published as a precedential opinion.[11] In

7 *See, e.g.*, 3d Cir. IOP 9.1 ("It is the tradition of this court that the holding of a panel in a precedential opinion is binding on subsequent panels. Thus, no subsequent panel overrules the holding in a precedential opinion of a previous panel."); 6th Cir. R. 32.1(b) ("Published panel opinions are binding on later panels. A published opinion is overruled only by the court en banc."); 7th Cir. R. 32.1(b) ("Opinions, which may be signed or per curiam, are released in printed form, are published in the Federal Reporter, and constitute the law of the circuit."); 9th Cir. R. 36-3(a) ("Unpublished dispositions and orders of this Court are not precedent, except when relevant under the doctrine of law of the case or rules of claim preclusion or issue preclusion"); 10th Cir. R. 32.1(A) ("Unpublished decisions are not precedential"); 11th Cir. R. 36-2 ("Unpublished opinions are not considered binding precedent, but they may be cited as persuasive authority").

8 See, *e.g.*, *United States v. Wurie*, 867 F.3d 28, 34 (1st Cir. 2017); *Lotes Co. v. Hon Hai Precision Industry Co.*, 753 F.3d 395, 405 (2d Cir. 2014); *In re Lemington Home for the Aged*, 659 F.3d 282, 294 n.6 (3d Cir. 2011); *Hoffman v. Hunt*, 126 F.3d 575, 584 (4th Cir. 1997); *Legendre v. Huntington Ingalls, Inc.*, 885 F.3d 398, 403 (5th Cir. 2018); *United States v. Lee*, 793 F.3d 680, 684 (6th Cir. 2015); *United States v. Wilson*, 315 F.3d 972, 973–74 (8th Cir. 2003); *State Bar v. Findley*, 593 F.3d 1048, 1050 (9th Cir. 2010); *Bates v. Department of Corrections*, 81 F.3d 1008, 1011 (10th Cir. 1996); *United States v. Gillis*, 938 F.3d 1181, 1198 (11th Cir. 2019); *New York-New York, LLC v. NLRB*, 676 F.3d 193, 194–95 (D.C. Cir. 2012); *Newell Co. v. Kenney Manufacturing Co.*, 864 F.2d 757, 765 (Fed. Cir. 1988).

9 *United States v. Reyes-Hernandez*, 624 F.3d 405, 412 (7th Cir. 2010) (internal citation and quotation marks omitted) (emphasis in original).

10 1st Cir. R. 36.0(b)(2)(B) (stating that with respect to cases decided by a unanimous panel with a single opinion, if any judge is of the view that the opinion should be published, "it must be"); 2d Cir. IOP 32.1.1(a); 5th Cir. R. 47.5.2 (the rule goes on to note that "[i]f any judge of the court or any party so requests the panel will reconsider its decision not to publish an opinion"); 6th Cir. IOP 32.1(b)(2) (the rule goes on to state that the court may also publish "on motion"); 9th Cir. Gen. Ord. 4.3 (the panel "should" publish if at least one member of the panel determines that a published decision is necessary).

11 3d Cir. IOP 5.1 (the rule states that "[a] majority of the panel determines whether an opinion is designated as precedential or not precedential, unless a majority of the active judges of the court decides otherwise."); 8th Cir. IOP IV(B) ("The panel determines whether the opinion in the case is to be published or unpublished"); 11th Cir. R. 36-2, IOP (6) ("An opinion shall

the Tenth Circuit, an opinion is "ordinarily" designated for "publication" as a precedential opinion if the opinion being reviewed from a district court, an administrative agency, or the Tax Court has been published.[12]

In the Seventh Circuit, any person may request by motion that an unpublished opinion (or "order") be reissued as a published opinion.[13]

In the Second Circuit, by IOP, a decision must be unanimous for a summary order to issue; if the decision includes a dissent, the majority writing must be converted to an opinion.[14] In the Federal Circuit, a dissenting judge may require the entire opinion to be precedential.[15]

8.4 CRITERIA FOR PRECEDENTIAL OPINIONS

Some circuits have detailed criteria for determining when an opinion is published as precedential. The criteria of the Fifth Circuit are as follows:

> An opinion is published if it: (a) Establishes a new rule of law, alters, or modifies an existing rule of law, or calls attention to an existing rule of law that appears to have been generally overlooked; (b) Applies an established rule of law to facts significantly different from those in previous published opinions applying the rule; (c) Explains, criticizes, or reviews the history of existing decisional or enacted law; (d) Creates or resolves a conflict of authority either within the circuit or between this circuit and another; (e) Concerns or discusses a factual or legal issue of significant public interest; or (f) Is rendered in a case that has been reviewed previously and its merits addressed by an opinion of the United States Supreme Court.[16]

Additionally, an opinion may be published if it is "accompanied by a concurring or dissenting opinion; or reverses the decision below or affirms it upon different grounds."[17]

The Sixth Circuit has similar criteria for publication of precedential opinions:

be unpublished unless a majority of the panel decides to publish it"); Fed. Cir. IOP 10(6) ("An election to issue a precedential opinion shall be by a majority of the panel, except that, when the decision includes a dissenting opinion, the dissenting judge may elect to have the entire opinion issued as precedential notwithstanding the majority's vote").

[12] 10th Cir. R. 36.2.

[13] 7th Cir. R. 32.1(c).

[14] 2d Cir. IOP 32.1.1 (though in extremely rare circumstances, a very short dissent might accompany a summary order).

[15] Fed. Cir. IOP 10(6).

[16] 5th Cir. R. 47.5.1.

[17] *Id.* R. 47.5.2.

> When determining whether a decision will be published in the Federal Reporter, panels consider whether the decision: (A) Establishes a new rule of law, modifies an existing rule of law, or applies an established rule to a novel factual situation; (B) Creates or resolves a conflict of authority within this circuit or between this circuit and another; (C) Discusses a legal or factual issue of continuing public interest; (D) Is accompanied by a concurring or dissenting opinion; (E) Reverses the decision below, unless: (i) the reversal was because of an intervening change in law or fact; or (ii) the reversal is a remand to the lower court or agency – without further comment – of a case reversed or remanded by the United States Supreme Court; (F) Addresses a published lower court or agency decision; or (G) Has been reviewed by the United States Supreme Court.[18]

The Ninth Circuit has slightly different criteria for published opinions: if the disposition –

> (a) Establishes, alters, modifies or clarifies a rule of federal law, or (b) Calls attention to a rule of law that appears to have been generally overlooked, or (c) Criticizes existing law, or (d) Involves a legal or factual issue of unique interest or substantial public importance, or (e) Is a disposition of a case in which there is a published opinion by a lower court or administrative agency, unless the panel determines that publication is unnecessary for clarifying the panel's disposition of the case, or (f) Is a disposition of a case following a reversal or remand by the United States Supreme Court, or (g) Is accompanied by a separate concurring or dissenting expression, and the author of such separate expression requests publication of the disposition of the Court and the separate expression.[19]

In the D.C. Circuit, several similar criteria are provided for determining when an opinion should be "published" as precedential, plus "a case of first impression," "it criticizes or questions existing law," or "it creates a conflict with another circuit."[20]

8.5 VOTING AND ASSIGNING AUTHORSHIP OF OPINIONS

In all circuits, the panel meets after oral argument to discuss the day's cases. Usually, at least a tentative vote is taken as to (1) the disposition of the appeal, (2) whether the appeal will be decided in a precedential opinion or in whatever form of non-precedential opinion the circuit uses, unless that decision

[18] 6th Cir. IOP 32.1(b)(1).
[19] 9th Cir. R. 36-2.
[20] D.C. Cir. R. 36(c)(2)(A), (D), (E).

has previously been made in a screening process (*see* Chapter 3), and (3) the writing assignment for precedential opinions. In the Third, Ninth, and Federal Circuits, local provisions specify that judges express a tentative view in reverse order of seniority,[21] and Judge Edwards's survey reported that this is true in four other circuits (not identified) and generally true in two others (also not identified).[22]

In the Second Circuit, until around 1990, the panel did not vote right after the argument. Instead, the three judges returned to their chambers and prepared two- or three-page voting memos, stating each judge's vote and reasoning.[23] The memos were sent to the other two judges within a day or two of the argument, and each judge refrained from reading the other judges' memos until sending one out. The panel then met at the end of the week. The availability of the three voting memos narrowed the discussion and facilitated an efficient conference. As volume increased, however, the use of voting memos declined and has largely disappeared. Today, the three judges who have heard arguments on consecutive days confer to decide the cases (or agree to exchange voting memos to facilitate a decision), and the writing assignments are made by the presiding judge, with senior judges usually offered a choice of what to write.

In nearly all circuits, the presider of the panel has authority to make the writing assignment if in the majority, and the Fifth, Sixth, and Ninth Circuits so provide in local rule or IOP.[24] In the Fourth Circuit, the panel presider recommends an authoring judge to the chief judge, who makes the final assignment. In the Sixth Circuit, the presiding judge makes a recommendation for writing assignments, but determination of the author varies from panel to panel based upon discussions in the voting conference.

In the Federal Circuit, for cases submitted on the briefs, the presiding judge may assign the writing responsibility to a panel member before the voting conference.[25]

Finally, there are special customs in some circuits regarding the assignment of opinions to senior judges. As noted previously, in the Second Circuit, by custom, when a panel meets after oral argument to discuss and tentatively vote

[21] 3d Cir. IOP 4.1; 9th Cir. R. Court Structure and Procedures E(8); Fed. Cir. IOP 8(1).

[22] Harry T. Edwards, *Collegial Decision Making in the US Courts of Appeals*, lecture presented at All Souls College, Oxford University 41 (question 3) (July 2017).

[23] *See* Wilfred Feinberg, *Unique Customs and Practices of the Second Circuit*, 14 HOFSTRA L. REV. 297, 298–303 (1986).

[24] 5th Cir. IOP Oral Argument (Case Conferences and Designation of Writing Judge); 6th Cir. IOP 32.1(a)(1); 9th Cir. R. Court Structure and Procedures E(8).

[25] Fed. Cir. IOP 8(4).

on the day's cases, the presiding judge usually asks a senior judge whether there is an opinion that the judge prefers to write or prefers not to write. The senior judge's choice is generally honored.

8.6 CONTENT OF OPINIONS

Some courts of appeals have rules concerning the content of their opinions – both what the opinions should include and general principles about how they should be fashioned. In the Third Circuit, "The face of an opinion states whether it is precedential or not precedential."[26] Also in the Third Circuit, a judgment order affirming a district court judgment in a criminal appeal includes a statement of the issues raised by the appellant and considered by the panel.[27]

The Eleventh Circuit has the following policy on opinions:

> The unlimited proliferation of published opinions is undesirable because it tends to impair the development of the cohesive body of law. To meet this serious problem it is declared to be the basic policy of this court to exercise imaginative and innovative resourcefulness in fashioning new methods to increase judicial efficiency and reduce the volume of published opinions. Judges of this court will exercise appropriate discipline to reduce the length of opinions by the use of those techniques which result in brevity without sacrifice of quality.[28]

The Federal Circuit has a policy that "all opinions and orders shall be as short and as limited to the dispositive issue as the nature of the cases or motions will allow."[29]

Separately, the Federal Circuit has a provision on decretal language, and distinguishes between "vacating" and "reversing": The court will vacate all or part of a judgment or order when it is being eliminated but not replaced with a contrary judgment or order of the court, and reverse when it is being replaced with a contrary judgment or order of the court.[30] Other circuits follow this practice by custom, although not always uniformly.[31]

The Federal Circuit has a unique policy stating that, in order to show respect for the tribunals whose judgments are being reviewed, references

[26] 3d Cir. IOP 5.1.
[27] *Id.* IOP 6.3.1.
[28] 11th Cir. R. 36, IOP(5).
[29] Fed. Cir. IOP 9(4).
[30] *Id.* IOP 9(9).
[31] *See generally* Jon O. Newman, *Decretal Language: Last Words of an Appellate Opinion*, 7 Brook. L. Rev. (Spring 2005).

should not be made to "the court below," "the lower court," or "the judge below," but should say "the district court," "the trial court," or "the district judge."[32]

The Federal Circuit does not say in precedential opinions that the court affirms on the basis of a trial court's opinion,[33] but the court may accept all or a part of a trial court's published opinion as its own opinion.[34]

8.7 PANEL PRIORITY TO ISSUE OPINIONS

In the Second Circuit, soon after a panel hears arguments, the presider sends to all judges a one- or two-paragraph summary of the significant issues in every appeal for which a precedential opinion will be prepared, and the court maintains a searchable "significant issues" database of those summaries; the panel that was first scheduled to hear argument or take an appeal on submission has priority, and the other panels with the same issue await the first panel's disposition.

In the Ninth Circuit, when pending cases raise the same legal issue, the first panel to whom the issue is submitted has priority.[35] Specifically, the panel with the earliest scheduled oral argument date has priority.[36] If two or more arguments are scheduled for the same day, the panel with the case with the earliest notice of appeal has priority.[37] Any dispute as to priority is resolved by the chief judge, but within seven days of that decision, any judge of the court may request review of that decision, and priority will be determined by a majority of the nonrecused active judges at the next scheduled court meeting.[38]

Normally, other panels will enter an order vacating submissions and advise counsel of the other pending case when "it appears that the first panel's decision is likely to be dispositive of the issue."[39] When the author of a proposed opinion knows that the disposition may decide a question pending before one or more other panels, the proposed opinion is circulated to all members of those panels, who have 14 days to respond.[40]

32 Fed. Cir. IOP 11(9).
33 *Id.* IOP 9(10)(a).
34 *Id.* IOP 9(10)(b).
35 9th Cir. R. 34-1 to 34-3, Cir. Adv. Comm. N. 1.
36 *Id.* Gen. Ord. 4.1(a).
37 *Id.*
38 *Id.*
39 *Id.* R. 34-1 to 34-3, Cir. Adv. Comm. N. 1.
40 *Id.* Gen. Ord. 4.1(a).

In the D.C. Circuit, a panel "occasionally" defers decision pending decision of another case in the circuit or "in another tribunal."[41]

8.8 CIRCULATION OF OPINIONS BEFORE FILING

Some circuits have provisions for circulating precedential opinions to all judges before filing. The Third, Fourth, Sixth, D.C., and Federal Circuits circulate proposed precedential opinions to all judges.[42]

The Third Circuit has an elaborate provision concerning circulation of draft opinions, which further states that a unanimous "not precedential" opinion will not be circulated to non-panel judges, but will be circulated to all judges if it contains a dissent.[43] In the Ninth Circuit, all judges receive a daily summary of soon to be filed opinions.

In the Eleventh Circuit, proposed opinions are normally not circulated to other judges, but a panel or one member may circulate a proposed opinion to the court.[44]

8.9 OPINIONS CONTEMPLATING RETURN AFTER REMAND

Three circuits have explicit provisions or practices when the case is remanded with a likelihood that it will return after the district court carries out a prescribed task, such as making a finding of fact.

In the Second Circuit, the court cites its opinion in *United States v. Jacobson*,[45] which remanded to a district court for explanation of the reasons for a sentence.[46]

In the Third Circuit, a panel opinion may hold an appeal in abeyance and remand, for example, to correct the record pursuant to Federal Rule of Appellate Procedure (FRAP) 10(e).[47] After a remand, a subsequent appeal is

[41] D.C. Cir. IOP XII (D).

[42] 3d Cir. IOP 5.5.4; 4th Cir. IOP 36.2; 6th Cir. IOP 32.1(a)(3); D.C. Cir. IOP XII(C); Fed. Cir. IOP 10(5).

[43] "Drafts of unanimous not precedential opinions do not circulate to non-panel judges. Drafts of not precedential opinions that contain a dissent circulate to non-panel judges. Drafts of not precedential opinions that contain a concurrence circulate to non-panel judges if a member of the panel requests that the opinion be circulated to all judges. Drafts of precedential opinions and not precedential opinions that are not unanimous are circulated to all active judges of the court after the draft opinion has been approved by all three panel members, concurring or dissenting opinions have been transmitted, or all members of the panel have had the time … to write separate opinions." 3d Cir. IOP 5.5.4.

[44] 11th Cir. R. 36, IOP(4).

[45] 15 F.3d 19 (2d Cir. 1994).

[46] *Id.* at 21.

[47] 3d Cir. IOP 7.1.

assigned to a new panel in the regular course unless the panel has directed assignment to it.[48]

In the Sixth Circuit, when a panel remands and "retains" jurisdiction, the case is assigned to the panel that ordered the retention of jurisdiction, unless the chief judge orders the case assigned to another panel.[49]

8.10 CORRECTING MISTAKES

In the Second Circuit, minor changes in an opinion can be made by filing an "errata sheet."

In the Ninth Circuit, when a district judge, magistrate judge, or bankruptcy judge is aware of a mistake in a disposition by the court of appeals involving an appeal from that judge's decision and believes that the parties might not point out the mistake – and believes "that justice will be disserved if the mistake is not corrected" – the judge may bring the mistake to the clerk of the court of appeals in a letter, which is distributed to the panel.[50]

8.11 POSTING OPINIONS ON A COURT'S WEBSITE

In 2016, Congress required all federal agencies, including courts, to "make available for public inspection in an electronic format – (A) final opinions, including concurring and dissenting opinions, as well as orders, made in the adjudication of cases."[51] Implementing this requirement, all circuits post opinions on their websites, located by opening variously worded tabs and links. Opinions generally are posted the day they are filed or the day after. Courts vary as to the links on their websites for locating opinions and as to how far back opinions are posted.

First Circuit: "Opinions & Oral Arguments" tab, then link to "Opinion Search." Opinions are searched by case number or short title. Search discloses links to opinions and docket sheets.

Second Circuit: "Decisions" tab, then links to "Recent Opinions" and "Recent Summary Orders." A search discloses links to docket numbers and shows the posting date. "Opinions" and "Summary Orders" are available since April 1, 2007. Receipt of all opinions can be obtained by using the Court's RSS link at the bottom of the court's website.

48 *Id.* IOP 7.2.
49 6th Cir. IOP 34(b)(3).
50 9th Cir. Gen. Ord. 12.10(a).
51 5 U.S.C. § 552(a)(2)(A).

Third Circuit: "Opinions & Oral Arguments" tab, then links to "Precedential Decisions Filed Today," "Recent Precedential Opinions," "Not Precedential Decisions Filed Today," "Recent Not Precedential Decisions," and "Villanova Opinion Archives" (which, "[a]s a recognized backup archive" for the court, "maintains digital copies of all opinions filed by the Court since May of 1994").

Fourth Circuit: "Opinions" tab, then links to "Search Opinions," "Daily Opinions," "Recent Opinions," "En Banc Cases," and "Pacer Orders/ Judgments & Opinions Search." Opinions from 1996 to date are returned through a text search on the "Search Opinions" page. The "Pacer Orders/ Judgments & Opinions Search" page returns opinions by dates since 2008. "Opinions" tab also includes a link to "U.S. Courts Opinions (govinfo)," which has opinions of all federal courts since 2008.

Fifth Circuit: "Opinions/Orders" link on the court's website leads to a way to search opinions (both published and unpublished) released from 1992 to the present. There is separately an RSS link, which enables one to link to RSS feeds, categorized by "Summary" or "Detail[ed]" "Published Opinions Only" or "All Opinions." Finally, the website has a "Latest Opinions" page that is updated regularly.

Sixth Circuit: "Opinions and Oral Argument" tab, then "Opinions" link, then links to "Today's Opinions," "Opinions Search," "Opinions Date Search," and "Opinions Last 10 Days." Published opinions are available since January 1, 2000; unpublished opinions are available since October 1, 2004. There is also a link to "National Opinions Search."

Seventh Circuit: "Opinions-Oral Arguments" tab, then "Opinions and Nonprecedential Dispositive Orders" link, searchable by date, author, or case name.

Eighth Circuit: "Opinions" tab, then links to "Today's Opinions," "Case Number," "Release Date," "Party Name," "Full Text Opinion Search," "Daily Descriptions" (brief summaries for each day's opinions), "Month/ Year," "Authoring Judge."

Ninth Circuit: "Opinions" link, then links to "Published" and "Unpublished," links for both by case name; link to "Status of En Banc Cases"; link to "RSS Feeds."

Tenth Circuit: "Decisions/Oral Arguments" tab, then links to "Today's Decisions" and "Search Decisions."

Eleventh Circuit: "Opinions/Oral Arguments" tab, then link to "Published Opinions," which has links to "Published Opinions Issued Today," "Published Opinion Logs by Case Name," "Search Published Opinions," and "Published Opinions RSS Feed,"; link to "Unpublished Opinions," which has links to "Unpublished Opinions Issued Today," "Unpublished Opinion Logs by Case Name," and "Search Unpublished Opinions."

D.C. Circuit: "Case Information" tab, "Opinion Locator" link, which has links to "Today," "This Week," "Last Week," "This Month," "Last Month," "Most Recent," and "Browse by Date."

Federal Circuit: "Case Information" tab, "Opinions & Orders" link, which has links to opinions back to October 1, 2004.

9

Non-Precedential Opinions

This chapter considers the courts of appeals' practices concerning those opinions that are not precedential. Unless a court has decided that an opinion is precedential (or "published"), as discussed in Chapter 8, the opinion is non-precedential.

9.1 CRITERIA FOR NON-PRECEDENTIAL OPINIONS

Some circuits specify criteria for a non-precedential opinion.

In the Second Circuit, a non-precedential "summary order" may be used when the decision is unanimous and "each judge believes that no jurisprudential purpose is served" by a precedential opinion.[1] In the Third Circuit, a "not precedential opinion" is used if it "appears to have value only to the trial court or the parties,"[2] even if the decision is not unanimous, and a "judgment order" is used where a written opinion "will have no precedential or institutional value," and the decision is unanimous.[3]

9.2 LABELING NON-PRECEDENTIAL OPINIONS

The courts of appeals use various labels for a non-precedential opinion in their local rules and internal operating procedures (IOPs). In the First, Fifth, Sixth, Eighth, and Eleventh Circuits, such an opinion is called an "unpublished opinion."[4] In the Second Circuit, it is called a "summary order";[5] in

1 2d Cir. IOP 32.1.1(a).
2 3d Cir. IOP 5.3.
3 *Id.* IOP 6.2.1.
4 1st Cir. R. 32.1.0(a); 5th Cir. R. 28.7; 6th Cir. R. 32.1; 8th Cir. R. 32.1A; 11th Cir. R. 36-2.
5 2d Cir. R. 32.1.1.

the Third Circuit, a "not precedential opinion"[6] or a "judgment order";[7] in the Fourth Circuit, an "unpublished opinion"[8] (or a "summary opinion" in IOPs);[9] in the Seventh Circuit, an "order" and labeled a "nonprecedential disposition";[10] in the Ninth Circuit, a "memorandum,"[11] "order,"[12] or "memorandum disposition";[13] in the Tenth Circuit, an "order and judgment";[14] in the D.C. Circuit, an "unpublished disposition"[15] or "unpublished order or judgment";[16] and in the Federal Circuit, a "nonprecedential disposition"[17] or "nonprecedential opinion or order."[18]

Because many circuits refer to non-precedential opinions as "unpublished," we will retain the words "published" and "unpublished" if their local rules and IOPs use these terms, with the understanding that "published" means "precedential" and "unpublished" means "non-precedential."

9.3 CONTENT OF NON-PRECEDENTIAL OPINIONS

In the Second Circuit, an unsigned "summary order" bears an elaborate legend set out in the margin,[19] and, to keep the order reasonably brief, often includes the following statement in the text: "We assume the parties' familiarity with the underlying facts, the procedural history of the case, and the issues on appeal."[20] In the Fourth Circuit, a "summary opinion" does not discuss

6 3d Cir. IOP 5.3.
7 *Id.* IOP 6.
8 4th Cir. R. 36(b).
9 *Id.* IOP 36.3.
10 7th Cir. R. 32.1(b).
11 9th Cir. R. 36-1.
12 *Id.*
13 *Id.* Gen. Ord. 4.3.a.
14 10th Cir. R. 35.2; *id.* R. 36.1.
15 D.C. Cir. R. 32.1(b)(1).
16 *Id.*
17 Fed. Cir. R. 32.1(a).
18 *Id.* R. 32.1.(b).
19 RULINGS BY SUMMARY ORDER DO NOT HAVE PRECEDENTIAL EFFECT. CITATION TO A SUMMARY ORDER FILED ON OR AFTER JANUARY 1, 2007, IS PERMITTED AND IS GOVERNED BY FEDERAL RULE OF APPELLATE PROCEDURE 32.1 AND THIS COURT'S LOCAL RULE 32.1.1. WHEN CITING A SUMMARY ORDER IN A DOCUMENT FILED WITH THIS COURT, A PARTY MUST CITE EITHER THE FEDERAL APPENDIX OR AN ELECTRONIC DATABASE (WITH THE NOTATION "SUMMARY ORDER"). A PARTY CITING TO A SUMMARY ORDER MUST SERVE A COPY OF IT ON ANY PARTY NOT REPRESENTED BY COUNSEL. 2d Cir. IOP 32.1.1(b).
20 *E.g.*, *Hund v. Bradley*, 845 F. App'x 78, 79 (2d Cir. 2021).

the facts or elaborate on the court's reasoning.[21] In the Seventh Circuit, every "order," that is, non-precedential decision, bears the legend "Nonprecedential disposition. To be cited only in accordance with Fed. R. App. P. 32.1."[22] In the Ninth Circuit, a memorandum disposition contains the notation, "This disposition is not appropriate for publication and is not precedent except as provided by Ninth Circuit Rule 36-3"[23] Also in the Ninth Circuit, a "memorandum" or "order" does not identify the author and is not designated "Per Curiam."[24]

9.4 PUBLISHING NON-PRECEDENTIAL OPINIONS

In the Eleventh Circuit, at any time before the mandate issues, a panel may, by unanimous vote, decide to publish a previously "unpublished" opinion.[25]

Sometimes a party, usually the winning party, requests a court of appeals to publish a non-precedential opinion to have it available as the law of the circuit. U.S. Attorneys' offices and government administrative agencies occasionally make such a motion.

In the First Circuit, any party or interested person may apply for good cause shown for publication of an "unpublished" opinion.[26] In the Seventh Circuit, any person, may, by motion, request that an "unpublished" order be reissued as an opinion.[27] In the Ninth Circuit, publication of any "unpublished" disposition may be requested by letter to the clerk, withing 60 days of the issuance of the court's disposition.[28] In the D.C. Circuit, any person may, within 30 days after judgment, request publication of an unpublished opinion (though such motions are not favored and will be granted only for compelling reasons).[29] In the Federal Circuit, any person may, within 60 days after issuance, move that a non-precedential opinion or order be reissued as precedential.[30]

9.5 CITATION OF NON-PRECEDENTIAL OPINIONS

Being non-precedential does not mean that an opinion may not be cited. Before 2007, some circuits prohibited citation of what they then called

21 4th Cir. IOP 36.3.
22 7th Cir. R. 32.1.
23 9th Cir. Gen. Ord. 4.5(b).
24 *Id.* R. 36-1.
25 11th Cir. R. 36-3.
26 1st Cir. R. 36.0(b)(2)(D).
27 7th Cir. R. 32.1(c).
28 9th Cir. R. 36-4.
29 D.C. Cir. R. 36(f).
30 Fed. Cir. R. 32.1(e).

"unpublished opinions," except with respect to certain purposes such as issue or claim preclusion; that prohibition continues with respect to non-precedential opinions issued before January 1, 2007.[31] The First, Fifth, Sixth, Tenth, D.C., and Federal Circuits permit citation of such opinions.[32] In the Fourth Circuit, citation of such opinions is "disfavored," except for the purpose of establishing issue or claim preclusion, or the law of the case.[33] Also, in the Fourth Circuit, if a party believes that an unpublished disposition issued prior to January 1, 2007 has "precedential value in relation to a material issue in the case" and that "there is no published opinion that would serve as well," the disposition may be cited.[34] Similarly, in the Eighth Circuit, such an opinion may be cited if a party believes the opinion "has persuasive value on a material issue" and that "no published opinion … would serve as well."[35]

Federal Rule of Appellate Procedure (FRAP) 32.1(a) was issued in 2006 to eliminate the publication prohibition prospectively: "A court may not prohibit or restrict the citation of federal judicial opinions, orders, judgments, or other written dispositions that have been: (i) designated as 'unpublished,' 'not for publication,' 'non-precedential,' 'not precedent,' or the like; and (ii) issued on or after January 1, 2007."[36] FRAP also provides, "If a party cites a federal judicial opinion, order, judgment, or other written disposition that is not available in a publicly accessible electronic database, the party must file and serve a copy of that opinion, order, judgment, or disposition with the brief or other paper in which it is cited."[37] Some circuits have provisions implementing FRAP 32.1(a) that permit citation of non-precedential opinions issued on or after January 1, 2007.[38]

Nevertheless, in the Third Circuit, the court "by tradition" does not cite its non-precedential opinions (regardless of the date).[39] In the Eleventh Circuit, "[t]he court generally does not cite to its 'unpublished' opinions."[40]

31 2d Cir. R. 32.1.1(b); 7th Cir. R. 32.1(d); 8th Cir. R. 32.1A ("Unpublished opinions issued before January 1, 2007, generally should not be cited"); 9th Cir. R. 36-3(c).

32 1st Cir. R. 32.1.0(a); 5th Cir. R. 28.7, 47.5.3, 47.5.4; 6th Cir. R. 32.1(a); 10th Cir. R. 32.1(A); D.C. Cir. R. 32.1(b)(1)(B)(entered on or after January 1, 2002); Fed. Cir. R. 32.1(c).

33 4th Cir. R. 32.1.

34 *Id.*

35 8th Cir. R. 32.1A.

36 Fed. R. App. P. 32.1.

37 *Id.*

38 2d Cir. R. 32.1.1(b); 8th Cir. R. 32.1A; 9th Cir. 36-3(b).

39 3d Cir. IOP 5.7.

40 11th Cir. R. 36-1, IOP 7.

9.6 EFFECT OF NON-PRECEDENTIAL OPINIONS ON SUBSEQUENT PANELS

No circuit requires a subsequent panel to be bound to follow a non-precedential opinion. Several circuits express this position in various ways in their local rules or IOPs.[41] Unique among the circuits, the Fifth Circuit considers an unpublished opinion (issued before January 1, 1996) as precedent.[42]

9.7 FORGOING ANY OPINION

There are times when, beyond resolving an appeal with an unpublished summary order or disposition, a court will forgo a written opinion altogether. In such instances, the panel simply "affirms" the judgment below.

In the Third Circuit, a judgment order[43] is filed when the panel unanimously determines to affirm the judgment or order of the district court or decision of the Tax Court, enforce or deny review of a decision or order of an administrative agency, or dismiss the appeal or petition for review for lack of jurisdiction or otherwise, and determines that a written opinion will have no precedential or institutional value.[44] Furthermore, a judgment order may be used when the judgment of the district court is based on findings of fact that are not clearly erroneous, sufficient evidence supports a jury verdict,

[41] 1st Cir. R. 32.1.0(a) ("The court will consider such dispositions for their persuasive value but not as binding precedent.); 2d Cir. R. 32.1.1(a) ("Rulings by summary order do not have precedential effect.); *id.* IOP 32.1.1(b) (Summary Order caption: "Rulings by summary order do not have precedential effect."); 3d Cir. I.O.P. 5.7 ("[N]ot precedential opinions … are not regarded as precedents that bind the court because they do not circulate to the full court before filing."); 5th Cir. R. 47.5.4 ("Unpublished opinions issued on or after January 1, 1996, are not precedent [with limited exceptions].)"; 7th Cir. R. 32.1(b) ("Orders … not published in the Federal Reporter … are not treated as precedents."); 8th Cir. R. 32.1A ("Unpublished opinions are decisions a court designates for unpublished status. They are not precedent."); 9th Cir. R. 36-3(a) ("Unpublished dispositions and orders of this Court are not precedent, except when relevant under the doctrine of law of the case or rules of claim preclusion or issue preclusion."); 10th Cir. R. 32.1(A) ("may be cited for their persuasive value"); 11th Cir. R. 36-3, IOP 6 ("Although unpublished opinions may be cited as persuasive authority, they are not considered binding precedent."); D.C. Cir. R. 36(e)(2) ("a panel's decision to issue an unpublished disposition means that the panel sees no precedential value in that disposition."); Fed. Cir. R. 32.1(d) ("The court may refer to a nonprecedential or unpublished disposition in an opinion or order and may look to a nonprecedential or unpublished disposition for guidance or persuasive reasoning but will not give one of its own nonprecedential dispositions the effect of binding precedent."). In the Sixth Circuit, a published opinion is "binding on later panels," implying that an unpublished (non-precedential) opinion is not. 6th Cir. R. 32.1(b).

[42] 5th Cir. R. 47.5.3.

[43] 3d Cir. IOP 6.

[44] *Id.* IOP 6.2.1.

substantial evidence supports an agency's decision, no error of law appears, the district court did not abuse its discretion, or the court of appeals lacks jurisdiction.[45]

In the Fifth Circuit, a judgment may be affirmed and an order enforced without opinion when the court determines that an opinion would have no precedential value and: (1) that a judgment of the district court is based on findings of fact that are not clearly erroneous; (2) that the evidence in support of a jury verdict is sufficient; (3) that the order of an administrative agency is supported by substantial evidence on the record as a whole; (4) in the case of a summary judgment, that no genuine issue of material fact has been properly raised by the appellant; or (5) no reversible error of law appears.[46]

In the Eighth Circuit, a judgment or order may be affirmed or enforced without opinion if the court determines that an opinion would have no precedential value and the judgment is based on findings of fact that are not clearly erroneous, the evidence in support of a jury verdict is sufficient, the order of an administrative agency is supported by substantial evidence, or no error of law appears.[47]

In the D.C. Circuit, the court may "dispense with published opinions where the issues occasion to need therefor, and confine its action to such abbreviated disposition as it may deem appropriate."[48]

In the Federal Circuit, the court may affirm without opinion when it determines that any of the following circumstances are met and that an opinion would have no precedential value: "(1) the judgment, decision, or order of the trial court appealed from is based on findings that are not clearly erroneous; (2) the evidence supporting the jury's verdict is sufficient; (3) the record supports summary judgment, directed verdict, or judgment on the pleadings; (4) the decision of an administrative agency warrants affirmance under the standard of review in the statute authorizing the petition for review; or (5) a judgment or decision has been entered without an error of law."[49]

45 *Id.* IOP 6.2.2.

46 5th Cir. R. 47.6.

47 8th Cir. R. 47B.

48 D.C. Cir. R. 36(d).

49 Fed. Cir. R. 36(a).

10

En Banc Procedures

This chapter considers courts of appeals' practices concerning rehearings en banc,[1] including initiating the en banc process, criteria for en bancs, composition of en banc panels, the effect of an en banc order on the panel's decision, and, as also explained in Chapter 13, the role of senior judges in the en banc process.

10.1 AUTHORITY FOR REHEARINGS EN BANC

A federal statute provides that courts of appeals will use panels of three judges to decide appeals and also provides that appeals may be decided by the full court,[2] known as the court sitting "en banc." The issue of whether a court of appeals was permitted to decide appeals en banc could not have arisen until 1902 when Congress first increased one court of appeals, the Second Circuit, from three to four judges,[3] and was not the subject of litigation until 1941, when a challenge was brought to the validity of the Third Circuit, then

[1] We will use the spelling "en banc" (without italics), which is used in almost all court opinions (unless the spelling is "in banc" in the document cited), but we note that the spelling of the phrase is a matter of some dispute. The relevant statute, 28 U.S.C. § 46(c), uses "in banc," but the relevant appellate rule, Fed. R. App. P. 35, uses "en banc." Fed. R. App. P. 35 was amended in 1998 to use "en banc" (without italics). The change is inferable from comparison of the 1998 and subsequent years' versions of Rule 35 (using "en banc") with the pre-1998 and previous years' versions (using "in banc") and comparison of the pre-1998 notes to Rule 35 (using "in banc"), *see* Fed. R. App. P. 35, Notes of Advisory Committee on Rules–1994, 1979, and 1967 Amendments, with the 1998 and subsequent years' notes (using "en banc"). The 1998 note acknowledged "changed language." Fed. R. App. P. 35, Committee Notes on Rules–1998 Amendment. For a discussion of the spelling dispute and some basis for doubting the authenticity of the "en banc" spelling, *see* Jon O. Newman, *In Banc Practice in the Second Circuit*, 1984–1988, 55 BROOK. L. REV. 355, 356 n.1 (1989) (explanation by the etymologist Sol Steinmetz).

[2] 28 U.S.C. § 46(c).

[3] Act of April 17, 1902, ch. 530, 57th Cong., 1st Sess., 32 Stat. 106.

consisting of five judges,[4] rehearing an appeal en banc. The Supreme Court, resolving a split between the Third and Ninth Circuits,[5] approved en banc rehearings in 1941 in *Textile Mills Securities Corp. v. Commissioner*,[6] and Congress authorized them in 1948.[7]

An en banc court may *rehear* an appeal considered and decided by a panel of three judges, and is authorized to *hear* an appeal or other proceeding as an original matter without a previous panel decision.[8] En banc rehearings occur infrequently. In the 12-month period ending September 30, 2022, of 28,504 appeals decided on the merits by the courts of appeals,[9] only 38 were reheard en banc.[10]

10.2 FREQUENCY OF REHEARINGS EN BANC

The circuits vary considerably in the frequency of rehearings en banc. Table 10.1 shows the number of en banc rehearings during the ten years 2011–20.[11]

An original en banc hearing of an appeal hardly ever occurs.[12] A notable example was the Second Circuit's original en banc hearing of the appeal in the so-called *Pentagon Papers* case.[13] The circuits' practices considered in this

4 The Third Circuit increased from four to five judges in 1936. Act of June 24, 1936, ch. 753, 74th Cong., 2d Sess., § 1, 49 Stat. 1903. The judgeship created in 1936 was temporary, *see id.* § 2, but the provision making it temporary was repealed in 1938, *see* Act of May 31, 1938, ch. 290, 75th Cong., 3d Sess., § 3, 52 Stat. 584, 585.

5 *Compare Commissioner v. Textile Mills Securities Corp.*, 117 F.2d 62, 67–71 (3d Cir. 1940) (approving rehearing en banc) (Biggs, J., with whom Jones, J., joins); *id.* at 71 (Clark, J., concurring on validity of en banc rehearing); *id.* at 75 (Maris, J., with whom Goodrich, J., joins, concurring on validity of en banc rehearing), *with Lang's Estate v. Commissioner*, 97 F.2d 867, 869 & n.2 (9th Cir. 1938) (disapproving rehearing en banc).

6 314 U.S. 326, 327–335 (1941).

7 Act of June 25, 1948, ch. 646, 80th Cong., 2d Sess. § 1, 62 Stat. 869, 871, (revising 28 U.S.C. § 46(c)).

8 28 U.S.C. § 46(c).

9 Administrative Office of the U.S. Courts (AO), "Statistical & Reports" tab, "Data Tables" link, Table B-10 (12-month periods ending September 30, 2022) (data excludes appeals decided by the Federal Circuit because the AO does not report rehearings en banc for that circuit).

10 *Id.*

11 *Id.*, Tables B-10 (12-month periods ending September 30, 2011–September 30, 2020). A call for Table B-10 for the 12-month periods ending September 30, 2011, 2012, and 2013 return Tables S-1. The AO does not report rehearings en banc for the Federal Circuit.

12 No data is reported for the frequency of original hearings en banc. The Third Circuit provides that an original hearing, which is called "extraordinary," is ordered only when a majority of the active judges who are not disqualified determines that the case is controlled by a prior decision of the court that should be reconsidered and the case is of such immediate importance that exigent circumstances require initial consideration by the full court. 3d Cir. IOP 9.2.

13 *United States v. New York Times Co.*, 444 F.2d 544 (2d Cir.) (en banc), *rev'd*, 403 U.S. 713 (1971).

TABLE 10.1 *Rehearings en banc, 2011–20*

1st	7
2nd	7[14]
3rd	30
4th	29
5th	58
6th	24
7th	33
8th	36
9th	166[15]
10th	9
11th	28
D.C.	18

chapter apply equally to rehearings en banc and original hearings en banc, but, to avoid repetition, we will refer only to rehearings.

The Federal Rules of Appellate Procedure (FRAP) implement the statutory authority for rehearings by providing that "[a] majority of the circuit judges who are in regular active service and who are not disqualified may order that an appeal or other proceeding be heard or reheard by the court of appeals en banc,"[16] and that "[a] vote need not be taken … unless a judge calls for a vote."[17] Several circuits have adopted detailed provisions for the en banc process in local rules and internal operating procedures (IOPs). Our discussion will consider these provisions in the order in which the various steps in the en banc process are taken.

10.3 A PARTY'S PETITION FOR A REHEARING EN BANC

The first step in the rehearing process is usually a party's petition for a rehearing en banc of a panel's decision.[18] FRAP 35(c) provides that the time limit

[14] Number reported by Second Circuit's Clerk's Office; the number reported for the Second Circuit by the AO's Table B-10 is inaccurate because of a coding error.

[15] An en banc court in the Ninth Circuit does not consist of all the active judges, as explained further in this chapter.

[16] Fed. R. App. P. 35(a).

[17] *Id.* 35(f).

[18] Before 1998, a party seeking a rehearing en banc filed a "suggestion" for such a rehearing along with a petition for a rehearing by the panel that originally heard the appeal. *See Western Pacific R. Corp. v. Western Pacific R. Co*, 345 U.S. 247, 262 (1953). Fed. R. App. P. 35(b) was amended in 1998 to change "suggestion" to "petition." *See* Fed. R. App. P. 35, Committee Notes on Rules–1998 Amendment.

for filing the en banc petition is the same as the time for a petition for panel rehearing,[19] which is 14 days after entry of judgment, or 45 days in a civil case in which a party is the United States, a United States agency, or a United States official sued in an official capacity.[20]

Some circuits have special provisions concerning a petition for rehearing en banc. In the First, Second, Fourth, and Federal Circuits, a petition for a rehearing en banc must be combined with a petition for panel rehearing (if filed),[21] but in the Fifth Circuit, such a combined filing is prohibited.[22] In the First, Fifth, Sixth, Eleventh, and Federal Circuits, a petition for rehearing en banc is treated as a petition for panel rehearing if no petition is filed.[23] In the Second, Fifth, Eighth, and Federal Circuits, local rules specify that costs may be assessed for filing a frivolous petition for rehearing en banc.[24]

In the Third Circuit, a petition for rehearing en banc is not permitted to rehear a denial of a petition to file a second or successive habeas corpus petition.[25] Also in the Third Circuit, the parties are cautioned that a petition for panel or en banc rehearing in a case where an execution is scheduled within 48 hours might not be distributed to members of the court in sufficient time for adjudication prior to the time of the execution.[26] Petitions for rehearing en banc filed within 48 hours of an execution will be processed and distributed by the "normal means of delivery" unless the panel has ordered expedited voting.[27]

In the Fifth Circuit, an IOP expresses that "[p]etitions for rehearing en banc are the most abused prerogative of appellate advocates in the Fifth Circuit."[28]

In the Sixth Circuit, the petition for rehearing en banc is sent to the panel, which has 14 days to comment to the en banc coordinator in the clerk's office.[29] If the panel alters its decision, it will provide the new decision to the en banc coordinator; that decision will be filed and counsel will be notified.[30] Counsel then has 14 days to "withdraw, modify, or maintain" their petition for rehearing

19 Fed. R. App. P. 35(c).

20 *Id.* 40(a)(1). The rule notes these time limits "[u]nless the time is shortened or extended by order or local rule[.]" *Id.*

21 1st Cir. R. 35.0(b); 2d Cir. R. 35.1(a); 4th Cir. R. 35(a); Fed. Cir. R. 35(d).

22 5th Cir R. 35.2.

23 1st Cir. IOP X(C); 5th Cir. IOP Handling of Petition by the Judges; 6th Cir. IOP 35(d)(1), (2); 11th Cir. R. 35, IOP 2; Fed. Cir. R. 35, Prac. N., Petition for Rehearing En Banc Referred to Panel.

24 2d Cir. R. 35.1(e); 5th Cir. 35.1; 8th Cir. R. 35A(2); Fed. Cir. R. 35(a)(2).

25 3d Cir. L.A.R. 111.7(d).

26 *Id.* L.A.R. 111.7(a).

27 *Id.*

28 5th Cir. IOP Petition for Rehearing En Banc (The Most Abused Prerogative).

29 6th Cir. IOP 35(d)(2).

30 *Id.* IOP 35(d)(2)(A).

en banc or file a new petition if they so choose.[31] In the Seventh Circuit, a judge has 14 days to request a response to a party's petition for rehearing.[32]

In the Ninth Circuit, a petition for rehearing en banc is circulated to all active judges and to those senior judges who have requested copies.[33] The petition will not be granted without giving other parties an opportunity to express their views.[34] The Ninth Circuit designates an active or senior judge as an en banc coordinator to supervise the en banc process.[35] In the Tenth Circuit, a petition for rehearing en banc is generally circulated to the full court.[36] In the Eleventh Circuit, the time for filing the petition in a nongovernment case is within 21 days after entry of judgment.[37] In the Federal Circuit, a party may ask a panel to overrule a precedent without filing a petition for rehearing en banc, and the panel will decide whether to ask the judges in regular active service to consider hearing the case en banc.[38]

10.4 A JUDGE'S REQUEST FOR A REHEARING EN BANC

In all circuits, an active judge of the court may request a poll of the active judges to determine if a majority of them favors a rehearing en banc. In addition, in the Second, Fourth, Fifth, Sixth, Seventh, Eighth, Tenth, D.C., and Federal Circuits,[39] a senior judge who served on the panel that originally heard the appeal may also request a poll.[40] In the Second Circuit, a senior judge who was not a member of the panel can ask the chief judge to request an en banc poll, a request usually honored. In the Ninth Circuit, any judge of the court can request an en banc poll.[41] Also in the Ninth Circuit, a judge can request an en banc rehearing of an order in a death penalty case denying an authorized second or successive motion for collateral relief.[42]

[31] *Id.*
[32] 7th Cir. OP 5.
[33] 9th Cir. Gen. Ord. 5.4(a).
[34] *Id.* R. 35-2.
[35] *Id.* Gen. Order 5.1(b)(2), 8.2 (Duties of En Banc Coordinator in Death Penalty Procedures).
[36] 10th Cir. R. 35.1(A).
[37] 11th Cir. R. 35-2.
[38] Fed. Cir. R. 35(a)(1).
[39] For the Federal Circuit, a senior judge can request a poll in situations of petitions for rehearing en banc but may not do so for petitions for hearing en banc or *sua sponte* requests for hearing or rehearing en banc. *Id.* IOP 14(2).
[40] 2d Cir. IOP 35.1(a); 4th Cir. R. 35(b) (in the Fourth Circuit, a visiting judge who was on the original panel may also request a poll); 5th Cir. IOP Handling of Petition by Judges; 6th Cir. IOP 35(e); 8th Cir. IOP IV(D) ¶ 5; D.C. Cir. Handbook of Practice and Internal Procedures XIII.B.2.
[41] 9th Cir. Gen. Ord. 5.4(c)(1).
[42] *Id.* R. 22-4(d).

10.5 TIME TO REQUEST A POLL

In all circuits, the opportunity to call for an en banc poll ends when the mandate issues,[43] but some courts of appeals have varied the time period. In the Second Circuit, an active judge requesting an en banc poll should make the request shortly after circulation of the petition, but a judge can obtain additional time up to 45 days by placing a "hold" on issuance of the mandate to afford that judge and other judges time to decide whether to request a poll. In the Third Circuit, an active judge who has written a dissent to the panel opinion is presumed to have voted for an en banc rehearing, absent notification in writing to the contrary;[44] non-panel active judges have eight days (ten days in August) to request a poll.[45] In the Fifth Circuit, a poll may be requested within ten days of the filing of a petition for rehearing en banc;[46] in the Sixth Circuit, within 14 days of the circulation of a petition for rehearing and the panel's comments;[47] in the Seventh Circuit, within 14 days of the filing of an en banc petition or 14 days of the filing of any answer to the petition if one is requested;[48] in the Eighth Circuit, the judges have two weeks to review the petition and request a poll or a response;[49] in the D.C. Circuit, within 30 days of the circulation of a petition for rehearing;[50] in the Federal Circuit, within ten working days of an ordered response, which must be requested within ten working days of the circulation of an en banc petition.[51]

In the Ninth Circuit, within 21 days after a petition for rehearing en banc is circulated, a judge may request the panel to make known its recommendation,[52] and the panel should respond as soon as possible and, in any event, within 90 days of the request or the petition for rehearing, whichever is later.[53] Upon receipt of the panel's recommendation, a judge has 14 days to request a poll.[54] If no petition for rehearing has been filed, a judge may, within seven

43 The mandate would normally issue seven days after the time for filing a petition for panel or en banc rehearing expires, or seven days after an order denying a petition for panel rehearing, a petition for en banc rehearing, or a motion to stay issuance of the mandate, whichever is later. Fed. R. App. P. 41(b). The time can be shortened or lengthened by court order or local rule. *Id.*

44 3d Cir. IOP 9.4.3.

45 *Id.* IOP 5.5.4. *See also id.* IOP 9.4.2 (permitting brief extension of time); *id.* IOP 9.5.5 (same).

46 5th Cir. IOP Handling of Petition by the Judges (Requesting a Poll).

47 6th Cir. IOP 35(d)(3).

48 7th Cir. OP 5(b); *id.* OP 9(e).

49 8th Cir. IOP IV(D) ¶ 4.

50 D.C. Cir. R. 35(a).

51 Fed. Cir. IOP 14(2).

52 9th Cir. Gen. Ord. 5.4(b)(2).

53 *Id.*

54 9th Cir. R. 35-3, Cir. Adv. Comm. N. (2), *see also id.* Gen. Ord. 5.4(c)(3).

days after the date such petition was due, request a vote on whether the case should be reheard by the full court.[55]

In the Eleventh Circuit, within 30 days after the clerk transmits a petition for rehearing en banc, an active judge may notify the opinion author (or the senior active judge on the panel if the author is a visitor) that, if panel rehearing is denied, an en banc poll is requested.[56] The request can also come from a senior judge who wrote the panel opinion. The judge requesting a poll notifies the clerk to place a hold on issuance of the mandate.[57]

10.6 JUDGES ELIGIBLE TO VOTE IN A POLL

A federal statute limits voting in an en banc poll to judges "who are in regular active service."[58] The Supreme Court has ruled that this limitation precludes even senior judges who were members of a panel whose decision is being reheard from voting in an en banc poll.[59]

Some circuits have transition provisions or customs concerning an active judge who takes senior status during the en banc process. In the First Circuit, if a judge takes senior status after a *sua sponte* request for a rehearing en banc, that judge is not eligible to vote in the poll. In the Second Circuit, a judge's status as an active or a senior judge, for purposes of voting in an en banc poll, is determined on the date of entry of the en banc order.[60]

In the Ninth Circuit, if a judge takes senior status during the vote, the vote is discontinued and a new voting period is established, in which the senior judge may not vote.[61]

In the Tenth Circuit, if a judge, while active, voted in an en banc poll, and then took senior status before the poll was completed, the judge's vote will not be counted in the poll.

In the D.C. Circuit, judges do not vote in an en banc poll regardless of when they took senior status with respect to the en banc process.

Two circuits have provisions concerning whether a judge who joins the court during the en banc process may vote in an en banc poll. In the Fourth Circuit, a judge who joins the court after a petition for rehearing en banc has been submitted and before an order has been entered is eligible to vote in the

55 *Id.* Gen. Ord. 5.8(b).
56 11th Cir. R. 35, IOP 3.
57 *Id.*
58 28 U.S.C. § 46(c).
59 *See Moody v. Albemarle Paper Co.*, 417 U.S. 622, 626 (1974).
60 2d Cir. IOP 35.1(b).
61 9th Cir. Gen. Ord. 5.1(a)(3).

poll.[62] In the Ninth Circuit, a judge who joins the court before a petition has been submitted is eligible to vote in the poll,[63] but a new judge may choose to recuse from voting in en banc polls for whatever transition period the judge selects.[64] After the self-selected transition period, the judge is eligible to vote in a new poll, including polls in which the voting period has already begun.[65]

10.7 TIME TO VOTE IN A POLL

If a poll has been requested, five circuits have time limits for the active judges to vote. In the Second Circuit, panel members have 14 days to respond to the call for a poll, and the active judges have 21 days after such a response to vote in the poll. In the Third Circuit, the active judges have ten days to vote;[66] in the Sixth Circuit, 14;[67] in the Federal Circuit, the tenth working day after distribution of the ballot.[68] In the Seventh Circuit, active judges must vote within 14 days of the later of a poll request or the filing of a party's answer.[69] In the Ninth Circuit, after memoranda have been exchanged, the en banc coordinator notifies judges to vote, and they have seven days to do so;[70] a failure to vote is considered a "no" vote.[71]

In the Fifth Circuit, when a rehearing petition is filed in a death penalty case in which the execution is scheduled within 22 days, the chief judge or "delegee" may order expedited consideration and set time limits for calling for, and voting in, an en banc poll.[72]

10.8 THE POLL BALLOT

In the Fifth and Eleventh Circuits, an en banc ballot provides an opportunity for a judge favoring a rehearing to indicate if oral argument is desired,[73] and, in

[62] 4th Cir. R. 35(b).
[63] 9th Cir. R. 35-3, Cir. Adv. Comm. N. (2).
[64] *Id.* Gen. Ord. 5.1(a)(3).
[65] *Id.*
[66] 3d Cir. IOP 9.5.4. If one judge has timely voted for rehearing, another judge may circulate a letter asking that the time for voting be extended by not more than five days beyond the original ten day period, and the request will result in an automatic extension. *Id.* IOP 9.5.5.
[67] 6th Cir. IOP 35(d)(3).
[68] Fed. Cir. IOP 14(5)(b). The Federal Circuit also limits when voting can commence – "[t]he voting period will begin on the third working day following the date of distribution of the ballot." *Id.*
[69] 7th Cir. OP 5(d)(2); *id.* OP 9(e).
[70] 9th Cir. Gen. Ord. 5.5(b).
[71] *Id.*
[72] 5th Cir. IOP Handling of Petition by the Judges (Capital Cases).
[73] *Id.* IOP Handling of Petition by the Judges (Polling the Court); 11th Cir. R. 35, IOP 6.

the Eleventh Circuit, oral argument is not scheduled if fewer than three judges request it (though appeals to be reheard en banc usually are argued).[74] In the Federal Circuit, an en banc ballot offers the active judges a choice of denying or granting en banc review or deferring voting pending a conference of the judges,[75] which can be easily convened in a court with all judges in the same building.

10.9 CONTENT OF AN EN BANC ORDER

Some circuits specify the content of the en banc order. If no poll was requested, in the Fourth, Fifth, and Eleventh Circuits the order denying en banc review reflects that.[76] If there was a poll, the Fourth Circuit requires that the order reflect the vote of each participating judge;[77] the Fifth Circuit requires that the order reflect the vote of each participating judge when the en banc poll fails, but not when the en banc is granted. In the Ninth Circuit, the vote, whether to grant or deny a rehearing, is not reported.[78] In the Federal Circuit, if a poll is unsuccessful, the order notes any dissenting votes.[79]

Sometimes, active judges who voted for a rehearing in an unsuccessful poll file an opinion, which occasionally prompts an opinion from an active judge who voted to deny a rehearing.[80] The Third Circuit explicitly permits such opinions.[81] In several circuits, a senior judge on the panel has filed an opinion or a "statement" with respect to the denial of the order,[82] and in the Eighth and Ninth Circuits a senior judge not on the panel has filed such a

[74] 11th Cir. R. 35, IOP 9(d).

[75] Fed. Cir. IOP 14(5)(a).

[76] 4th Cir. R. 35(b); 5th Cir. IOP Handling of Petition by the Judges (No Poll Request); 11th Cir. R. 35, IOP 4.

[77] 4th Cir. R. 35(b).

[78] 9th Cir. R. 35-1 to 3, Cir. Adv. Comm. N. (2), (3).

[79] Fed. Cir. IOP 14(2)(g)(ii).

[80] *See, e.g., Jolly v. Listerman*, 675 F.2d 1308, 1309 (D.C. Cir. 1982) (statement of Judges Tamm and Wilkey, setting forth reasons for voting to deny rehearing en banc); *id.* at 1311 (statement of Judge Edwards, setting forth reasons for voting to grant rehearing en banc).

[81] 3d Cir. IOP 9.5.8 (any active judge may file an opinion concerning the denial of the petition for rehearing and direct its publication).

[82] *Brzozowski v. Correctional Physician Services, Inc.*, 362 F.3d 876, 876 (3d Cir. 2004) (opinion of Garth, senior judge); *United States v. Houston*, 691 F. App'x 751, 751 (4th Cir. 2017) (statement of Davis, senior judge); *Coastal Production Services, Inc. v. Hudson*, 567 F.3d 752, 752 (5th Cir. 2009) (opinion of DeMoss, senior judge); *Smith & Lee Associates, Inc. v. City of Taylor*, 13 F.3d 920, 920 n.* (6th Cir. 1994) (footnote stating that Contie, senior judge, would grant rehearing en banc); *Trinh v. Citibank, N.A.*, 850 F.2d 1164, 1164 (6th Cir. 1988) (statement in syllabus that Brown, senior judge, would have voted for rehearing en banc); *United States v. Arpaio*, 906 F.3d 800, 812 (9th Cir. 2018) (statement of Tallman, senior judge, agreeing with dissent from denial of rehearing en banc); *but see Becker v. Thompson*, 463 F.2d 1338, 1339 (5th Cir.

statement.[83] The Second Circuit permits a senior judge, not on the panel, to file a statement concerning a denial of rehearing en banc if a judge dissenting from the denial filed an opinion.

10.10 DETERMINING A MAJORITY IN A POLL

It might seem that determining whether a majority favors a rehearing requires only counting the votes in the poll, but two problems can arise. The first is whether the majority voting for a rehearing en banc must be composed of judges all of whom are active judges at the time a majority votes for the rehearing, or only that each judge forming the majority voting for a rehearing must be or have been an active judge at the time that judge voted. The issue appears not to have been litigated. In the Second Circuit, an IOP appears to provide that all the judges who formed a majority in favor of a rehearing en banc must be in regular active service not only when each voted, but also when the order is entered directing that the case will be reheard en banc.[84]

The second problem concerns identification of the base for determining whether a majority of active judges favors a rehearing. In *Western Pacific R. Corp. v. Western Pacific R. Co.*,[85] the Supreme Court left this issue for each circuit to decide.[86]

Before 2005, eight circuits included a disqualified active judge in the base for calculating a majority of active judges, and five circuits did not.[87] In 2005, FRAP Rule 35 was amended to provide that disqualified active judges are not counted in the base.[88] That amendment left open the issue of whether active

1972) (opinion of Brown, C.J., noting that (senior) Judge Tuttle, a member of the panel, did not have an opportunity to respond to views expressed in an opinion concurring in denial of rehearing en banc).

83 *Jenkins ex rel. Agyei v. Missouri*, 19 F.3d 393, 393 (8th Cir. 1994) (opinion of Gibson, senior judge, who was not on the panel but who was an active judge on the court when the petition for rehearing en banc was filed, concurring in the denial of rehearing en banc); *United States v. Recio*, 270 F.3d 845, 851 (9th Cir. 2001) (statement of Hall, senior judge, who was not on the panel, agreeing with views of those voting to deny rehearing en banc).

84 2d Cir. IOP 35.1(a) ("A judge's status as an active or senior judge for the purpose of an en banc poll is determined on the date of entry of the en banc order").

85 345 U.S. 247 (1953).

86 "The court is left free to devise its own administrative machinery to provide the means whereby a majority may order such a hearing." *Id.* at 250.

87 Marie Leary, *Defining the "Majority" Vote Requirement in Federal Rule of Appellate Procedure 35(a) for Rehearing En Banc in the United States Courts of Appeals* 8–9 Table 1 (Federal Judicial Center 2002).

88 Fed. R. App. P. 35, Committee Notes on Rules–2005 Amendment. This amendment appears to abrogate 1st Cir. R. 35.0(a)(1), which states that the judges voting for a rehearing en banc must be a majority of all the active judges.

judges who are not disqualified but who do not participate in an en banc poll for some other reason, such as illness or unavailability, are included in the base. The Third Circuit has ruled by court decision, with the approval of the Supreme Court, that such judges are included in the base,[89] a position confirmed by local rule.[90]

By custom, active judges who are unavailable (but not recused) are also included in the base in the Second, Fifth, Eighth, Ninth, Eleventh, and Federal Circuits, but are not included in the base in the Sixth and Seventh Circuits.[91] The First, Fourth, Tenth, and D.C. Circuits have not encountered the issue.

10.11 GROUNDS FOR REHEARING EN BANC

FRAP 35(a) first states that en banc rehearings are not favored,[92] and then identifies two criteria for a rehearing en banc: (1) "to secure or maintain uniformity of the court's decisions" or (2) "the proceeding involves a question of exceptional importance."[93] With respect to the first factor, all circuits, with varying degrees of consistency, endeavor to consider panel precedential decisions to establish the law of the circuit and to bind subsequent panels considering the same issue.

The Eleventh and Federal Circuits have reenforced the FRAP criteria by requiring counsel seeking a rehearing en banc to state that, in counsel's professional judgment, the panel decision is contrary to identified decisions of the Supreme Court or the circuit or requires an answer to identified precedent-setting questions of exceptional importance.[94]

In the Fifth and Eleventh Circuits, a ground for rehearing is conflict with prior decisions of the Supreme Court or the circuit.[95] The Fifth Circuit

89 *Shenker v. Baltimore & Ohio R. Co.*, 303 F.2d 596, 600 (3d Cir. 1962) (rehearing en banc denied), *rev'd on merits after approval of this point*, 374 U.S. 1, 4 (1963) (pointing out that four of eight active judges voted in favor of rehearing en banc, two voted against, and two abstained, and ruling that the Third Circuit was entitled to decide that the four who voted for rehearing were not a majority of eight active judges, thus ruling that the base for the required majority included two who had not participated, although they were apparently not disqualified).

90 3d Cir. L.A.R. 35.3 ("For purposes of determining the majority number necessary to grant a petition for rehearing, all circuit judges currently in regular active service who are not disqualified will be counted.").

91 In the Seventh Circuit, a footnote would be added to the order reporting the judge's unavailability.

92 Fed. R. App. P. 35(a).

93 *Id.* 35(a)(1), (2).

94 11th Cir. R. 35-5(c); Fed. Cir. R. 35(b)(2).

95 5th Cir. IOP Petition for Rehearing En Banc (Extraordinary Nature of Petitions for Rehearing En Banc); 11th Cir. R. 35-3.

adds conflict with a state law precedent.[96] In the Ninth Circuit, a ground for rehearing is the fact that a panel opinion conflicts with an opinion of another circuit and substantially affects a rule of national application in which there is an overriding need for national uniformity.[97] In the Third and Sixth Circuits, rehearing is not ordered when the panel's statement of the law is correct and the controverted issue is solely the application of the law to the circumstances of the case.[98] Additionally, the Third Circuit ordinarily does not grant a rehearing when the only issue presented is one of state law.[99] The Eleventh Circuit precludes a rehearing of administrative or interim orders and unpublished (non-precedential) orders.[100]

10.12 EFFECT OF GRANTING REHEARING EN BANC ON A PANEL OPINION

In the First Circuit, when an en banc rehearing petition is granted, the opinion and judgment of the panel is "usually" vacated.[101] In the Second Circuit, the effect, if any, of an order for a rehearing en banc on a panel's opinion or judgment is stated in the decision of the en banc court. In the Third, Fourth, and Sixth Circuits, the granting of a petition for rehearing en banc vacates the panel opinion and the judgment,[102] and does so in the Fifth and Eleventh Circuits unless otherwise expressly provided.[103] In the Ninth Circuit, once the chief judge enters an order taking the case en banc, the panel's opinion may not be cited as precedent by the court of appeals or a district court in the circuit (except to the extent adopted by the en banc court).[104] In the Tenth Circuit, the grant of a rehearing en banc vacates the panel's judgment and stays the mandate, but does not vacate the panel's opinion unless the court so orders.[105] In the D.C. Circuit, the grant of a rehearing en banc vacates the panel's judgment, but "ordinarily" not its opinion.[106]

96 5th Cir. IOP Petition for Rehearing En Banc (Extraordinary Nature of Petitions for Rehearing En Banc).
97 9th Cir. R. 35-1.
98 3d Cir. IOP 9.3.2; 6th Cir. IOP 35(b).
99 3d Cir. IOP 9.3.3.
100 11th Cir. R. 35-4.
101 1st Cir. IOP X(D).
102 3d Cir. IOP 9.5.9; 4th Cir. R. 35(c); 6th Cir. R. 35(b).
103 5th Cir. R. 41.3; 11th Cir. R. 35-10, 41-1(d).
104 9th Cir. Gen. Ord. 5.5(d).
105 10th Cir. R. 35.6.
106 D.C. Cir. R. 35(d).

10.13 MEMBERS OF AN EN BANC COURT

By statute, an en banc court consists of all the active judges of the court and any senior judge who was a member of the panel whose decision is being reheard,[107] except that a court with more than 15 active judges may prescribe by local rule the number of active judges that serve on an en banc court.[108] Although the Fifth, Sixth, and Ninth Circuits have more than 15 active judges,[109] only the Ninth Circuit has implemented this exception. An en banc court in that circuit consists of the chief judge and ten other judges, selected at random from the active judges of the court and any senior judge who was a member of the original panel whose decision is being reviewed and who elects to be eligible.[110] The court may order a rehearing by the full court following a hearing or rehearing by the (limited) en banc court.[111]

Some circuits have transition provisions concerning participation on an en banc court by active judges who take senior status during the en banc process and by new judges. By federal statute, a judge in regular active services who takes senior status after a case is reheard en banc may continue to participate in the decision,[112] which some circuits reaffirm by rule,[113] or IOP.[114] In the Third, Fifth, and Seventh Circuits, an active judge who takes senior status after voting in the poll can serve on the en banc court.[115] In the Sixth Circuit, if there is no oral argument, an active judge who took senior status after the en banc court agreed to decide the case without oral argument can be a member of the en banc court.[116] In the Ninth Circuit, an active judge who has been chosen for the randomly selected 11-member en banc court and then takes senior status may remain on the court until the case is disposed of;[117] but if the judge took senior status after the call for an en banc poll and before the members of the limited en banc are selected, the judge cannot be a member

[107] 28 U.S.C. § 46(c). Senior judges on the panel have the option of serving on the en banc court. *Id.*

[108] Public Law No. 95-486, § 6, 92 Stat. 1629, 1633 (set out at 28 U.S.C. § 41, Historical and Statutory Notes, Appeals Court Administrative Units).

[109] 28 U.S.C. § 44.

[110] 9th Cir. R. 35-3; *id.* 35-3, Cir. Adv. Comm. N. (2). In the absence of the chief judge, the local rules specify that an 11th active judge should be drawn by lot, and then the most senior active judge will preside. *Id.* R. 35-3.

[111] *Id.* R. 35-3.

[112] 28 U.S.C. § 46(c).

[113] 1st Cir. R. 35.0(a)(2)(A); 4th Cir. R. 35(c); 5th Cir. R. 35.6; 11th Cir. R. 35-9.

[114] 2d Cir. IOP 35.1(c); 3d Cir. IOP 9.6.4; Fed. Cir. IOP 14(7).

[115] 3d Cir. IOP 9.6.4.

[116] 6th Cir. IOP 35(c).

[117] 9th Cir. R. 35-3, Cir. Adv. Comm. N. (2); *id.* Gen. Ord. 5.1(a)(4).

of the en banc court, unless that judge was a member of the original panel whose decision is being reviewed and chooses to be eligible.[118] In the Federal Circuit, a senior judge who was a member of the original panel "will participate in consideration and disposition" of a petition for rehearing en banc.[119]

Three circuits have en banc provisions concerning new judges. In the Second and Fourth Circuits, a judge who joined the court after a case was reheard en banc is not eligible to participate in the decision,[120] but in the Fourth Circuit, a judge who joined the court after a case was submitted to an en banc court without oral argument "will participate in the decision of the case."[121] In the Federal Circuit, a new judge joining the court after a case is reheard en banc is eligible to participate in the decision.[122]

10.14 SCHEDULING A REHEARING EN BANC

In the Third, Fourth, Fifth, Sixth, Seventh, Eighth, Ninth, Tenth, Eleventh, and D.C. Circuits, multiple en banc hearings are sometimes (if rarely) scheduled for a single day. In the Eighth Circuit, this is usually done in September, October, January, or April, when all the judges hear cases in one location. In the Third Circuit, rehearings are normally held at a regularly scheduled en banc session of the court, unless a majority of the active judges has voted to expedite.[123] In the Ninth Circuit, the chief judge sets the date, time, and place of oral argument, or, if there will not be oral argument in a rehearing en banc, the date, time, and place of a court conference;[124] oral arguments and conferences are normally scheduled on a quarterly basis in conjunction with court meetings.[125]

10.15 ISSUES IN A REHEARING EN BANC

In the Second Circuit, the chief judge, after consulting the proponent of the en banc and the panel, is authorized to identify the issues to be considered at the rehearing and provide for a conference immediately after the rehearing argument. In the Third Circuit, the chief judge, when requested by a majority

118 *Id.* R. 35-3, Cir. Adv. Comm. N. (2).
119 Fed. Cir. IOP 12(5)(c).
120 2d Cir. IOP 35.1(d); 4th Cir. 35(c).
121 4th Cir. R. 35(c).
122 Fed. Cir. IOP 14(7).
123 3d Cir. IOP 9.6.2.
124 9th Cir. R. 35-3, Cir. Adv. Comm. N. (3).
125 *Id.* Gen. Ord. 5.6.

of the en banc court, directs the clerk to advise counsel to submit supplemental briefs on specific issues or to be prepared to discuss at oral argument any other relevant issues.[126] In the Eleventh Circuit, "appeal managers" circulate to the en banc court a proposed notice to the parties,[127] advising which issue(s) should be briefed, the length limits of the briefs, and whether there will be oral argument; if no member of the en banc court objects, the notice is sent to counsel.[128] In the Federal Circuit, when a rehearing is ordered, the chief judge appoints a committee of judges (which normally will include the judge who initiated the poll), who prepare and transmit to the en banc court an order setting forth the questions proposed to be considered by the en banc court.[129]

10.16 THE EN BANC PROCESS

In the Second Circuit, the chief judge sets a briefing schedule, normally 30 days for the appellant, 30 days for the appellee, and ten days for the appellant's reply.

In the Third Circuit, there is oral argument in an en banc case if it is requested by at least one judge of the en banc court.[130] Four members of the en banc court may permit an amicus to argue.[131]

In the Ninth Circuit, the chief judge appoints an active or senior judge to serve as an en banc coordinator.[132] The en banc coordinator supervises the en banc process, including time limits, circulates periodic reports on the status of en banc cases, and may, in a particular case, alter time limits, suggest modification of en banc provisions, and for good cause may suspend en banc proceedings.[133] The en banc coordinator or the clerk's office records the votes in the en banc poll,[134] and circulates the tally to the court.[135]

In the Eleventh Circuit, the chief judge appoints a group of active judges to serve as appeal managers, normally including (if not in senior status) the judge who authored the panel opinion, the judge who called for the poll, and a judge who dissented from, or specially concurred in, the panel opinion.[136]

[126] 3d Cir. IOP 9.6.3.
[127] *See* discussion regarding appeal managers in "The En Banc Process," Section 10.16; 11th Cir. R. 35, IOP 9(a).
[128] 11th Cir. R. 35, IOP 9(c).
[129] Fed. Cir. IOP 14(2)(f).
[130] 3d Cir. IOP 2.2.
[131] *Id.*
[132] 9th Cir. Gen. Ord. 5.1(a)(5); *see also id.* R. 35-3, Cir. Adv. Comm. N. (2).
[133] *Id.* Gen. Ord. 5.1(b)(2).
[134] *Id.* Gen. Ord. 5.1(b)(3).
[135] *Id.*
[136] 11th Cir. R. 35, IOP 9(a).

In the D.C. Circuit, an amicus curiae brief in response to, or in support of, a petition for rehearing en banc will not be received unless invited by the court.[137]

10.17 AFTER AN EN BANC ARGUMENT

In the Second Circuit, the en banc court meets immediately after oral argument for a brief discussion to identify issues to be resolved and tentative votes so that a majority opinion can be assigned. At that conference the judges speak in reverse order of seniority. Members of the en banc court have 14 days to circulate memos and must vote within 21 days of the argument. The majority opinion is normally circulated 30 days after voting is completed, and a dissenting opinion 30 days after that circulation. The chief judge is authorized to set a deadline for filing final versions of opinions.

In the Ninth Circuit, after the case has been submitted, the most senior judge voting with the majority assigns the writing of the majority opinion; and if more than one judge expresses a minority view, the most senior judge sharing that view assigns the dissenting opinion.[138] A judge should not be selected to write a majority or dissenting opinion in an en banc case unless the judge's workload permits the judge to circulate the opinion within 45 days.[139]

If the judge assigned the majority opinion ultimately is unable to circulate it within 45 days, that judge is expected to circulate a memorandum explaining why the deadline was not met and when the draft will circulate.[140] A judge must notify the court within 14 days of receiving the majority opinion that the judge plans to write a concurring or dissenting opinion and circulate that opinion within 30 days.[141] The chief judge establishes the time for voting on an opinion.[142]

Proposed opinions are circulated only to judges of the 11-member en banc court, but all members of the court – senior and active – and any visiting judges who participated in the original panel decision are kept informed of en banc calls, responsive memoranda, and votes.[143]

137 D.C. Cir. R. 35(f).
138 9th Cir. Gen. Ord. 5.7(a).
139 *Id.*
140 *Id.* Gen. Ord. 5.7(b)(1).
141 *Id.* Gen. Ord. 5.7(b)(2).
142 *Id.* Gen. Ord. 5.7(b)(3).
143 *Id.* Gen. Ord. 5.1(b)(1).

10.18 AN EVENLY DIVIDED VOTE

In the D.C. Circuit, an IOP provides that if the en banc court consists of an even number of judges and the result is an evenly divided vote, a judgment affirming the order or judgment being reviewed is entered (following Supreme Court practice[144]), and the court may publish the en banc court's divided views[145] (not following Supreme Court practice).[146] By caselaw, in most circuits an evenly divided vote results in affirmance of the judgment under review, sometimes without publication of divided views,[147] and occasionally with publication of divided views.[148]

10.19 REJECTING A PRECEDENTIAL DECISION WITHOUT A REHEARING EN BANC

Some circuits have a procedure for rejecting a precedent of the court,[149] or obtaining the full court's approval of a panel's ruling without invoking the formal en banc process. In the Second Circuit, a panel circulates its proposed opinion to the active judges of the court, with copies to the senior judges, and, in the absence of objection or call for an en banc poll, files the opinion with a footnote stating, "Prior to filing, this opinion has been circulated to all the judges of this Court."[150] The Second Circuit calls this

[144] E.g., *Morgan Stanley & Co. v. Pacific Mutual Life Insurance Co.*, 511 U.S. 658 (1994).

[145] D.C. Cir. Handbook of Practice and Internal Procedures XIII(B)(2).

[146] E.g., *Morgan Stanley & Co. v. Pacific Mutual Life Insurance Co.*, 511 U.S. 658 (1994).

[147] *See, e.g.*, *Kiman v. New Hampshire Department of Corrections*, 332 F.2d 29, 29 (1st Cir. 2003) (en banc); *Allegheny Corp. v. Kirby*, 340 F.3d 311, 312 (2d Cir. 1965) (en banc); *Commonwealth v. Local Union* 542, 648 F.2d 923, 924 (3d Cir. 1981) (en banc); *Griffin v. Martin*, 795 F.2d 22, 22 (4th Cir. 1986) (en banc); *Baris v. Sulpicio Lines, Inc.*, 101 F.3d 367, 368 (5th Cir. 1996) (en banc); *Marchwinski v. Howard*, 60 F. App'x 601, 601 (6th Cir. 2003) (en banc); *Schultz v. Frisby*, 822 F.2d 642, 642 (7th Cir. 1987) (en banc); *United States v. Waterman*, 732 F.2d 1527, 1533 (8th Cir. 1984) (en banc); *Zuni Public School District No. 89 v. United States Department of Education*, 437 F. 3d 1289, 1290 (10th Cir. 2006) (en banc); *Penthouse International, Ltd. v. McAuliffe*, 717 F.2d 517, 517 (11th Cir. 1983) (en banc); *Ginsburg, Feldman & Bress v. Federal Energy Administration*, 591 F.2d 752, 753 (D.C. Cir. 1978) (en banc).

[148] *See, e.g.*, *Jean v. Collins*, 221 F.3d 656, 658, 663, 678 (4th Cir. 2000) (en banc); *United States v. McFarland*, 311 F.3d 376, 377, 377, 410, 416 (5th Cir. 2002) (en banc).

[149] *See* Chapter 8, discussing how courts of appeals determine whether an opinion has precedential effect.

[150] E.g., *United States v. Crosby*, 397 F.3d 103, 105 n.1 (2d Cir. 2005). The Second Circuit divides circulated opinions into three categories. One category covers opinions where a panel concludes that a circuit precedent has clearly been abrogated by an intervening Supreme Court decision or legislation, predicts that all the active judges will agree that

procedure a "mini en banc."[151] In the Seventh Circuit, a proposed opinion that would overrule a prior decision or create a conflict between or among circuits may not be filed unless it is circulated to the active judges and a majority does not vote to rehear the case en banc;[152] if a proposed opinion would establish a new rule or procedure, a panel may also use this procedure.[153] An opinion published under these procedures contains a footnote stating that the opinion has been circulated to all judges in regular active service, and no judge favored or a majority did not favor a rehearing en banc.[154]

In the D.C. Circuit, a policy statement provides that a panel may seek court endorsement of a proposed decision.[155] Among the decisions appropriate for this procedure are those:

(1) resolving an apparent conflict in the prior decisions of panels of the court;
(2) rejecting a prior statement of law which, although arguably dictum, warrants express rejection to avoid future confusion;
(3) overruling an old or obsolete decision which, although still technically valid as precedent, has plainly been rendered obsolete by subsequent legislation or other developments; and
(4) overruling a more recent precedent which, due to an intervening Supreme Court decision, or the combined weight of authority from other circuits, a panel is convinced is clearly an incorrect statement of current law.[156]

the circuit precedent should be abandoned, and that a rehearing en banc is not needed. A second category covers opinions like those in the first category except that abrogation has occurred for other reasons; for example, to prescribe a procedure for the district court to follow. A third category covers opinions not in the first two categories where a panel concludes that the full court should have an opportunity to see and comment on the proposed opinion before filing. Non-panel judges have 14 days to respond. For opinions in the first two categories, if one or more active judges object to filing, the panel must either adhere to the precedent proposed to be abandoned or call for an en banc poll. An objection to the filing of an opinion in the third category does not prevent filing the opinion, unless an en banc poll is requested.

[151] *Shipping Corp. of India Ltd. v. Jaldhi Overseas Pte Ltd.*, 585 F.3d 58, 67 n.9 (2d Cir. 2009).

[152] 7th Cir. R. 40(e).

[153] *Id.*

[154] *Id.*

[155] D.C. Circuit website, "Rules & Procedures" tab, "*En Banc* Endorsement of Panel Decisions (Irons footnote)" link.

[156] *Id.* POLICY STATEMENT ON *EN BANC* ENDORSEMENT OF PANEL DECISIONS (January 17, 1996).

The policy statement requires that prior to filing, the panel opinion is circulated to the full Court: "[T]he panel must obtain the affirmative agreement of every member of the court not recused," and "those voting to endorse the panel's decision must constitute an absolute majority of the active members of the court."[157] The statement also requires that "the panel shall announce the en banc court's endorsement of its decision [in] a footnote[.]"[158]

[157] *Id.* Thus, the policy cannot be used if several recusals leave the court without a majority of active judges endorsing the panel decision.

[158] *Id.*

11

Promoting the Expeditious Disposition of Appeals

This chapter considers how the courts of appeals endeavor to promote the expeditious disposition of appeals. It includes time limits or at least target dates for circulation of opinions (majority, concurring, and dissenting), issuance of reports on the status of opinions not filed, and what remedial steps have been taken when applicable time limits or target dates have not been observed. The chapter also reports the circuits' median disposition times, which to some extent reflect their success in the expeditious disposition of appeals.

Although the Federal Rules of Civil Procedure, governing litigation in the district courts, provide that they should be "construed, administered, and employed by the court and the parties to secure the just, *speedy*, and inexpensive determination of every action and proceeding,"[1] the Federal Rules of Appellate Procedure, applicable to the courts of appeals, have no counterpart provision referring to speedy disposition of appeals. Nevertheless, all courts of appeals endeavor to minimize delays in issuing opinions. As pointed out in Chapter 1, all chief judges consider monitoring the expeditious decision of appeals an important part of their job. Some courts have deadlines or target dates for circulating and responding to opinions, all have some form of reporting system to alert judges that assigned opinions have not been timely circulated to panel members, and some have practices for remedying delinquencies.[2]

[1] Fed. R. Civ. P. 1 (emphasis added). Reenforcing this direction, Congress enacted the Civil Justice Reform Act of 1990, Pub. L. No. 101-650, 104 Stat. 5089, 5093, which requires the Director of the Administrative Office of the U.S. Courts (AO) to prepare a semiannual report disclosing for each district judge and magistrate judge (1) the number of motions pending for more than six months and the name of each case in which such a motion is pending, (2) the number of bench trials submitted for more than six months and the name of each case, and (3) the number of cases that have not been terminated within three years after filing and the name of each case (codified at 28 U.S.C. § 476). There is no comparable requirement for court of appeals judges.

[2] Because federal judges have constitutionally assured life tenure (subject only to impeachment), penalties for chronic delinquencies in writing opinions cannot be as severe as those

The Supreme Court has noted, with apparent approval, that many federal courts have "informal, unpublished rules" providing that a judge with "a given number of cases under submission … will not be assigned more cases until opinions and orders issue on his 'backlog,'" and stated in dictum that "[t]hese are reasonable, proper, and necessary rules, and the need for enforcement cannot reasonably be doubted."[3] The time limits or target dates, reporting systems, and practices for remedying delinquencies in the circuits vary considerably.

11.1 TIME LIMITS AND TARGETS FOR CIRCULATING AND RESPONDING TO OPINIONS

The circuits generally have "targets" for circulating and responding to opinions – some by custom, some by internal operating procedure (IOP), and some by general order.

In the First Circuit, there has been an effort to circulate opinions within 45 days of assignment.

In the Third Circuit, it is the "aspirational goal" of the court that the judge assigned an opinion circulates a draft within 60 days after assignment or receipt of supplemental briefs (except in complex cases).[4] The non-writing judges have eight calendar days to respond that they approve or disapprove the circulated opinion (ten days during August).[5] After a second judge of the panel approves the draft opinion, the third judge has 45 days to circulate a concurring or dissenting opinion if the judge chooses to write separately.[6] These time limits also apply to opinions in en banc cases (though the court's IOPs specify that "judges will give preparation of en banc opinions priority over preparation of panel opinions").[7]

In the Fourth Circuit, the target date for circulating an opinion is 75 days.

In the Fifth Circuit, the majority opinion should be circulated within 60 days of assignment, and any concurrences or dissents should be circulated within 30 days thereafter. For civil cases, opinions should issue within 75 days of submission in summary calendar cases and within 90 days of oral argument. For criminal cases, the opinion should issue within 45 days of the date of submission for summary calendar cases and within 60 days of the date of oral argument.

that have occurred in some non-Article III courts, where such failures have contributed to decisions to deny reappointment.

3 *Chandler v. Judicial Council of Tenth Circuit*, 398 U.S. 74, 85 (1970).

4 3d Cir. IOP 5.5.3(a).

5 *Id.* IOP 5.5.2.

6 *Id.* IOP 5.5.3.(b).

7 *Id.* IOP 5.5.5.

In the Sixth Circuit, in calendared cases, opinions should be circulated within 45 days of the hearing date, with work pending as of the end of the summer arguments to be completed by the October sitting. In non-oral argument cases, work is expected to be circulated within 14 days, and ultimately all work of the panel should be completed within 30 days of the conclusion of the panel's three-month existence.

In the Seventh Circuit, in a case to be decided by non-precedential order, a draft opinion should be circulated to other members of the panel within 21 days of the date the case was argued or submitted,[8] and in a case to be decided by precedential opinion, a draft opinion should be circulated within 90 days of the date the case was argued or submitted (or 180 days if the case is unusually complex).[9] Responding to circulated drafts is "the first order of business" according to the court's operating procedures,[10] and a judge should respond within 14 days of submission with approval, suggestions, or notice that a separate opinion is being considered.[11] Concurring or dissenting opinions should be circulated within 28 days of receiving an initial opinion.[12] If a panel member needs additional time, the judge must notify the other members of the panel, and, if more than 30 days are needed for an opinion or more than 14 days are needed for other actions, must notify the chief judge of the delay and the reasons for it.[13] Also in the Seventh Circuit, the operating procedures note that: "Each judge should establish a tickler system designed to ensure adherence to these norms. When one chambers does not receive a draft, vote or response within the time presumptively established, secretaries or law clerks should inquire."[14] This provision concludes that such a step "not only catches communications lost in transmission but also serves as a backup reminder system."[15]

In the Ninth Circuit, in non-complex cases, non-precedential memorandum dispositions are normally to be circulated within seven days of submission, and precedential published opinions are normally to be circulated within 30 days of submission.[16] Judges "shall" give priority to responding to a circulated opinion,[17] and "should normally" inform the panel within seven

[8] 7th Cir. OP 9(a).
[9] *Id.* OP 9(b).
[10] *Id.* OP 9(c).
[11] *Id.*
[12] *Id.* OP 9(d).
[13] *Id.* OP 9(g).
[14] *Id.* OP 9(f).
[15] *Id.*
[16] 9th Gen. Ord. 9.2.
[17] *Id.*

days after the opinion has been circulated whether they intend to concur or dissent.[18] Dissenting or other separate opinions are normally to be circulated within 14 days after the proposed majority opinion is circulated.[19]

In the D.C. Circuit, the court expects judges to make every effort to circulate an opinion within 90 days of assignment.

In the Federal Circuit, there is a 30-day rule for circulating dissents.

11.2 REPORTING THE STATUS OF OPINIONS NOT CIRCULATED OR FILED

The circuits use various time limits for reporting to their judges information on draft opinions not yet circulated or filed.

First Circuit: A report is generated each month listing all of the assigned opinions that are pending 90 days, which is circulated to all judges of the court. The report is presented at the court's staff meetings, which are attended by all judges of the court and the unit heads.

Second Circuit: A list of all cases with opinions not circulated to panel members 60 days after submission is circulated to all judges before the court's quarterly meetings. At each meeting, the chief judge reads the list. The list groups the cases into four categories: (1) cases awaiting another decision, either from the Supreme Court, a panel of the Second Circuit, or a state supreme court to which a question of state law has been certified; (2) opinions circulated prior to the previous court meeting and awaiting votes from panel members; (3) opinions circulated after the previous court meeting and awaiting votes from panel members; (4) all other cases in which opinions have yet to be circulated. In each category, cases are listed in the order in which they were argued or submitted, and the list shows the name of each case, the date of submission, the number of days since submission, a brief statement of the principal issues in the appeal, the initials of the panel members, the initials of the writing judge, the writing judge's comment from the last time the list was read if the case was then listed, and a blank space for the writing judge's report at the current court meeting.

Third Circuit: Three different reports are used: (1) "Opinions Not Drafted," (2) "Pending Cases Without Writing Assignments," and (3) "Pending Cases With Writing Assignments." The report on "Opinions Not Drafted" displays the number of precedential and not precedential opinion assignments not drafted (excluding per curiam opinions). The report provides an overview of

[18] *Id.*
[19] *Id.*

cases assigned to an individual judge with a list of case numbers, captions, and a notation whether 60 days has lapsed since the case was argued or submitted. The report on "Pending Cases Without Writing Assignments" displays cases that have been assigned to merits panels, but for which a writing assignment judge has not been entered. (There are a number of reasons as to why a case would be before a merits panel, but a writing assignment should be deferred (i.e., the case was recently argued or submitted, the case is a death penalty case which has not yet been argued or submitted, the case is held CAV (*Curia Advisari Vult*), or the case contains a question of law that has been certified to a state court).) This report tracks cases until a writing assignment has been made. The report on "Pending Cases With Writing Assignments" provides a complete picture of cases assigned to a judge to draft the opinion, providing elapsed time and status of the opinion.

Two monthly emails are sent to the entire court. The first is a reminder for chambers to update the status of their opinions in CM/ECF (the courts' electronic docketing system). The second contains hyperlinks to the listed reports and is sent after the initial reminder to update the status of opinions.

Fourth Circuit: A monthly report is circulated to the full court listing any cases in which the opinion has not been filed within 75 days of assignment to an authoring judge. The report reflects the date of circulation if an opinion has been circulated.

Fifth Circuit: The clerk prepares monthly detailed reports on various matters, including the status of all submitted cases. The clerk provides each judge with a list of pending cases, which notes the writing judge and fellow panelists.

Sixth Circuit: Several reports are available to the court concerning the status of cases under submission. Judges have individual reports on their assignments available only to them. There are also reports accessible to all judges. These reports list all cases pending more than 90, 180, 360 days, or longer. The clerk and the circuit executive have access to all reports. A monthly summary is circulated to the judges. The "Report of Cases Under Submission For More than Ninth Months" is considered at the court meetings.

Seventh Circuit: A list of all cases pending before a panel after submission is circulated monthly to all judges and considered at semiannual court meetings. The list groups the cases by the name of the assigned writing judge. At the court meeting, judges are asked about each case pending more than three months after submission in which they have been assigned an opinion. As in some other circuits, the chief judge contacts judges who have opinions outstanding before the court meeting, by telephone or by email, to ask about the cases on the list.

Eighth Circuit: Every month, judges submit one report of all cases assigned to them that have been under submission more than 90 days. The reports are sent to the circuit executive, with a copy to every judge and to the clerk. The report is rarely considered at court meetings. A chief judge noting a problem will typically take it up with the assigned judge or the presiding judge of the panel.

Ninth Circuit: Quarterly, each judge is sent a list of all cases assigned to that judge which have been under submission but not yet circulated for more than six months or that have not been filed within nine months of submission. These reports (as updated) are then included as part of the quarterly court meeting agendas and each judge reports orally on the status of those cases.[20]

Tenth Circuit: Once a month, the clerk's office prepares and circulates a list of pending cases under submission. Each judge receives a list of the pending cases under submission that are assigned to that judge. The chief judge, clerk of court, and circuit executive receive a list that includes opinions assigned to all the judges on the court. The chief judge might pay particular attention to cases that have been under submission for more than six months, and to judges who have more than ten opinions that have not been circulated. The report is not considered at court meetings.

Eleventh Circuit: A monthly report of opinions not circulated is sent to all judges, which shows how each judge is doing compared with other judges. At the court's three meetings each year, a report is considered showing how the court compares with other circuits in median time from notice of appeal to filing of appellant's brief and from filing of last brief to disposition.

D.C. Circuit: Each month, there is a report on the status of every case that has been argued but not yet assigned.[21] Each judge reports on the status of every opinion assigned to him or her that has not been circulated or is waiting to be cleared by other members of the panel.[22]

Federal Circuit: A report is prepared that shows the number of outstanding cases and their respective ages, by judge. The report is sent to all judges, but not discussed at court meetings.

11.3 REMEDYING DELAYS IN DISPOSITION OF APPEALS

Some circuits endeavor to remedy noncompliance with time limits for circulating opinions or responding to circulated opinions, beyond circulating and sometimes discussing reports.

[20] *Id.* Gen. Ord. 9.1.

[21] D.C. Cir. Handbook of Practice and Internal Procedures XII(D), Making the Decision, Timing of Decisions.

[22] *Id.*

In the Second Circuit, on one known occasion an additional law clerk was provided to the chambers of a delinquent judge. On another occasion, the chief judge removed sitting days from a delinquent judge and restored some of them when the judge became almost current. No one but the chief judge and the delinquent judge were aware that this had occurred.

In the Third Circuit, on one occasion, a chief judge provided support from a staff attorney to a delinquent judge.

In the Fourth Circuit, on one occasion, a chief judge provided calendar relief to a judge who had fallen behind to allow him to catch up on his work.

In the Fifth Circuit, the opinions proctor, or sometimes the chief judge, will have discussions with a judge who is behind in his or her work. A provision, unique among the circuits, authorizes the chief judge to appoint one or more panels "to review pending cases for appropriate assignment or disposition."[23]

In the Seventh Circuit, if original and extended time limits for circulating an opinion have not been complied with, the presiding judge of a panel is supposed to reassign the opinion, unless, in consultation with the assigned writer and the chief judge, the presiding judge determines that reassignment will cause further delay.[24] If two members of a panel have agreed to an opinion and the third member does not comply with the time limits to respond or circulate a separate opinion, the writing judge is supposed to inquire of the third judge whether a response is imminent, and if further delay is anticipated, the majority is supposed to issue the opinion with a notation that the third judge reserves the right to file a separate opinion later.[25]

In the Ninth Circuit, when two judges of a panel have agreed to a written disposition but the third judge has not agreed to a circulated opinion or circulated a concurring or dissenting opinion within 60 days of receiving the main and any separate opinion, the author of the main opinion is to submit the disposition to the clerk of court and send a copy of the cover memo to the third judge.[26] Ten days later, the clerk is to file the opinion with a notation that the third judge may file a separate opinion later; the two judges may grant the request of the third judge to delay filing for 14 days, or more in extraordinary circumstances.[27]

Also in the Ninth Circuit, if a judge falls behind in preparing opinions, the chief judge may relieve the judge of further calendar duties until

23 5th Cir. R. 34.1.
24 7th OP 9(h).
25 *Id.* OP 9(i).
26 9th Cir. Gen. Ord. 4.5(a).
27 *Id.*

the judge becomes "more current" or assign the judge to fewer panels.[28] A prima facie case for relieving a judge consists of one or more of the following criteria: (1) two or more cases not circulated after nine months, (2) five or more cases not circulated after six months, or (3) 15 or more cases not circulated after three months.[29] The assigned judge may rebut the prima facie case by showing that within one month the judge will no longer meet any of the criteria (or that there is good cause for remaining on the calendar).[30]

Unique among the circuits, the Ninth Circuit has a local rule providing that parties are encouraged to contact the clerk if a motion has been pending for more than four months, decision on the merits of an appeal has not been issued within nine months after submission, or a petition for rehearing has been pending longer than six months.[31]

In the Eleventh Circuit, sometimes a panel presider will not assign opinions in a particular week to a delinquent judge.

In the D.C. Circuit, if a judge has more than two opinions not circulated by August 15, that judge cannot sit when the new term begins in September.

In the Federal Circuit, the court has informal policies that set out the conditions under which judges may not sit. If a judge has more than one opinion that is more than one year old, that judge cannot sit; and if a judge has more than four opinions that are more than 180 days old, that judge cannot sit. The chief judge enforces those rules. Panels are expected to enforce on their own the target date of 30 days for circulating dissents.

11.4 MEDIAN DISPOSITION TIMES OF APPEALS

The various practices of the courts of appeals in monitoring the status of uncirculated opinions and remedying failure to observe time limits might have contributed to significant differences among the circuits in the median times from oral argument to disposition or from submission on briefs to disposition, as Table 11.1 indicates (for the 12-month period ending September 30, 2022).[32]

These differences among the circuits in the intervals from argument or submission on briefs to disposition contribute to the significant differences

[28] *Id.* Gen. Ord. 3.2(j).

[29] *Id.*

[30] *Id.*

[31] *Id.* R. 25-2, Cir. Adv. Comm. N. (1), (3), (5).

[32] AO, "Statistics & Reports" tab, "Data Tables" link, Table B-4 (September 30, 2022). The AO does not report these time intervals for the Federal Circuit.

TABLE 11.1 *Median time intervals from oral argument to disposition and from submission on briefs to disposition*

Circuit	Median time in months from oral argument to disposition	Median time in months from submission on briefs to disposition
1st	4.1	2.0
2nd	1.0	0.2
3rd	4.2	1.2
4th	2.8	0.3
5th	1.2	0.4
6th	2.9	1.1
7th	3.1	0.2
8th	3.9	0.2
9th	1.6	0.2
10th	4.2	1.4
11th	3.2	0.8
D.C.	4	0.7

TABLE 11.2 *Median time intervals from notice of appeal to disposition, from notice of appeal to filing of appellee's last brief, and from filing of appellee's last brief to argument or submission on briefs*

Circuit	Median time in months from notice of appeal or docket date to disposition	Median time in months from notice of appeal or docket date to filing of appellee's last brief	Median time in months from filing of appellee's last brief to argument or submission on briefs
1st	14.0	6.9	3.3
2nd	12.2	7.0	5.8
3rd	9.0	5.8	3.2
4th	7.9	4.9	8.5
5th	9.2	4.7	4.8
6th	8.5	4.5	3.6
7th	9.5	5.2	3.0
8th	4.6	3.9	4.5
9th	13.2	7.8	6.2
10th	9.5	5.0	4.1
11th	9.2	5.0	4.0
D.C.	11.6	7.2	3.8

among the circuits in the aggregate median times from notice of appeal to disposition, although the major variables in these aggregate median times are the differences in the median times from notice of appeal to filing of appellee's last brief and in the median times from filing of appellee's last brief to argument or submission on briefs. Table 11.2 shows the differences among the

TABLE 11.3 *Appeals not decided 12 or more months after submission*

Circuit	Appeals not decided 12 or more months after submission
1st	19
2nd	9
3rd	21
4th	2
5th	32
6th	2
7th	13
8th	2
9th	10
10th	14
11th	2
D.C.	3
Fed.	0

circuits for these three intervals (for the 12-month period ending September 30, 2022).[33]

A final indicator of the pace of dispositions among the circuits is the number of appeals not decided 12 or more months after oral argument or submission on briefs, as shown in Table 11.3 (for the 12-month period ending September 30, 2022).[34]

Some of the differences reflected in these three tables are likely attributable, at least in part, to differences during the 12-month period reported in the number of judicial vacancies in the circuits, the aggregate number of months the vacancies have existed, the number of senior judges, and the percentage of workload undertaken by senior judges.

[33] *Id.* The AO does not report these time intervals for the Federal Circuit.

[34] AO, "Statistics & Reports" tab, "Data Tables" link, Table B-20 (September 30, 2022).

12

Death Penalty Cases

This chapter considers the courts of appeals' practices concerning death penalty cases. This category includes appeals in federal criminal cases in which the defendant is sentenced to death and habeas corpus cases challenging such sentences, usually those imposed in state courts, raising constitutional claims after state court appeals have been exhausted.

All circuits, except the D.C. Circuit (and the Federal Circuit, which has no jurisdiction over criminal cases), have special rules and internal operating procedures (IOPs) for death penalty cases.[1] These concern a variety of topics.

12.1 PANELS FOR DEATH PENALTY CASES

In most circuits, local rules or IOPs specify that the panel assigned the first filing in a death penalty case is assigned all matters concerning that case.[2]

Additionally, several of the courts note how the panels for hearing death panels are formed outside of the normal panel configuration process. In the First Circuit, capital cases are randomly assigned to a panel of three judges (of whom at least one is an active judge) from the "capital case pool."[3] That pool consists of all active judges and the senior judges who have filed with the clerk of court a statement of willingness to serve on capital case panels.[4]

1 1st Cir. R. 48.0; *id.* IOP VII(E); 2d Cir. R. 47; *id.* IOP 47; 3d Cir. L.A.R. Misc. 111.1-.9; *id.* IOP ch. 16; 4th Cir. R. 22(b), (c); *id.* IOP 22.1; 5th Cir. R. 8; 6th Cir. R. 8, 22(c), 31(c), 32(b)(2); *id.* IOP 22; 7th Cir. R. 22; 8th Cir. R. 22A; 9th Cir. R. 22-2, 22-3, 22-4(c), (e), 22-6, 27-5; *id.* Gen. Ord. 8; 10th Cir. R. 22.2; 11th Cir. R. 22-4; *id.* IOP 2 Oral Argument in Capital Cases.

2 1st Cir. IOP VII(E)(2); 2d Cir. IOP 47.1(b)(6); 3d Cir. IOP 16.2; 4th Cir. IOP 22.1; 5th Cir. R. 8.2; 6th Cir. IOP 22(b)(1); 7th Cir. R. 22(a)(2); 8th Cir. R. 22A; 9th Cir. R. 22-2(c), (e); 10th Cir. R. 22.2; 11th Cir. R. 22-4.

3 1st Cir. IOP VII(E)(1).

4 *Id.*

In the Second Circuit, a panel for a death penalty case is drawn from the "death penalty case pool," which is made up of all active judges of the court and the senior judges who have filed a statement of willingness to serve on death penalty case panels.[5] A judge who serves on a death penalty case is not eligible to serve on another such case until the pool of eligible judges is exhausted.[6]

In the Third Circuit, the clerk of court uses a computer program to "randomly select a panel from a pool of all possible three-judge combinations" consisting of circuit judges in active service and any senior judges who have said they are willing to hear death penalty cases.[7] But the computer is designed to minimize the possibility of assignment of any judge to successive panels.[8]

In the Fifth Circuit, special panels are selected in rotation from the court's regular screening panels.[9]

In the Sixth Circuit, the court maintains a roster of active judges and any senior judges who "so elect for making panel assignments in all death penalty cases[.]"[10] The clerk of court assigns the panel as soon as the case is docketed.[11]

In the Ninth Circuit, the clerk of court assigns the appeal in capital cases to a death penalty panel composed of active judges and senior judges willing to serve on death penalty panels.[12]

In the Eleventh Circuit, capital cases are randomly assigned from a roster of active judges of the court.[13]

12.2 SENIOR JUDGES

By local provision or custom, senior judges may opt out of assignment to panels considering death penalty cases in the First, Second, Third, Fourth, Sixth, Eighth, and Ninth Circuits.[14] In the Fifth and Eleventh Circuits, senior judges do not serve on death penalty panels.[15]

5 2d Cir. IOP 47.1(b)(1).
6 *Id.* IOP 47.1(b)(4).
7 3d Cir. IOP 16.2.
8 *Id.*
9 5th Cir. R. 8.2.
10 6th Cir. IOP 22(b)(1).
11 *Id.*
12 9th Cir. R. 22-2(a).
13 11th Cir. R. 22-4.
14 1st Cir. IOP VII(E)(1); 2d Cir. IOP 47.1(b)(1); 3d Cir. IOP 16.2; 6th Cir. IOP 22(b)(1); 9th Cir. R. 22-2(a).
15 5th Cir. R. 8.2 (death penalty panels are selected from members of administrative panels, which are composed of active judges, 5th Cir. IOP, Motions Panels (after R. 27); once a judge takes senior status, that judge can continue on the cases the judge has already been assigned or opt out); 11th Cir. R. 22-4.

12.3 PROMPT NOTIFICATION

Some circuits provide for prompt notification to the court of appeals of cases with death penalty sentences so that a panel will be ready for emergency motions. In the First Circuit, each party, upon filing in a district court a proceeding challenging a sentence of death imposed pursuant to a federal or state court judgment, must file with the court of appeals a "Certificate of Death Penalty Case" containing pertinent information.[16] The U.S. Attorney must file such a certificate with the court of appeals upon notifying the district court of intent to seek the death penalty in a federal criminal case, and must update the certificate immediately upon the return of a verdict of a death sentence.[17]

In the Second Circuit, within seven days after initiation in the court of appeals or a district court of a proceeding challenging a death sentence imposed by a federal or state court, each party and the government must file with the clerk of the court of appeals a "Certificate of Death Penalty form."[18]

In the Third Circuit, each party, upon filing in a district court a proceeding challenging a sentence of death imposed pursuant to a federal or state court judgment, must file with the district court a "Certificate of Death Penalty Case" containing pertinent information.[19] The U.S. Attorney must file such a certificate upon the return of a verdict of a death sentence in a federal criminal case.[20] Upon docketing, the clerk of the district court transmits a copy of the certificate with a copy of the petition to the clerk of the court of appeals.[21] Finally, upon entry of an order setting an execution date, the clerk of the court of appeals monitors the status of the execution and any pending litigation and establishes communication with all parties and relevant courts.[22]

In the Fourth Circuit, whenever a petition for writ of habeas corpus or motion to vacate a federal sentence in which a sentence of death is involved is filed in the district court or the court of appeals, the petitioner files with the petition a statement certifying the existence of a death sentence and the emergency nature of the proceedings and listing any proposed date of execution.[23]

[16] 1st Cir. R. 48.0(b)(1).

[17] *Id.*

[18] 2d Cir. R. 47.1(b). For the form, *see id.* website, "Rules" link, "Forms and Instructions" link, "Death Penalty Cases" link, Certificate of Death Penalty Case form.

[19] 3d Cir. L.A.R. Misc. 111.2(a).

[20] *Id.*

[21] *Id.*

[22] *Id.* L.A.R. Misc. 111.2(c).

[23] 4th Cir. R. 22(b)(1).

The clerk of the district court immediately forwards a copy of any such statement to the court of appeals.[24]

In the Sixth Circuit, counsel must notify the clerk by telephone at the earliest possible time that an appeal is coming, even before filing a notice of appeal if possible.[25]

In the Seventh Circuit, the clerk of the district court must notify the clerk of the court of appeals immediately upon the filing of a notice of appeal.[26]

In the Eighth Circuit, a state attorney general or the U.S. Attorney must notify the clerk when a warrant of execution has been issued.[27]

In the Ninth Circuit, upon the filing of a notice of appeal in a case in which a district court has denied a stay of execution, the clerk of the district court must immediately notify the clerk of the court of appeals promptly by telephone or electronic filing.[28]

In the Tenth Circuit, when a petitioner has a scheduled execution date at the time the notice of appeal is filed, a separate notice regarding the date must be filed with the clerk.[29]

12.4 STAY OF EXECUTION

Federal law provides that upon the appointment of counsel for an indigent defendant sentenced to death and the filing of a petition for a writ of habeas corpus, an order setting an execution date shall be stayed; the stay expires if the petition for habeas corpus is not filed, the defendant waives the right to file the petition, or the petition is filed but the petitioner fails to make a substantial showing of the denial of a federal right.[30]

Some circuits have local provisions supplementing the federal provision. In the First Circuit, the filing of a notice of appeal automatically stays an execution.[31] In the Second Circuit, in any case in which a death sentence has been imposed by a federal or state court in the circuit, the sentence is stayed upon the filing of a direct appeal from the judgment imposing the sentence or the filing of a notice of appeal from the denial of the first collateral attack on the judgment.[32] Unless vacated or modified, the stay remains in effect until

24 *Id.*
25 6th Cir. R. 22(c)(2).
26 7th Cir. R. 22(b)(1).
27 8th Cir. R. 22A(a).
28 9th Cir. R 22-6(a).
29 10th Cir. R. 22.2(B)(1).
30 28 U.S.C. § 2262.
31 1st Cir. R. 48.0(c)(2).
32 2d Cir. R. 47.1(c)(1).

the issuance of a mandate in the appeal.[33] Also in the Second Circuit, when a notice of appeal is filed in a death penalty case, the clerk designates a staff member to receive emergency stay motions during nonbusiness hours, and the staff member immediately notifies the panel assigned to the appeal of the filing of an emergency motion.[34]

In the Third Circuit, in a direct appeal of conviction or sentence in a criminal case in which the district court has imposed the death penalty, an order is entered staying the sentence;[35] the stay remains in effect until issuance of the mandate in the appeal.[36]

In the Fifth Circuit, the filing of a petition for rehearing (or hearing) en banc does not operate as a stay of execution.[37] (If an en banc poll results in a grant of rehearing (or hearing) en banc, the chief judge will enter an order staying the execution pending further order of the court.[38])

In the Sixth Circuit, an appellant moving for a stay in a death penalty case must file the motion as soon as possible after filing a notice of appeal.[39] The court may conclude it can address the merits of the case on a motion for a stay; if so, the court will order the parties to address the merits in expedited briefs and may grant a temporary stay pending consideration of the merits.[40] In the Seventh Circuit, a movant filing a motion for a stay must immediately notify opposing counsel by telephone.[41] In the Ninth Circuit, counsel must notify the clerk by telephone or email as soon as it becomes evident that emergency relief will be sought, and if the case has not yet been assigned to a death penalty panel, a motions panel may grant a stay.[42] In the Tenth Circuit, a motion for a stay of execution may be filed before filing a notice of appeal; counsel should also contact the clerk of court "as soon as feasible" regarding anticipated motions for stay.[43]

12.5 MISCELLANEOUS DEATH PENALTY PROVISIONS

In the Third Circuit, the clerk of the court of appeals notifies the clerk of the Supreme Court when a case involving the suspension or stay of execution

33 *Id.*
34 *Id.* R. 47.1(c)(7).
35 3d Cir. L.A.R. 8.3.
36 *Id.* Misc. L.A.R. 111.7(c)(3).
37 5th Cir. IOP Handling of Petition by the Judges (Capital Cases).
38 *Id.*
39 6th Cir. R. 8(a)(1); *id.* R 22(c)(3)(A).
40 *Id.* R. 8(a)(2); *id.* R 22(c)(3)(B).
41 7th Cir. R. 22(h)(3).
42 9th Cir. R. 22-2(e).
43 10th Cir. R. 22.2(C)(2).

of the judgment of a state or federal court is filed.[44] The Third Circuit also warns counsel that a petition for rehearing en banc filed within 48 hours of a scheduled execution might not be delivered to all the judges in time for adjudication before the execution, and such a petition will be distributed by the normal means of delivery unless the panel hearing the case has ordered expedited voting.[45]

The Fourth Circuit has designated a coordinator of death penalty cases in the clerk's office to act as a liaison with district court personnel and counsel to "aid in the expeditious treatment of appeals involving a sentence of death."[46]

In the Sixth Circuit, an emergency motion must be filed with the clerk, not an individual judge.[47] As for briefing, the deadline for the appellant's brief is set by the clerk, then the appellee's brief must be filed within 60 days after service of the appellant's brief, and the appellant has 14 days to file a reply brief (but it must be filed at least seven days before argument).[48] In habeas corpus death penalty cases and appeals from a federal sentence of death, the briefs may not exceed one-and-a-half times the length specified in Federal Rule of Appellate Procedure (FRAP) 32(a)(7)(A) and (B).[49]

In the Seventh Circuit, unless the court sets another schedule, the following time limits apply. On a direct appeal in a federal criminal prosecution, the appellant's brief is due within 63 days of the date when the appeal is docketed, the appellee's brief is due within 49 days after service of the appellant's brief, and a reply brief is due within 21 days after service of the appellee's brief.[50] In all other appeals in death penalty cases, the applicable time limits are 28 days, 21 days, and 7 days, respectively.[51] In appeals in death penalty cases, oral argument will be held expeditiously after filing of the reply brief.[52]

In the Eighth Circuit, all pleadings filed after notification of a death penalty warrant will be treated as emergency matters.[53]

In the Ninth Circuit, the chief judge appoints an active or senior judge to serve as the capital case coordinator for a particular death penalty case or for all such cases in which an execution date has been set.[54] The capital case

44 3d Cir. IOP 16.5.
45 *Id.* Misc. L.A.R. 111.7(a).
46 4th Cir. IOP 22.1.
47 6th Cir. R. 22(c)(4).
48 *Id.* R. 31(c)(3).
49 *Id.* R. 32(b)(2).
50 7th Cir. R. 22(c)(1)(A).
51 *Id.* R. 22(c)(1)(B).
52 *Id.* R. 22(d)(2).
53 8th Cir. R. 22A(b).
54 9th Cir. Gen. Ord. 8.1(a).

coordinator may establish deadlines for various procedural steps.[55] A principal brief in a capital case may not exceed 21,000 words, and a reply brief may not exceed 9,800 words.[56]

Also in the Ninth Circuit, an active or senior judge may request a rehearing en banc of an order denying an authorized second or successive motion for collateral relief.[57] Such a request will result in en banc review if a majority of active judges votes in favor of en banc review; a judge's failure to vote within the stated timeframe shall be considered a "yes" vote in favor of en banc review.[58]

In the Tenth Circuit, upon receipt of a docketing statement in death penalty cases arising under 28 U.S.C. § 2254 or any federal criminal statute, the clerk enters an order directing the parties to schedule a video or telephone conference with the chief deputy clerk or other designated court representative to discuss procedural matters and a briefing schedule.[59] Also in the Tenth Circuit, if an execution date has been set, the clerk of the district court notifies the clerk of the court of appeals of any new habeas corpus petition.[60]

55 *Id.* Gen. Ord. 8.1(b).
56 *Id.* R. 32-4.
57 *Id.* R. 22-4(d).
58 *Id.*
59 10th Cir. R. 22.2(A)(1), 2.
60 *Id.* R. 22.2(B)(2).

13

Senior Judges

This chapter considers various aspects of the role of senior judges on the courts of appeals, including eligibility for senior status, what senior judges are entitled to vote on, their role in en banc rehearings, and other distinctions between senior and active judges.

13.1 SENIOR STATUS

Federal judges serving full time are known as "active" judges.[1] Those who have "retire[d] from regular active service" at an eligible age and after a sufficient number of years of service,[2] and continue to serve either full- or part-time, as they choose, are known as "senior judges."[3] Those who have left the bench are said to have "resigned."[4]

Federal judges are eligible to become senior judges after reaching age 65 with 15 years of service or age 70 with ten years of service.[5] Between ages 65 and 70, the "rule of 80" permits an active judge to take senior status when the judge's age and years of service total 80 (e.g., age 67 + 13 years of service = 80).[6]

1 *See, e.g.*, 2d Cir. IOP 35-1(a).
2 28 U.S.C. § 371(b).
3 *Id.* § 371(e)(2). In 1958, Congress first used the term "senior judge" to mean a judge who had retired from regular active service. Pub. L. No. 85-755 § 5, 72 Stat. 848, 849 (1958) (amending 28 U.S.C. § 294(b)). They were previously called "retired judges." *See, e.g.*, *Steckel v. Lurie*, 185 F.2d 923, 924 (6th Cir. 1950).
4 *See, e.g.*, *In re Judicial Misconduct*, 747 F.3d 869, 871 (U.S. Jud. Conf. 2014). Although a judge who has left the bench is properly said to have "resigned," the term has also (and confusingly) been applied to a judge who had taken senior status and receives only the salary of the office at the time of leaving active service because the judge has not performed sufficient work to qualify for the salary of the office, that is, a salary that includes pay raises, 28 U.S.C. § 371, Historical Notes. *See Booth v. United States*, 291 U.S. 339, 348–50 (1934) (distinguishing between a judge "retiring" and "resigning").
5 28 U.S.C. § 371 (a), (c).
6 *Id.* § 371(c).

Senior judges may continue to perform such judicial duties as they are willing and able to undertake *within* their circuit when designated and assigned by the chief judge or judicial council of their circuit and such judicial duties within their court when designated and assigned by the chief judge.[7] They may also perform such "special" judicial duties *outside* their circuit when designated and assigned by the Chief Justice of the United States.[8]

Each senior judge reports to the chief circuit judge the number of months in which the senior judge has performed judicial and/or administrative duties in the previous year, a number that may vary up or down from year to year.[9] In all of the numbered circuits and the D.C. Circuit in 2022, there were 111 sitting senior judges.[10] Resident senior judges (meaning judges performing service in their own circuit) participated in 21.8 percent of all appeals in that year.[11]

Taking senior status creates a vacancy to be filled by appointment of a new active judge;[12] resigning from a court of appeals after becoming a senior judge does not create a vacancy and therefore has no effect on the number of a court's active judges.

Supplementing statutory provisions affecting senior judges, there are variations in circuit local rules, internal operating procedures (IOPs), other documents, and customs concerning several topics.

13.2 PRECEDENCE

Circuits vary in the precedence accorded senior judges. In most circuits, when determining where judges will sit on three-judge oral argument panels, after the presiding judge, the other two panel members are seated based on strict seniority (regardless of the judge's senior or active status). However, active judges have precedence over senior judges in seating on three-judge panels by an IOP in the Third Circuit,[13] and by custom in the Fourth, Eleventh, and

7 *Id.* § 294(c).

8 *Id.* § 294(d).

9 Neither the average number of months all senior judges work nor the average percentage of active judges' workload undertaken by all senior judges is reported, but the latter has been estimated to be about 50 percent for senior circuit and district judges combined. *See* Frederic Block, *Senior Status: An "Active" Senior Judge Corrects Some Common Misunderstandings*, 92 Cornell L. Rev. 533, 540 (2007).

10 Administrative Office of the U.S. Courts (AO), "Statistics & Reports" tab, "Federal Court Management Statistics" link, "U.S. Court of Appeals–Federal Court Management Statistics–Profiles" link (December 31, 2022).

11 AO, "Statistics & Reports" tab, "Federal Court Management Statistics" link, "U.S. Court of Appeals–Federal Court Management Statistics–Case Participation" link (December 31, 2022).

12 28 U.S.C. § 371(d).

13 3d Cir. IOP 3.2.

D.C. Circuits (not in the First, Second, Fifth, Sixth, Seventh, Eighth, Ninth, Tenth, and Federal Circuits). In rehearings en banc, active judges have precedence over senior judges in seating in the Third, Eleventh, and D.C. Circuits, but not in the First, Second, Fourth, Fifth, Sixth, Seventh, Eighth, Ninth, Tenth, and Federal Circuits. In a provision unique among the circuits, the Seventh Circuit explicitly provides that no distinction is made between active and senior judges with respect to precedence, except as required by law.[14]

In the Second, Fifth, Sixth, Seventh,[15] and Ninth Circuits, senior judges are listed on orders and opinions in order of precedence, that is, ahead of active judges with less seniority (apart from the chief judge). In the First, Eighth, Tenth, and Federal Circuits, the presider (the active judge with most seniority) is listed first, followed by the other two judges in order of commission date. In the Third, Fourth, Eleventh, and D.C. Circuits, senior judges are listed after active judges.

At ceremonial events such as installations of a new judge, memorial sessions for a deceased judge, and portrait unveilings, in the First, Second, Third, Fourth, Fifth, Sixth, Seventh, Eighth, Ninth, Tenth, and Federal Circuits, the presiding judge (typically the chief judge) has precedence over the remaining judges, who are then seated based on strict seniority (regardless of a judge's senior or active status). This almost always means that after the presiding judge, senior judges sit ahead of active judges. The Eleventh and D.C. Circuits, by custom, gives precedence in seating to active judges.

13.3 COMPENSATION

Implementing the Constitution's provision that federal judges "hold their Offices during good Behaviour,"[16] Congress in 1948 authorized senior judges to continue to receive their salary (considered to be an annuity) for the rest of their lives, whether they remain in the judiciary or resign from it.[17] However, Congress also provided that to be eligible for "the salary of the office," that is, compensation that includes pay raises, senior judges must perform in the preceding year judicial duties in a courtroom or administrative work in the court to which the judge is assigned equal to, or greater than, judicial or administrative work performed by an active judge in three months.[18] Alternatively,

14 7th Cir. OP 2(a).
15 *Id.* OP 2(c).
16 U.S. Const. art. III, § 1.
17 28 U.S.C. § 371(a).
18 *Id.* § 371(e)(1)(A)–(C).

the judge can perform duties for a state or local governmental entity equal to the full-time work of a judicial branch employee.[19] The chief judge of the circuit certifies a senior judge's compliance with these requirements.[20] A senior judge unable to meet these requirements because of a disability is also entitled to receive the salary of the office.[21]

Also related to compensation is the exemption of senior judges from the limitation on outside income from teaching to 15 percent of the judge's salary that is in effect for active judges.[22] Another compensation consequence of assuming senior status is that the payment to senior judges is an annuity,[23] which is exempt from social security taxes.[24]

13.4 STAFF

In 1948, Congress authorized active circuit judges to appoint "necessary" law clerks and secretaries (now called "judicial assistants"),[25] and authorized the Director of the Administrative Office (AO) of the United States Courts to set their compensation.[26] For senior judges, authority for staff depends on work performed, which "shall be made pursuant to rules promulgated by" the Judicial Conference of the United States (JCUS).[27]

In 1950, the JCUS instructed the Director of the AO "to permit retired [*i.e.*, senior] judges to retain their personnel … provided that they continue to perform substantial judicial work [and concluded] that the question as to whether or not the services performed are substantial will be a matter for determination by the particular circuit judicial council involved."[28] In 1980, the JCUS learned that a report of a House Appropriations Subcommittee stated that "the number of supporting personnel (secretaries and law clerks) authorized for senior judges should be related directly to workload performed, and that 'the Judicial Councils should not only certify that a senior judge is

19 *Id.* § 371(e)(1)(D). If the work performed under this subsection is less than that of a full-time judicial employee, one-half of such work may be aggregated with work performed pursuant to subsections 371(e)(1)(A)–(C). *Id.* § 371(e)(1)(D).

20 *Id.* § 371(e)(1).

21 *Id.* § 371(e)(1)(E).

22 *See* 5 U.S.C. § 502(b)(2), exempting senior judges from the limitation imposed by 5 U.S.C. § 501(a)(1).

23 28 U.S.C. § 371(a).

24 26 U.S.C. § 3121(i)(5).

25 62 Stat. 869, 920, § 712 (codified at 28 U.S.C. § 712).

26 62 Stat. 869, 914 § 604 (a)(5) (codified at 28 U.S.C. § 604(a)(5)).

27 Pub. L. No. 101-194 § 705 (1989) (codified at 28 U.S.C. § 371(e)(2)).

28 Report of the Proceedings of the Judicial Conference of the United States 22 (September 25, 1950), www.uscourts.gov/sites/default/files/1950-09.pdf.

performing "substantial judicial duties," but also should determine the number of supporting positions necessary based on actual workload.'"[29] That report prompted the JCUS to state that "the judicial councils of the circuits will be asked to provide this information."[30] The councils usually accept the representations of the amount of work reported by each senior judge and approved by the chief circuit judge.

A few circuits have local provisions concerning staff for senior judges. In the Second Circuit, a senior circuit judge with a workload of at least 80 percent of that of an active circuit judge is presumed to be entitled to five staff positions; if at least 50 percent, four staff positions; and if at least 25 percent, three staff positions.[31] Additionally, if staff assigned to a senior judge are not used, the chief judge may reassign them (full time or part time) to other judges.[32] In the Third Circuit, senior judges are permitted to volunteer their law clerks to assist active judges, especially for work that can be performed in the senior judge's chambers, and to assist the staff attorney's office.[33] Senior judges taking an extended absence from chambers usually notify the active judges that their law clerks are available (unless the law clerks will be fully occupied with court work in that time).[34] In the Eighth Circuit, senior judges are "generally" allotted two law clerks.[35]

13.5 PANEL ASSIGNMENTS

All circuits, by custom or local provision,[36] offer senior judges the opportunity to indicate the workload they will undertake each year. Some circuits are particularly solicitous of the scheduling needs and preferences of their senior judges. For example, in the Second Circuit, senior judges' requests for sitting days are given priority when the annual sitting calendar is assembled. The Ninth Circuit provides that senior judges will not be assigned to hear appeals away from their home stations unless they are willing to do so,[37] and more generally can elect the number of days and the cities in which they will sit. Moreover, senior judges in the Ninth Circuit may elect not to serve on panels

[29] Report of the Proceedings of the Judicial Conference of the United States 81 (September 22–23, 1982), www.uscourts.gov/sites/default/files/1982-09.pdf.
[30] *Id.*
[31] 2d Cir. Staffing Guidelines for Senior judges, H(I) (2012).
[32] *Id.* at F.
[33] 3d Cir. IOP 15.
[34] *Id.*
[35] 8th Cir. IOP 1(C)(2).
[36] *See, e.g.*, 9th Cir. R. Court Structure and Procedures E(5).
[37] *Id.* Gen. Ord. 3.2(c).

screening for oral argument or considering certificates of appealability[38] (i.e., permission by a court of appeals, on a showing of a substantial question, to appeal a district court's denial of a petition for a writ of habeas corpus[39]). In the Tenth Circuit, for oral argument cases heard during a regularly scheduled term of court, senior judges specify the number of days they want to sit, and whether they want to hear civil cases, criminal cases, or a mix of both.

In the First, Second, Third, Sixth, Seventh, Ninth, Tenth, and Eleventh Circuits, two senior judges may serve on a merits panel. In the Fourth and D.C. Circuits, two senior judges may serve on a merits panel, but we were informed that they rarely do so. In the Fifth Circuit, court policy prohibits the assignment of two senior judges to a panel absent judicial emergency. In the Eighth Circuit an effort is made to avoid two senior judges serving on the same panel, but this has happened over the years, particularly when there were vacancies. In the Federal Circuit, panels hearing oral arguments will generally not include more than one senior judge.[40]

By local provision or custom, in the First, Second, Third, Fourth, Sixth, Eighth, and Ninth Circuits, senior judges hear death penalty cases only if they elect to do so,[41] and do not serve on death penalty panels in the Fifth and Eleventh Circuits.[42]

In the Fourth Circuit, senior judges may elect not to hear emergency motions. In the Sixth Circuit, senior judges may opt out of election-related and other time-sensitive matters. In the Ninth Circuit, senior judges can opt out of hearing motions and/or screening cases. In the D.C. Circuit, senior judges may opt out of "special panel" service and may also opt out of "complex cases."

13.6 VOTING AT COURT MEETINGS

Federal Rule of Appellate Procedure (FRAP) 47 limits voting on local rules to active judges. In the First, Seventh, Eighth, Ninth, Tenth, and D.C. Circuits, by custom or local provision, senior judges can vote on matters considered at court meetings,[43] and in the Second, Third, Fourth, Fifth, Sixth, and Federal Circuits,

[38] *Id.* Gen. Ord. 6.2(b).

[39] 28 U.S.C. § 2253(c)(2).

[40] Fed. Cir. R. 47.2(a).

[41] 1st Cir. IOP VII(E)(1); 2d Cir. IOP 47.1(b)(1); 3d Cir. IOP 16.2; 6th Cir. IOP 22(b)(1), 9th Cir. R. 22-2(a).

[42] 5th Cir. R. 8.2 (death penalty panels are selected from members of administrative panels, which are composed of active judges, 5th Cir. IOP, Motions Panels (after R. 27); once a judge takes senior status, that judge can continue on the cases the judge has already been assigned or opt out); 11th Cir. R. 22-4.

[43] 9th Cir. Gen. Ord. 10.2(a); D.C. Cir. Handbook of Practice and Internal Procedures I(C)(2).

by custom or local provision, they do not. In the Eleventh Circuit, senior judges "do not normally participate in the administrative work of the court."[44]

13.7 REHEARINGS EN BANC

Two provisions of federal law make distinctions between active and senior judges concerning the conduct of rehearings en banc. First, FRAP 35(a) provides that senior judges on courts of appeals may not vote in a poll to determine whether a majority of judges (not disqualified) favor a rehearing en banc.[45] Second, 28 U.S.C. § 46(c) provides that senior judges are not eligible to be members of an en banc court, except that any senior judge who was a member of the panel whose decision is being reheard en banc is eligible to serve on an en banc court.[46] Section 46(c) has a transition provision specifying that an active judge who takes senior status after a case is reheard en banc may continue to participate in the decision of that case.[47]

Several circuits have additional provisions concerning senior judges' participation in the en banc process and the significance of when they take senior status, as explained in Chapter 13. These provisions concern requesting an en banc poll, eligibility to vote in an en banc poll, and membership of an en banc court.

13.8 JUDICIAL MISCONDUCT INVESTIGATING COMMITTEES

Federal law provides that active judges serving on a committee to investigate complaints of judicial misconduct may continue to serve after taking senior status,[48] which implies that a judge already in senior status may not serve on such a committee. Nevertheless, Rule 12(a) of the JCUS's model rules on misconduct complaints authorizes senior judges to serve on such committees.

13.9 MISCELLANEOUS PROVISIONS CONCERNING SENIOR JUDGES

The Second Circuit provides a special benefit to senior judges. By custom, when a panel meets after oral argument to discuss and tentatively vote on the

44 11th Cir. R. 47, IOP 2.
45 Fed. R. App. P. 35.
46 28 U.S.C. § 46(c).
47 *Id.*
48 *Id.* § 353(b).

day's cases, the presiding judge usually asks a senior judge whether there is an opinion that the judge prefers to write or prefers not to write. The senior judge's choice is generally honored.

In the Third Circuit, senior judges can serve as mediators in the court's appellate mediation program.[49] Also in the Third Circuit, when drafts of precedential opinions and non-precedential opinions that are not unanimous are circulated to the active judges before filing, senior judges may request to receive them.[50]

In the Fourth Circuit, petitions for rehearing en banc are circulated to senior judges who request them (and any senior judge who was on the original panel).[51]

In the D.C. Circuit, the clerk designates one member of the panel each day to have primary responsibility for screening cases (the screening function is concerned with alignment of parties and issues, and allotment of time for the arguments), and senior judges are not eligible for this assignment.[52]

* * * * *

With respect to compensation, work assignments, and choice of where to hear cases, senior judges are treated well, but in some respects in some circuits, they are slightly disadvantaged.[53] The attitude of those circuits treating senior judges well was summed up by a former chief judge in these words: "We do whatever we can to make senior status attractive so that active judges will elect senior status as soon as they are eligible, thereby securing additional judges for the court." In the Second Circuit, "It is the policy of the Second Circuit Judicial Council that senior judges should be treated for all purposes exactly like active judges, except for those differences incident to statutes or required by the judge's reduction in workload."[54]

49 3d Cir. R. 33.1.
50 *Id.* IOP 5.5.4.
51 4th Cir. R. 35(a).
52 D.C. Cir. Handbook of Practice and Internal Procedures XI(C)(1).
53 *See* Marin K. Levy, *The Promise of Senior Judges*, 115 Nw. U. L. Rev. 1227 (2021).
54 2d Cir. Staffing Guidelines for Senior Judges (2012).

14

Judicial Councils and Judicial Conferences

This chapter considers the circuits' practices for their judicial councils and their judicial conferences.

14.1 CIRCUIT JUDICIAL COUNCILS

Federal law provides for the creation of a judicial council in each circuit, consisting of the chief judge and an equal number of circuit and district judges of the circuit.[1] The chief judge of each circuit is required to call a meeting of the judicial council of the circuit at least twice a year.[2]

14.1.1 *Functions of Circuit Councils*

A judicial council is the governing body of the circuit, with administrative authority over the court of appeals and the district courts within the circuit. A council's power is potentially very broad. Since 1948, 28 U.S.C. § 332(d)(1) has provided that each council "shall make all necessary and appropriate orders for the effective and expeditious administration of justice within its circuit,"[3] a power the Supreme Court has stated explicitly is constitutional.[4] Any "general order" concerning practice or procedure can be issued only after giving the public notice and an opportunity to comment.[5] But once issued,

1 28 U.S.C. § 332(a)(1). Congress created the Judicial Councils in 1939, when they were composed of only the judges of a court of appeals. Act of Aug. 7, 1939, ch. 501, 76th Cong., 1st Sess., § 1, 53 Stat. 1223, 1224 (adding § 306 to the Judicial Code).

2 28 U.S.C.§ 332(a)(1).

3 *Id.* § 332(d)(1).

4 *Chandler v. Judicial Council of the Tenth Circuit*, 398 U.S. 74, 86 n.7 (1970) ("We see no constitutional obstacle preventing Congress from vesting in the Circuit Judicial Councils, as administrative bodies, authority to make 'all necessary orders for the effective and expeditious administration of the business of the courts within [each] circuit.'").

5 28 U.S.C. § 332(d)(1).

"[a]ll judicial officers and employees of the circuit shall promptly carry into effect all orders of the judicial council,"[6] an obligation enforceable by the contempt power.[7]

Judicial councils have used their section 332 power in various ways. By statute, councils have the authority to make "the necessary orders" "[i]f the district judges in any district are unable to agree upon the adoption of rules" for the division of "business of a court having more than one judge."[8] And judicial councils have used their section 332 power to recommend to all district courts in their circuit adoption of a model rule needed to maintain the proper handling of bankruptcy cases,[9] in the wake of the Supreme Court's decision in the *Northern Pipeline* case.[10]

In addition to the broad section 332 power to issue necessary orders, a judicial council has several specific responsibilities. The one with potentially the most direct effect on judges is the role of the judicial council in the administration of the Judicial Conduct and Disability Act of 1980.[11] The Act permits complaints against a judge for misconduct or disability to be filed with the chief judge of the judge's circuit.[12] Most are dismissed because they relate to the merits of a case, meaning that the person filing the complaint thought that the judge's decision was incorrect. This type of complaint is excluded from the coverage of the Act.[13] A chief judge may also conclude the proceedings if the chief judge finds that "appropriate corrective action has been taken" or that "action on the complaint is no longer necessary because of intervening events."[14] (A complainant or a judge aggrieved by an order of a chief judge may seek review by the judicial council.[15])

If a complaint has sufficient merit to survive dismissal, the chief judge appoints an investigating committee consisting of the chief judge and an equal number of circuit and district judges.[16] The committee's report is sent to the judicial council, which can investigate further, dismiss the complaint,

6 *Id.* § 332(d)(2).
7 *Id.*
8 *Id.* § 137(a).
9 *E.g., In re Q1 Corp.*, 28 B.R. 647, 649 (E.D.N.Y. 1983) (recounting a Second Circuit Council order).
10 *Northern Pipeline Co. v. Marathon Pipe Line Co.*, 458 U.S. 50 (1982).
11 28 U.S.C. §§ 351–364.
12 *Id.* § 351(a). The complaint may allege that a judge "has engaged in conduct prejudicial to the effective and expeditious administration of the business of the courts" or "is unable to discharge all the duties of office by reason of mental or physical disability." *Id.*
13 *Id.* § 352(b)(1)(A)(ii).
14 *Id.* § 352(b)(2).
15 *Id.* § 352(c).
16 *Id.* § 353(a)(1).

or, for misconduct, take any of several disciplinary actions.[17] The council can order that for a limited time no further cases be assigned to the judge, censure or reprimand the judge privately or publicly,[18] or "certify" to the Judicial Conference of the United States (JCUS) that the judge "may have engaged in conduct … which might constitute one or more grounds for impeachment."[19] The JCUS may transmit the recommendation to the House of Representatives.[20] A complainant or a judge aggrieved by an order of a judicial council may petition for review of the order by the JCUS Committee on Judicial Conduct and Disability.[21]

In the event of a judge's disability, a council can certify disability pursuant to the judicial disability statute,[22] and recommend that the judge voluntarily retire.[23] If the judge does not voluntarily retire, a council can present a certificate of disability to the President, and if the President finds that the judge is unable to discharge the duties of office and that the appointment of an additional judge is necessary for the efficient dispatch of business, the President may appoint a judge, subject to Senate confirmation.[24] The judge "whose disability causes the appointment of an additional judge" is treated "as junior in commission" to the other judges of the court.[25]

Courts and individual judges have expressed various views on the disciplinary power of judicial councils.[26] Whether a judicial council has power to order

[17] *Id.* § 354(a)(1).

[18] *See, e.g.*, *In re Complaint of Judicial Misconduct*, 751 F.3d 611, 623 (U.S. Jud. Conf. 2014) (order publicly reprimanding a district judge and prohibiting assignment of new cases for 180 days as punishment for derogatory emails).

[19] 28 U.S.C.§ 354(a)(2), (b)(2)(A). The D.C. Circuit has upheld the power of a judicial council and the JCUS to certify to the House of Representatives that circumstances may warrant impeachment of a district judge. *Hastings v. Judicial Conference of the U.S.*, 829 F.2d 91, 94 (D.C. Cir. 1987).

[20] 28 U.S.C. § 355 (b)(1).

[21] *See* Rules for Judicial-Conduct and Judicial-Disability Proceedings 21(a), 249 F.R.D. 662 (2008).

[22] 28 U.S.C. § 372(b).

[23] *Id.* § 354(a)(2)(B).

[24] *Id.* 372(b).

[25] *Id.*

[26] *See Hastings v. Judicial Conference of the United States*, 770 F.2d 1093, 1100 (D.C. Cir. 1985) ("As to each of the investigatory and disciplinary powers conferred by the Act, there may be a question of whether Congress may lawfully vest such power in an administrative organ of the federal judiciary composed of Article III judges."); *id.* at 1107 (Edwards, J., concurring) ("[I]n order for Article III's guarantee of independence to be fulfilled, the Constitution must be interpreted to designate impeachment as the *exclusive* mechanism for disciplining or removing federal judges."). The Fifth Circuit has stated that section 332 does not authorize a judicial council to censure a judge to remedy judicial misconduct. *In re McBryde*, 117 F.3d 208, 228 (5th Cir. 1997).

reassignment of a district judge's cases to other judges has divided the courts considering the issue.[27] By statute a council has authority to order the assignment of cases among district judges in the absence of agreement among the judges.[28]

A judicial council is required periodically to review district court rules for consistency with rules promulgated by the Supreme Court and can abrogate or modify any district court rule found to be inconsistent.[29] District court rules "remain in effect unless modified or abrogated" by a judicial council.[30] A council also reviews the validity of a district court's plan (1) for the random selection of members of grand juries and petit (trial) juries,[31] (2) for the speedy disposition of criminal cases,[32] and (3) for furnishing representation to those unable to afford counsel in criminal cases.[33] Judicial councils have also used their section 332 powers (1) to promulgate plans for death penalty cases,[34] (2) to issue interim rules to avoid a judicial emergency,[35] (3) to issue statements

[27] *Compare Utah-Idaho Sugar Co. v. Ritter*, 461 F.2d 1100, 1101 (10th Cir. 1972) (upholding a judicial council's authority to assign cases when district judges disagree) *with McBryde*, 117 F.3d at 222 ("Nothing in 28 U.S.C. §§ 331–335 ... can be read to empower the Council to issue a self-executing order transferring cases from one district court judge to another," but acknowledging a council's power to order that no further cases be assigned to a district judge, *id.* at 229). *Compare also Chandler*, 398 U.S. at 123–25 (Harlan, J., concurring) (approving a council order prohibiting the assignment of new cases to a district court judge), *with id.* at 141 (Douglas, J., with whom Black, J. joins, dissenting) ("It is time to put an end to the monstrous practices that seem about to overtake us, by vacating the orders of the Judicial Council that brand Judge Chandler as unfit to sit in oncoming cases." *and id.* at 142 (Black, J., with whom Douglas, J., joins, dissenting) (rejecting the power of a council to prohibit the assignment of new cases to a district judge). But a council can reassign a case pursuant to section 332 for administrative reasons. *See Jimenez v. Aristeguieta*, 311 F.2d 547 (5th Cir. 1962).

[28] 28 U.S.C. § 137(a).

[29] *Id.* § 332(d)(4).

[30] *Id.* § 2071(c)(1).

[31] *Id.* § 1863(a). *See, e.g.*, *In re Jury Plan of the Eastern District of New York*, 61 F.3d 119, 121–22 (2d Cir. Jud. Council 1995) (giving a jury plan conditional approval). When sitting as a panel for reviewing jury plans, the council includes the chief judge of the relevant district or an active district judge designated by the chief judge. 28 U.S.C. § 1863(a).

[32] 18 U.S.C. §§ 3165(a), 3165(c), 3166(f). *See, e.g.*, *Government of the Virgin Islands v. Bryan*, 818 F.2d 1069, 1074–75 (3d Cir. 1987).

[33] 18 U.S.C. § 3006A(a).

[34] *See, e.g.*, *Truesdale v. Moore*, 142 F.3d 749, 758 (4th Cir. 1998) (upholding a judicial council's promulgation pursuant to section 332 of a plan for death penalty cases that directed the court of appeals and district courts to identify competent counsel experienced in death penalty cases and directed district courts to dispose of petitions collaterally challenging death penalty sentences within 180 days of filing (shorter than the statutory limit of 450 days) and the court of appeals to render a decision within 120 days of the petitioner's reply brief).

[35] *See White Motor Corp. v. Citibank, N.A.*, 704 F.2d 254, 261–64 (6th Cir. 1983). The emergency arose in the wake of *Northern Pipeline Construction Co. v. Marathon Pipeline Co.*, 458 U.S. 50, 84–87 (1982) (invalidating the grant of jurisdiction to bankruptcy courts of civil proceedings arising under Title 11 of the Judicial Code).

to accompany court of appeals rules in plans regarding prompt disposition of criminal cases,[36] and (4) to approve a chief district judge's request for suspension of Speedy Trial Act time limits if a district court is unable to comply with those time limits.[37]

A judicial council may require a district judge to live at or near a place for holding court,[38] and may approve the furnishing of chambers for circuit judges at locations other than where regular sessions of court are held.[39]

A judicial council may approve a district court's request to pretermit a session of the court for insufficient business or other good cause.[40]

A judicial council identifies and evaluates the needs of district courts for interpreters and may request the Director of the Administrative Office of the U.S. Courts (AO) to certify the need for interpreters in a particular language.[41]

A judicial council has three functions with respect to senior judges. A council certifies whether a "retired" judge, that is, a senior judge (*see* Chapter 13), who has rendered "substantial service" in the previous year is entitled to retain staff and chambers,[42] can assign a senior judge to perform services within the circuit (the chief circuit judge can also do this),[43] and certifies a senior district judge's need for court reporters.[44]

A judicial council has several functions with respect to bankruptcy judges. A council (1) evaluates bankruptcy judge candidates and recommends finalists to the court of appeals for appointment,[45] (2) may approve the temporary transfer of a bankruptcy judge to another district,[46] (3) may approve the designation of a bankruptcy judge to serve all or the remainder of such judge's 14-year term in another district,[47] (4) may recall a retired bankruptcy judge to service with the judge's consent,[48] (5) may certify a bankruptcy court's need for a court clerk,[49] (6) may establish conditions and limitations on the use of

36 *See Hilbert v. Dooling*, 476 F.2d 355, 358 (2d Cir. 1973) (en banc).
37 18 U.S.C. § 3174(a).
38 28 U.S.C. § 134(c).
39 *Id.* § 462(c).
40 *Id.* § 140(a).
41 *Id.* § 1827(b)(1).
42 Report of the Proceedings of the Judicial Conference of the United States 21–22 (September 1950).
43 28 U.S.C. § 294(c).
44 6 AO, Guide to Judicial Policies ("Guide") § 280.30.
45 28 U.S.C. § 152(a)(1). The statute says "recommendations of the Judicial Conference," but the Guide makes clear that recommendations come from a Judicial Council, *see* 10 Guide § 1010.20(1)(3).
46 28 U.S.C. § 155(a).
47 *Id.* § 152(c).
48 *Id.* § 155(b).
49 *Id.* § 156(b).

facilities and services that a court may use (either on or off the court's premises) where the costs are paid from assets of an estate,[50] and (7) may establish a bankruptcy appellate panel composed of three bankruptcy judges to hear appeals from another bankruptcy judge.[51] Such panels currently exist in the First, Sixth, Eighth, Ninth, and Tenth Circuits.[52]

A judicial council also has several functions with respect to magistrate judges. It recommends to the JCUS necessary expenses, including compensation for legal, clerical, and secretarial assistance for magistrate judges,[53] and may approve their requests to the Director of the AO for courtroom and office space within courthouses or office buildings.[54]

A judicial council's approval is necessary for construction projects within a circuit if the cost exceeds $100,000,[55] and may authorize exceptions to the space standards in the U.S. Courts Design Guide.[56]

A judicial council may direct that the records of district courts and courts of appeals be kept at locations other than those designated by the respective courts.[57]

A judicial council has authority to appoint a circuit executive,[58] but in practice a council usually ratifies the choice made by the chief circuit judge.

14.1.2 *Composition of Circuit Councils*

The circuits vary in the composition of their judicial councils and the terms of the circuit and district judge members. The number of circuit and district judges and their terms are determined by a vote of the active circuit and district judges of the circuit.[59] In all circuits, the chief judge is a member and

50 *Id.* § 156(c).
51 *Id.* § 158(b)(1).
52 1st Cir., "United States Bankruptcy Appellate Panel for the First Circuit," www.bap1.uscourts.gov; 6th Cir., "United States Court of Appeals for the Sixth Circuit, Bankruptcy Appellate Panel," www.ca6.uscourts.gov/bankruptcy-appellate-panel; 8th Cir. "United States Court of Appeals for the Eighth Circuit, Bankruptcy Appellate Panel," www.ca8.uscourts.gov/bankruptcy-appellate-panel; 9th Cir. "Bankruptcy Appellate Panel for the Ninth Circuit," www.ca9.uscourts.gov/bap/; 10th Cir. "United States Bankruptcy Appellate Panel for the Tenth Circuit," www.bap10.uscourts.gov.
53 28 U.S.C. § 635(a).
54 *Id.*
55 16 Guide § 320.20.10(2).
56 Report of the Proceedings of the Judicial Conference of the United States 39 (September 20, 2005); *id.* 35 (March 16, 1999).
57 28 U.S.C. § 457.
58 *Id.* § 332(e).
59 *Id.* § 332(a)(1), (2).

presiding officer of the judicial council and serves during the term of chief judgeship.[60] The chief judge appoints a successor if any council member is unable to complete a term.[61] The number, selection, and terms of circuit and district judge members of the councils are as follows:

First Circuit: The chief circuit judge, five active circuit judges, and five district judges (one from each of the five districts), serving two-year terms. Nonvoting members (observers) include one bankruptcy judge and one magistrate judge, each serving two-year terms.

Second Circuit: The chief circuit judge, the six most senior active circuit judges, and the six chief judges of the six district courts in the circuit.

Third Circuit: The chief circuit judge, the five most senior active circuit judges, and the chief judges of the five district courts in the circuit.

Fourth Circuit: The chief circuit judge, four active circuit judges, and four chief district judges. The circuit judges, selected on the basis of seniority, come from each of the states within the circuit, other than the state of the chief judge's duty station. The first four chief district judges were chosen first by drawing by lot four of the five states in the circuit and then, because three states had more than one district, selecting the chief judge from each of these three states with the most seniority, plus the chief district judge from the single-district state. The circuit and district judges (apart from the chief circuit judge) serve four-year terms. Upon the completion of a circuit judge's term, membership rotates among the circuit judges of the state in order of seniority. Upon the completion of a chief district judge's term, membership goes to the chief district judge of the state that has just gone one year without membership, and within that state, membership goes to the chief district judge with the most seniority, measured by date of commission, who has not previously served on the council. Nonvoting members are the district judge representative to the JCUS, and a bankruptcy judge and a magistrate judge, selected by their colleagues, who serve three-year terms.

Fifth Circuit: The chief circuit judge, the circuit judge next eligible to become chief circuit judge, eight other circuit judges, and nine district judges – one from each district in the circuit, selected by the judges of the district. The chief circuit judge and the active circuit judge next in seniority to the chief judge serve what are said to be "permanent" terms; all other council members serve staggered three-year terms. Nonvoting members are a magistrate judge and a bankruptcy judge.

60 *Id.* § 332(a)(1).
61 *Id.* § 332(a)(5).

Sixth Circuit: The chief circuit judge, the circuit judge next eligible to become chief circuit judge, nine circuit judges, and the chief judge of each of the nine district courts in the circuit. Nonvoting members include one bankruptcy judge, selected by the circuit's bankruptcy judges, and one magistrate judge, selected by the circuit's magistrate judges.

Seventh Circuit: The chief circuit judge, ten active circuit judges, the chief judges of the seven district courts in the circuit, and three district court judges from the Northern District of Illinois (the circuit's largest district), selected by the judges of that district, who serve staggered three-year terms. Nonvoting members include one chief bankruptcy court judge and one magistrate judge.

Eighth Circuit: The chief circuit judge, ten circuit judges, and ten district judges. The district judges come from each of the circuit's ten districts, are selected by the judges of their district, and serve for three-year terms. Nonvoting members are one magistrate judge, chosen by all the magistrate judges; one bankruptcy judge, chosen by all of the bankruptcy judges; and the Eighth Circuit district judge representative to the JCUS.

Ninth Circuit: The chief circuit judge, the circuit judge next eligible to become chief circuit judge, one senior circuit judge, three circuit judges (one each representing the Northern, Middle (Central), and Southern administrative units of the court of appeals), the chief district judge of the Central District, and three other chief district judges (one each representing the Northern, Middle (Central), and Southern group of district judges), along with one senior district judge. Attending as observers are the President of the Ninth Circuit District Judges Association (serving a two-year term), the district judge representative to the JCUS (for the duration of the term on the JCUS), the chair of the Conference of Chief District Judges (serving a one-year term), the chair of the Conference of Chief Bankruptcy Judges (serving a one-year term), the chair of the Magistrate Judges Executive Board (serving a two-year term), a district court clerk (serving a one-year term), a bankruptcy court clerk (serving a one-year term), a chief probation officer (serving a one-year term), and a chief pretrial services officer (serving a one-year term). The council has an executive committee that consists of the chief judge, a circuit judge, and a chief district judge.

Tenth Circuit: The chief circuit judge, four active circuit judges, and four active district judges. The circuit judges and district judges serve two-year terms; the circuit judges rotate based on seniority. One district judge is a chief district judge, selected by all the chief district judges of the circuit; the other three district judges are selected by vote of all the active judges of the circuit, with only one district judge from any one district. Nonvoting members are the district judge representative to the JCUS, the chief judge of the bankruptcy appellate panel, and one magistrate judge and one bankruptcy judge selected by their colleagues.

Eleventh Circuit: The chief circuit judge, nine active circuit judges, and the chief judge of each of the nine district courts in the circuit. Nonvoting members are a magistrate judge and a bankruptcy judge, selected by their colleagues, who serve two-year terms.

D.C. Circuit: The chief circuit judge, four active circuit judges and four active district judges, all of whom are selected on the basis of seniority and serve two-year terms.

Federal Circuit: All circuit judges in regular active service.

14.1.3 *Staff of Circuit Councils*

A judicial council is authorized to appoint a circuit executive,[62] but the appointment is usually made by the chief judge with the council's approval. The circuit executive exercises administrative control of all nonjudicial activities of the court of appeals and has responsibility for administering the personnel system and the budget of the court of appeals.[63] The circuit executive may appoint necessary employees, with the approval of the council.[64]

14.2 CIRCUIT JUDICIAL CONFERENCES

Federal law provides that the chief judge of each circuit may summon biennially or annually the circuit, district, magistrate, and bankruptcy judges of the circuit in active service to a conference at a time and place the chief judge designates "for the purpose of considering the business of the courts and advising means of improving the administration of justice" within each circuit.[65]

14.2.1 *Functions of Circuit Judicial Conferences*

There is no prescribed format for circuit conferences. It is customary for the chief judge to give a report on the state of the circuit, discussing such matters

62 *Id.* § 332(e).

63 *Id.* § 332(e)(1)–(3).

64 *Id.* § 332(f)(3).

65 *Id.* § 333. Congress authorized circuit judicial conferences in 1939, which were then required to be held annually. Act of Aug. 7, 1939, ch. 501, 76th Cong., 1st Sess., § 1, 53 Stat. 1223, 1224 (adding § 307 to the Judicial Code).

as caseload volume in the court of appeals and the district courts, judicial vacancies, and prospects for nominations and confirmations of new judges.

The director of the AO, or a designee, usually reports on national developments affecting the federal judiciary, such as congressional appropriations for the judicial branch. The Director of the Federal Judicial Center (FJC), or a designee, usually reports on research projects being undertaken by the FJC and the availability of training sessions and seminars for judges and court staff.

At the circuit conference, the judges of the court of appeals and the district courts select the district court representative of the circuit to the JCUS,[66] considered in Chapter 2, and determine the representative's term (between three and five years).[67]

Many circuits present programs on current and historical topics at their conferences. The conference also promotes bench–bar relationships.

14.2.2 *Attendance at Circuit Judicial Conferences*

All circuits hold annual judicial conferences to which all judicial officers of the circuit are invited. There are variations in who else may attend – often members of the bar, including academics, are also invited, though some circuits (the Second, Sixth, Eighth, and Tenth) hold some conferences with only judicial officers.[68] The following shows the differences in the circuits' provisions for those invited to attend.

First Circuit: Members from within the circuit are presidents of bar associations of states and commonwealths within the circuit, the dean or faculty member designated by the dean of each accredited law school within the circuit, all U.S. Attorneys of the circuit, all federal defenders designated by the chief circuit judge, and lawyers in such number as the planning committee determines, selected by a committee of each district, or if there is no such committee, by the district judges as determined by each district court.[69]

Second Circuit: Lawyers, including academics, are invited in accordance with rules prescribed by the judicial council.[70] But the chief judge may hold a conference limited to judges,[71] and has done so, often in alternate years.

66 28 U.S.C. § 331.

67 *Id.*

68 2d Cir. IOP I(c)(2); 6th Cir. R. 205(a)(2) (odd-numbered years); 8th Cir. IOP 1(b)(3) (alternate years); 10th Cir. R. 37.3(A) (may hold in alternate years).

69 1st Cir. R. 47.1(c).

70 2d Cir. IOP I(c)(2).

71 *Id.*

Third Circuit: An "open invitation policy" is used, which permits, at the discretion of the chief judge, any member of the bar of any court within the circuit "interested in the work of the courts and the administration of justice in the circuit" to attend.[72]

Fourth Circuit: Invitees include the Attorney General of the United States (or a designee), the Solicitor General of the United States (or a designee), presidents of the state bar associations of the states of the circuit, one representative of the federal bar association elected to the Federal Bar Council from the Fourth Circuit, all U.S. Attorneys in the circuit, all federal public defenders of the circuit, all chief justices of the courts of last resort of the states within the circuit, all chief justices of the courts of last resort of federally recognized Native American Nations within the circuit, the chief judge of the United States Court of Appeals for the Armed Forces, the chief judge of the United States Tax Court, one representative of each accredited law school within the circuit, and one representative of the clerks of court of the circuit.[73] Additionally, invitees include one nominee by each active and senior circuit and district judge, two nominees by each Program Committee Chair, and three nominees by each new circuit and district judge to that judge's first two conferences.[74] Lawyers who have attended two conferences as nominees by judges become permanent conference members, entitled to attend all future conferences.[75]

Fifth Circuit: The court's rule for representation and participation by members of the bar is available from the clerk or the circuit executive.[76]

Sixth Circuit: Attendees include members of the bar admitted to a federal court within the circuit and "delegates."[77] A delegate must be an attorney who has demonstrated a "willingness to work to improve the judicial system" and has practiced actively for at least five years in one or more federal courts of the circuit, in a manner that reflects "integrity, honesty, capability, and civility."[78] Delegates consist of two or more lawyers appointed by the chief judge of the circuit, two by each other circuit judge, and one by each district judge.[79] An attorney who has attended three conferences in various capacities, such as a delegate, the president or president-elect of the state bar association of a state

[72] 3d Cir. L.A.R. 105.1.
[73] 4th Cir. IOP 47.2(A).
[74] *Id.* IOP 47.2(B)(1).
[75] *Id.* IOP 47.2(B)(2).
[76] 5th Cir IOP, Other Internal Operating Procedures (Judicial Conference).
[77] 6th Cir. R. 205(c).
[78] *Id.* R. 205(d)(1).
[79] *Id.* R. 205(d)(2).

within the circuit, a dean of a law school within the circuit, the U.S. Attorney for a judicial district in the Sixth Circuit, the federal public defender, and various other public officials, is a life member of the conference.[80] Additionally, any lawyer who has attended three conferences since 2000 may petition the chief judge to become a life member.[81] A life member may attend all open conferences.[82] But the Sixth Circuit holds "judges-only" conferences in odd-numbered years.[83]

Seventh Circuit: Those encouraged to attend include various court staff, law clerks to all circuit, district, bankruptcy, and magistrate judges, the clerks of these courts, U.S. Attorneys in the circuit and their legal staff, public defenders in the circuit and their legal staff, members of the Seventh Circuit Bar Association, United States Trustees in the circuit and their legal staff, and special guests invited by the chief judge or by the president of the Seventh Circuit Bar Association with the approval of the chief judge.[84]

Eighth Circuit: Circuit conferences alternate between conferences for judges (only) and conferences "open to the bar."[85]

Ninth Circuit: In addition to all judges, the circuit has an elaborate method of selecting lawyers to be invited. An order of the judicial council provides (1) in each district the number of lawyers invited is 1.28 times the number of authorized judgeships, (2) the bar in each district nominates to a committee of district judges three times the number of authorized lawyers, and the committee makes selections, (3) a committee of judges in each district nominates to the bar of the district three times the number of authorized lawyers, and the bar makes selections.[86]

Tenth Circuit: Regarding attendees, the Tenth Circuit states only that "[i]n alternate years, the circuit may hold a conference for judges only."[87]

Eleventh Circuit: The judicial council is responsible for planning and conducting the judicial conference.[88] The members of the conference, in addition to all judges of the circuit, senior staff, include, among others, the presidents and presidents-elect of the state bars of the states within the circuit, three representatives chosen by each state bar association, the chief justices of

80 *Id.* R. 205(e)(1).
81 *Id.* R. 205(e)(3).
82 *Id.* R. 205(e)(4).
83 *Id.* R. 205(a)(2).
84 7th Cir. R. 60(b).
85 8th Cir. IOP I(B)(3).
86 9th Cir. Council Order, Judicial Conference of the Ninth Circuit (November 1994).
87 10th Cir. R. 47.3(A).
88 11th Cir. R. Addendum One (a).

the state supreme courts within the circuit, the lawyers advisory committee of the circuit, each U.S. Attorney of the circuit, the federal public defender of any district within the circuit, the deans of all accredited law schools within the circuit, any retired Justice of the Supreme Court of the United States residing or practicing within the circuit, any current or former Attorney General of the United States residing or practicing within the circuit, the president of the American Bar Association (ABA), former presidents of the ABA residing or practicing within the circuit, state attorneys general, and any lawyer who has been nominated to a judgeship within the circuit.[89] Judges of the courts may also designate one or more lawyers, who actively practice in the federal courts of the circuit, to attend (with limits on the number of designees per court).[90] From time to time the court of appeals may conduct a judicial conference that is open to any attorney who practices in a district court within the circuit or the Eleventh Circuit Court of Appeals.[91]

D.C. Circuit: The judicial conference consists of the circuit, district, magistrate, and bankruptcy judges and various officials, including court staff, the chief judge of the Tax Court, the directors of the AO and the FJC, the U.S. Attorney for the District of Columbia, and Federal Public Defender for the District of Columbia, the director of the District of Columbia Public Defender Service, the deans of law schools located within the District of Columbia, the Attorney General of the District of Columbia, "members of the bar in such numbers as will permit and promote participation by those engaged in the various fields of federal court practice," and "other individuals whose background, position, or achievement, will contribute to the purpose and program of the conference."[92]

Federal Circuit: All members of the bar of the court may be members of the conference.[93]

89 *Id.* R. Addendum One (b)(1).
90 *Id.* R. Addendum One (b)(2).
91 *Id.* R. Addendum One (c).
92 D.C. Cir. R. 47.3(c).
93 Fed. Cir. R. 53.

15

Information on Websites

This chapter reports on the various types of information that can be located from the websites of the courts of appeals.

In 1982, Congress required that "[t]he rules for the conduct of the business of each court of appeals, including the operating procedures of such court, shall be published."[1] In 2002, Congress enacted the E-Government Act of 2002,[2] which included a provision requiring federal courts to establish websites containing several categories of information.[3] The Administrative Office of the U.S. Courts (AO) has implemented this provision with a website identifying for the courts of appeals categories of information that are "required," "highly recommended," "recommended," and "useful information to consider" for posting on court websites.[4] Although all circuits comply with the

[1] Federal Courts Improvement Act of 1982, Pub. L. No. 97-164, 96 Stat. 25, 54 (codified at 28 U.S.C. § 2077).

[2] Pub. L. No. 107-347, 116 Stat. 2899.

[3] *Id.* § 205, 116 Stat. at 2913–14. Section 205 requires that the websites of the Supreme Court, the courts of appeals, the district courts, the Court of Federal Claims, and the bankruptcy courts contain:

(1) Location and contact information for the courthouse, including the telephone numbers and contact names for the clerk's office and justices' or judges' chambers.
(2) Local rules and standing or general orders of the court.
(3) Individual rules, if in existence, of each justice or judge in that court.
(4) Access to docket information for each case.
(5) Access to the substance of all written opinions issued by the court, regardless of whether such opinions are to be published in the official court reporter, in a text searchable format.
(6) Access to documents filed with the courthouse in electronic form, to the extent provided under subsection (c). (Subsection (c) permits exceptions to protect privacy and security concerns.)

[4] *See* Required Website Content: U.S. Court of Appeals, available via the judiciary's internal network at https://JNet.ao.dcn. The "required" category for courts of appeals includes, in addition to information required by the E-Government Act, the local Employee Dispute Resolution ("EDR") plan, information on judges' attendance at privately funded seminars, and rules implementing the Judicial Conduct and Disability Act of 1980, 28 U.S.C. §§ 351–64.

E-Government Act and the AO's recommendations by creating websites with links to many kinds of documents, the formats of these websites, the documents linked to them, and the labeling of the documents vary considerably.

15.1 LINKS TO COURT RULES, IOPS, AND ORDERS

All circuits have links on their websites to the Federal Rules of Appellate Procedure (FRAP),[5] and their Local Rules,[6] called "Local Appellate Rules" in the Third Circuit,[7] and "Circuit Rules" in the D.C. Circuit.[8] The First, Second, Third, Fourth, Fifth, Sixth, Seventh, Eighth, Eleventh, D.C., and Federal Circuits have links on their websites to internal operating procedures (IOPs), called "Operating Procedures" in the Seventh Circuit,[9] and "Internal Procedures" in the D.C. Circuit.[10,11] The Third Circuit website has a link to Standing Orders.[12] The Fourth, Ninth, Tenth, and Eleventh Circuits' websites have links to General Orders.[13] The Fourth Circuit website also has a link to Related Standing Orders.[14] The Fifth Circuit has a link to the orders of

[5] All circuits' websites, "Rules" or "Rules & Forms" or "Rules & Procedures" or "Rules and Procedures" tab.

[6] *Id.*

[7] 3d Cir. website, "Rules & Procedures" tab, "Local Rules" link.

[8] D.C. Cir. website, "Rules & Procedures" tab, "Circuit Rules" link.

[9] 7th Cir. website, "Rules and Procedures" tab, "Operating Procedures" link.

[10] D.C. Cir. website, "Rules & Procedures" tab, "Handbook of Practice and Internal Procedures" link.

[11] 1st Cir. website, "Rules & Procedures" tab, "Internal Operating Procedures" link; 2d Cir. website, "Rules" link, "Internal Operating Procedures of the Second Circuit" link; 3d Cir. website, "Rules & Procedures" tab, "Internal Operating Procedures" link; 4th Cir. website, "Rules & Procedures" tab, "Federal & Local Rules of Appellate Procedure" link, "Federal & Local Rulebook with Internal Operating Procedures" link; *id.* website, "Rules & Procedures" tab, "Federal & Local Rules of Appellate Procedure" link, "Local Rulebook with Internal Operating Procedures" link; 5th Cir. website, "Rules & Procedures" tab, "Rules" link, "Federal and 5th Circuit Rules of Appellate Procedure and IOPs" link; *id.* website, "Rules & Procedures" tab, "Rules" link, "5th Circuit Rules of Appellate Procedure and IOPs" link; 6th Cir. website, "Rules and Procedures" tab, "Local Rules: F.R.A.P., Local Rules, I.O.P.'s" link; 7th Cir. website, "Rules and Procedures" tab, "Operating Procedures" link; 8th Cir. website, "Rules & Procedures" tab, "Internal Operating Procedures" link; 11th Cir. website, "Rules & Procedures" tab, "FRAP, 11th Circuit Rules, and IOPs" link; D.C. Cir website, "Rules & Procedures" tab, "Handbook of Practice and Internal Procedures" link; Fed. Cir. website, "Rules & Forms" tab, "Internal Operating Procedures" link.

[12] 3d Cir. website, "Rules & Procedures" tab, "Standing Orders" link.

[13] 4th Cir. website, "Rules & Procedures" tab, "General Orders" link; 9th Cir. website, "Rules" link, "General Orders" link; 10th Cir. website, "Rules and Instructions" heading, "General Orders" link; 11th Cir. website, "Rules & Procedures" tab, "General Orders" link.

[14] 4th website, "Rule & Procedures" tab, "Related Standing Orders" heading.

its judicial council (*see* Chapter 14).[15] The Sixth, Ninth, and Federal Circuits' websites have a link to Administrative Orders.[16] The D.C. Circuit's website has a link to General Notices,[17] and the Federal Circuit has a link to all Notices.[18]

15.2 LINKS TO OTHER INFORMATION

All circuits' websites have links to employee rights.[19]

The First, Second, Fourth, Seventh, Ninth, Tenth, and D.C. Circuits' websites have links to a rulebook, handbook, or practitioner's guide to local practices.[20]

The Second, Third, Fourth, Eighth, Ninth, Tenth, Eleventh, D.C., and Federal Circuits' websites have links to information for *pro se* litigants.[21]

15 5th Cir. website, "Rules & Procedures" tab, "Rules" link, "Judicial Council Orders" link.

16 6th Cir. website, "Rules and Procedures" tab, "Administrative Orders" heading; 9th Cir. website, "Rules" link, "Administrative Orders" link; Fed. Cir. website, "The Court" tab, "Administrative Orders" link.

17 D.C. Cir. website, "Rules & Procedures" tab, "General Notices" link.

18 Fed. Cir. website, "The Court" tab, "Notices & Announcements" link.

19 1st Cir. website, "Court Links" heading, "Employee Rights and Reporting Wrongful Conduct" link; 2d Cir. website, "About The Court" tab," "EDR Plan" link; 3d Cir. website, "About the Court" tab, "Workplace Relations" link; *id.* website, "Other Resources" heading, "Your Employee Rights and How to Report Wrongful Conduct" link; 4th Cir. website, "Your Employee Rights & How to Report Wrongful Conduct" link; 5th Cir. website, "Other Resources" heading, "Your Employee Rights and How to Report Wrongful Conduct" link; 6th Cir. website, "Quick Links" heading, "Your Employee Rights and How to Report Wrongful Conduct" link; 7th Cir. website, "Other Resources" heading, "Your Employee Rights and How to Report Wrongful Conduct" link; *id.* website, "Workplace Relations" link (bottom of webpage); 8th Cir. website, "About the Court" tab, "U.S. Court of Appeals for the 8th Circuit EEO and EDR Plan" link; *id.* website, "Quick Links" heading, "Your Employee Rights and How to Report Wrongful Conduct" link; 9th Cir. website, "Workplace Relations" link; *id.* website, "Employment" tab, "Workplace Relations" link; 10th Cir. Website, "General" heading, "Your Employee Rights and How to Report Wrongful Conduct" link; 11th Cir. website, "Rules & Procedures" link," "Your Employee Rights and How to Report Wrongful Conduct" link; D.C. Cir. website, "Your Employee Rights and How to Report Wrongful Conduct" link; Fed. Cir. website, "The Court" tab, "Human Resources" link, "Your Employee Rights and How to Report Wrongful Conduct" link.

20 1st Cir. website, "Rules & Procedures" tab, "First Circuit Rulebook" link; 2d Cir. website, "Case-Filing" tab, "Quicklinks" heading, "Forms and Instructions" link, "How to appeal a case in the Second Circuit" heading; 4th Cir. website, "Information For…" tab, "Attorneys" link, "Rules & Procedures" heading, "Appellate Procedure Guide" link; 7th Cir. website, "Rules and Procedures" tab, "Handbook" link; 9th Cir. website, "Legal Guides" link, "Appellate Practice Guide and Resources" link; 10th Cir. website, "Guides/Resources" tab, "Practitioner's Guide" link; D.C. Cir. website, "Rules & Procedures" tab, "Handbook of Practice and Internal Procedures" link.

21 2d Cir. website, "Case-Filing" tab, "Quicklinks" heading, "Forms and Instructions" link, "How to appeal a case in the Second Circuit" heading, "How to appeal as a pro se party" link; 3d Cir. website, "Attorneys & Litigants" tab, "Pro Se Litigant Information & 28 U.S.C. § 2244"

The First, Third, Fifth, Sixth, Seventh, and Ninth Circuits' websites have links to their court's history.[22]

The Second and Fifth Circuits' website have links to guidelines,[23] and a checklist,[24] for handling cases under *Anders v. California*.[25]

The Fifth, Ninth, and Federal Circuits' websites have links to court statistics.[26] The First, Second, Fourth, Seventh, Eighth, Tenth, Eleventh, and Federal Circuits' websites have links to assistance for visitors with disabilities.[27]

The Fifth and Federal Circuits' websites have links concerning wireless internet access.[28]

All of the circuits' websites have links to obtain RSS feeds to receive information about the court, including about cases.[29]

link; 4th Cir. website, "Information For…" tab, "Pro Se Parties" link; 8th Cir. website, "Site Map" link, "Filing Without An Attorney" link; 9th Cir. website, "Pro Se Litigants" link; 10th Cir. website, "How to File" tab, "Pro Se Filing" link; 11th Cir. website, "Forms & Information" tab, "Pro Se Forms and Information" link, "Pro Se Handbook" link; D.C. Cir. website, "Attorneys, Pro Se, and Media" tab, "Information for Litigants Representing Themselves (Pro Se)" link; Fed. Cir. website, "Information For…" tab, "Unrepresented Parties" link, "Guide for Unrepresented Parties" link.

22 1st Cir. website, "About the Court" tab, "Court History" link; 3d Cir. website, "About the Court" tab, "Circuit History" link; 5th Cir. website, "About the Court" tab, "Circuit History" link; 6th Cir. website, "About the Court" tab, "Circuit History" link; 7th Cir. website, "About the Court" tab, "Court History" link"; 9th Cir. website, "About the Court" tab, "History" heading, "History of the Court" link.

23 2d Cir. website, "Case-Filing" tab, "Quicklinks" heading, "Forms and Instructions" link, "How to appeal a case in the Second Circuit" heading, "How to file an *Anders* brief" link; 5th Cir. website, "Forms, Fees & Guides" tab, "*Anders* Guidelines" link.

24 2d Cir. website, "Case-Filing" tab, "Quicklinks" heading, "Forms and Instructions" link, "How to appeal a case in the Second Circuit" heading, "How to file an *Anders* brief" link, "Appendix A: Checklist for filing an *Anders* brief" link; 5th Cir. website, "Forms, Fees & Guides" tab, "Anders Checklist" link.

25 386 U.S. 738 (1967) (permitting counsel in criminal appeals to withdraw after reporting that no nonfrivolous issue exists).

26 5th Cir. website, "About the Court" tab, "Court Statistics" link"; 9th Cir. website, "About the Court" tab, "General Information" heading, "Caseload Statistics" link; Fed. Cir. website, "The Court" tab, Reports & "Statistics" link.

27 1st Cir. website, "About the Court" tab, "Court Calendar" link, "Access Coordinator" link; *id.* "Opinions & Oral Arguments" tab, "Access Coordinator" link; 2d Cir. website, "About the Court" tab, "Disabilities Accommodations" link; 4th Cir. website, "Oral Argument" tab, "Visiting the Court" link, "Access Coordinator" link; 7th Cir. website, "Forms, Fees, Guides" tab, "Guides" link, "Services to the Hearing Impaired and Others with Communication Disabilities" link; 8th Cir. website, "About the Court" tab, "ADA Accommodations" link; 10th Cir. website, "About the Court" tab, "Disability Access" link; 11th Cir. website, "Forms & Information" tab, "Disability Access Information" link; Fed. Cir. website, "Oral Argument" tab, "Access Coordinator" link.

28 5th Cir. website, "About the Court" tab, "Visitors Guide" link, "Wireless Internet Access" heading; Fed. Cir. website, "Oral Argument" link, "Attending Oral Arguments" link.

29 1st Cir. website, "Opinions & Oral Arguments" tab, "Sign Up for Opinions and Oral Argument Feed" links; 2d Cir. website, "RSS" link (bottom of webpage); 3d Cir. website, "RSS" symbol;

The Second and Ninth Circuits' websites have links to guidelines concerning cameras in the courtroom.[30]

The Fourth, Tenth, and Eleventh Circuits' websites have links to how to register to receive notice of activity in particular cases.[31]

The Third, Fifth, Sixth, Seventh, Eighth, Eleventh Circuits' websites have links to model jury instructions.[32]

The First, Second, Third, Sixth, Eighth, and Ninth Circuits' websites have links to a glossary of legal terms or filings events.[33]

15.3 LINKS TO UNIQUE SUBJECTS

The websites of a few circuits have links unique to their circuits.

The First Circuit's website has a link to civics initiatives in the circuit, including information about the Justice Stephen G. Breyer Community Learning Center on Courts and the Constitution.[34]

The Second Circuit's website has links to emergency information,[35] the Justice for All – Courts and the Community Initiative,[36] a virtual tour of the courthouse,[37] and a videotaped conversation about the history of the courthouse.[38]

4th Cir. website, "RSS" link; 5th Cir. website, "RSS" link; 6th Cir. website, "RSS" symbol; 7th Cir. website, "Subscribe to Seventh Circuit Opinion RSS" link; 8th Cir. website, "RSS" link; 9th Cir. website, "RSS Feeds" Link; 10th Cir. website, "Subscribe to Our RSS Feed" link; 11th Cir. website, "Court Links" heading, "Published Opinions RSS Feed" link; D.C. Cir. website, "RSS" link; Fed. Cir. website, "RSS" symbol.

30 2d Cir. website, "Rules" link, "Appendix to Local Rules of the Second Circuit [Parts A–B]" heading, "Part B. Second Circuit Guidelines Concerning Cameras in the Courtroom" link; 9th Cir. website, "Policies & Initiatives" heading, "Cameras and Electronic Devices Policy" link.

31 4th Cir. website, "Case Information & eFiling" tab, "Cases of Interest" link; 10th Cir. website, "How to File" tab, "File a Document (CM/ECF)" link, "How to Receive Notices for Cases of Interest" link; 11th Cir. website, "E-Filing Information (CM/ECF)" tab, "Cases of Interest" link.

32 3d Cir. website, "About the Court" heading, "Model Jury Instructions" link; 5th Cir. website, "Other Resources" heading, "Pattern Jury instructions" link; 6th Cir. website, "Pattern Jury Instructions" link; 7th Cir. website, "Pattern Jury Instructions" link; 8th Cir. website, "Quick Links" heading, "8th Circuit Jury Instructions" link; 11th Cir. website, "Pattern Jury Instructions" link; *id.* website, "Forms and Information" tab, "Pattern Jury Instructions" link.

33 1st Cir. website, "Glossary of Legal Terms" link (bottom of webpage); 2d Cir. website, "Decisions" tab, "Filing Events Glossary" link; 3d Cir. website, "Glossary of Legal Terms" link (bottom of webpage); 6th Cir. website, "Glossary of Legal Terms" link (bottom of webpage); 8th Cir. website, "Glossary of Legal Terms" link (bottom of webpage); 9th Cir. website, "Forms, FAQs, and Other Instructions" link, "Glossary" link.

34 1st Cir. website, "Civics Outreach" tab; *id.* website, "Civics Outreach" tab, "The Justice Stephen G. Breyer Community Learning Center on Courts and the Constitution" link.

35 2d Cir. website, "About the Court" tab, "Emergency Information" link.

36 *Id.* website, "Justice for All" photo.

37 *Id.* website, "A Virtual Tour" photo.

38 *Id.* website, "Here in Foley Square" photo.

The Third Circuit's website has links to Smart Scan (a service of the Federal Records Center that enables scanning of various documents),[39] to BrowseAloud (a program that speaks text),[40] and to the reports of the circuit's task forces on eye-witness identification,[41] and selection of class counsel.[42]

The Fourth Circuit's website has links to a Courtroom Protocol for Counsel, informing them that tea and coffee will be available when they arrive for an argument,[43] and that after an argument, "[t]he judges come down from the bench to shake hands with counsel and thank them for their advocacy before calling the next case."[44] The Fourth Circuit's website also has a link to its civics program, Courts4Civics.[45]

The Seventh Circuit's website has links to a Statement on Confidentiality of Court Materials,[46] a Report on Civility in the Seventh Circuit,[47] a detailed analysis of typography,[48] and Standards of Professional Conduct applicable to judges and lawyers in the Seventh Circuit.[49]

The Eighth Circuit's website has links to opinions written by each judge.[50]

The Ninth Circuit's website has a link to a mission statement,[51] and links to several guides on such topics as appellate jurisdiction, appellate practice, immigration litigation, section 1983 litigation, and social security cases.[52]

The Tenth Circuit's website has a chat function and a link to local rules from the last few years.[53]

The Eleventh Circuit's website has links to the orders entered after en banc rehearing polls,[54] and to the issues to be argued in en banc rehearings.[55]

39 3d Cir. website, "Case Information" Tab, "Smart Scan" link.

40 *Id.* website, "BrowseAloud" link (bottom of webpage).

41 *Id.* website, "Forms, Fees & Info Sheets" tab, "Task Force on Eye-Witness Identifications" link.

42 *Id.* website, "Forms, Fees & Info Sheets" tab, "Task Force on Selection of Class Counsel" link.

43 4th Cir. website, "Oral Argument" tab, "Courtroom Protocol for Counsel" link.

44 *Id.* website, "Oral Argument" tab, "Attending Oral Argument" link.

45 *Id.* website, "Courts4Civics" link.

46 7th Cir. website, "Rules and Procedures" tab, "Confidential Court Materials" link.

47 *Id.* website, "Forms, Fees, Guides" tab, "Guides" link, "Report on Civility in the Seventh Federal Judicial Circuit" link.

48 *Id.* website, "Forms, Fees, Guides" tab, "Guides" link, "Requirements and Suggestions for Typography in Briefs and Other Papers" link.

49 *Id.* website, "Rules and Procedures" tab, "Standards for Professional Conduct Within the Seventh Federal Judicial Circuit" link.

50 8th Cir. website, "Opinions" tab, "Authoring Judge" link.

51 9th Cir. website, "About the Court" tab, "Clerk's Office" heading, "Mission Statement" link.

52 *Id.* website, "Home" tab, "Legal Guides" link.

53 10th Cir. website, "Rules" tab, "Rules Archive" link.

54 11th Cir. website, "En Banc Matters" tab, "En Banc Poll Orders" link.

55 *Id.* website, "En Banc Matters" tab, "En Banc Issues" link.

The D.C. Circuit's website has links to orders of public interest (orders or judgments in high-profile cases),[56] orders concerning Guantanamo cases,[57] and a policy statement on en banc endorsement of panel decisions.[58]

The Federal Circuit's website has links to a description of the court's jurisdiction,[59] resources for staff, law clerks, and interns,[60] and a page on civic education and outreach,[61] with links to "Resources for Teachers" and "Resources for Students."[62]

* * * * *

Every circuit might usefully examine the websites of all other circuits to see the variety of information displayed and the differing arrangements of it. Although all websites contain a large number of links, conveniently grouped by topics, the sitemap links of the Second, Fourth, Seventh, Eighth, Eleventh, D.C., and Federal Circuits are especially helpful.[63] While several courts' websites have a search feature enabling users to search for a topic, a sitemap tab that provides a list of all available links would indicate the availability of many topics of which users might not be aware.

56 D.C. Cir. website, "Online Services" heading, "Orders of Public Interest" link.

57 *Id.* website, "Rules & Procedures" tab, "Guantanamo Cases – Orders Having General Application" link.

58 *Id.* website, "Rules & Procedures" tab, "En Banc Endorsement of Panel Decisions" link.

59 Fed. Cir. website, "The Court" tab, "About the Court" link, "Court Jurisdiction" link.

60 *Id.* website, "The Court" tab, "Human Resources" link, "Employee Forms & Resources" links.

61 *Id.* website, "Information for…" tab, "Civic Education and Outreach" link.

62 *Id.*

63 2d Cir. website, "Site Map" link (bottom of webpage); 4th Cir. website, "Site Map" link (bottom of webpage); 7th Cir. website, "SITEMAP" tab; 8th Cir. website, "Site Map" link (bottom of webpage); 11th Cir. website, "Site Map" link (bottom of webpage); *id.* "search this site" box; D.C. Cir. website, "Site Map" link; Fed. Cir. website, "Sitemap" link (bottom of webpage).

16

Miscellaneous Provisions

This chapter reports the practices of the courts of appeals on miscellaneous topics: attorney discipline, bar admission fees, certificate of interested persons, certification of state law questions, civic education, confidentiality, court reporter discipline, Criminal Justice Act plans, disposition of judges' personal papers, former court employees, immigration cases, *in forma pauperis*, judges' duties to each other, judges entering the courtroom for oral argument, law clerks, mandates, mediation programs, sabbaticals, sealed documents, terms of court, and three-judge district courts.

16.1 ATTORNEY DISCIPLINE

Federal Rules of Appellate Procedure (FRAP) 46(b) provides for the suspension or disbarment from the bar of a court of appeals of an attorney who "has been suspended or disbarred from practice in any other court" or "is guilty of conduct unbecoming a member of the court's bar." All circuits, except the Eighth Circuit,[1] have attorney discipline rules implementing FRAP 46(b), but their terms slightly vary.[2] A common feature, if discipline is considered,

[1] Although the Eighth Circuit has a local rule on "Admitting, Suspending, and Disciplining Attorneys," the substance of the rule pertains only to being admitted to the bar of the court. *See* 8th Cir. R. 46A.

[2] 1st Cir. R. 46(b); *id.* Rules of Attorney Disciplinary Enforcement for the Court of Appeals for the First Circuit; 2d Cir. R. 46.2; 3d Cir. website, "Rules & Procedures" tab, "Attorney Discipline Rules" link; 4th Cir. R. 46(g); 5th Cir. R. 46.2; *id.* IOP, Disciplinary Action; 6th Cir. R. 46(g); 7th Cir. R. 46(d); 9th Cir. R. 46-2; *id.* R. 46-2 (1)–(9), Cir. Adv. Comm. N.; 10th Cir. R. 46.6; *id.* Addendum III (Plan for Attorney Disciplinary Enforcement); 11th Cir. R. 46-10; *id.* website, "Rules & Procedures" tab, "Addenda to 11th Circuit Rules" link, Addendum 8 (Rules Governing Attorney Discipline in the U.S. Court of Appeals for the Eleventh Circuit); D.C. Cir. R. 46(b); *id.* website, "Attorney, Pro Se, and Media" tab, "Attorney Rules of Disciplinary Enforcement" link; Fed. Cir. R. 46(f); *id.* Federal Circuit Attorney Discipline Rules.

is to order the attorney to show cause why discipline should not be imposed. Without a local rule, the Eighth Circuit does this by custom.

Additionally, in the Third Circuit, if counsel fails to comply with a court order or rule, the clerk issues a show cause order requiring counsel to appear before a staff attorney designated as an "attorney-hearing officer" who endeavors to obtain compliance; if compliance is not achieved, the attorney-hearing officer sets the matter for hearing before the next available judge for possible imposition of sanctions.[3]

In the Ninth Circuit, a judge or the appellate commissioner may issue an order requiring a lawyer or a party to show cause why a sanction, in an amount to be determined by the court, should not be imposed for violation of FRAP or circuit rules.[4] After a response, the matter may be referred to a motion or a merits panel for a determination as to the propriety of sanctions.[5]

In the Tenth Circuit, the court may impose sanctions against attorneys (or parties) "who unreasonably increase the cost of litigation."[6]

16.2 BAR ADMISSION FEES

By statute, the fees charged in each court of appeals for bar admission are prescribed by the Judicial Conference of the United States (JCUS) and "shall be reasonable and uniform in all the circuits."[7] The JCUS has set a base fee of $199 for counsel to become members of the bar of a court of appeals.[8] All circuits add a local fee, in eight different amounts. The basic fee is sent to the Administrative Office of the U.S. Courts; the local fee remains with each court of appeals and is placed in their Attorney Admission Fee Fund. The local and total fees are shown in Table 16.1.

In some circuits, various exceptions to these payments are made. The First,[9] Fourth,[10] Fifth,[11] Sixth,[12] Seventh,[13] and Eighth[14] Circuits exempt attorneys

3 3d Cir. Standing Orders, Designating Hearing Officer for Show Cause Proceedings.

4 9th Cir. Gen. Ord. 12.9(a).

5 *Id.*

6 10th Cir. R. 46.6(A).

7 28 U.S.C. § 1913.

8 Administrative Office of the U.S. Courts, "Court of Appeals Miscellaneous Fee Schedule," www.uscourts.gov/services-forms/fees/court-appeals-miscellaneous-fee-schedule.

9 1st Cir. website, "Attorneys & Litigants" tab, "Attorney Admissions" link, "Application and Oath for Admission to Practice" link.

10 4th Cir. website, "Forms & Fees" tab, "Fee Schedule" link.

11 5th Cir. R. 46.1.

12 6th Cir. R. 46(a)(2); *id.* website, "Attorneys" tab, "Attorney Admission Instructions" link.

13 7th Cir. R. 46(b).

14 8th Cir. website, "Appeal Information" tab, "Attorney Admission" link.

TABLE 16.1 *Bar admission fees*

Circuit	Local fee	Total fee
1st	$50	$249[15]
2nd	$33	$232[16]
3rd	$40	$239[17]
4th	$40	$239[18]
5th	$50	$249[19]
6th	$50	$249[20]
7th	$15	$214[21]
8th	$40	$239[22]
9th	$31	$230[23]
10th	$26	$225[24]
11th	$40	$239[25]
D.C.	$50	$249[26]
Fed.	$101	$300[27]

appointed for indigent parties. The Second Circuit permits a lawyer who represents a CJA client or a person who has received *in forma pauperis* status to seek *pro hac vice* admission (to appear in a particular proceeding without formally applying for admission or paying the admission fee).[28] The Sixth Circuit also exempts attorneys employed by federal public defender organizations or

15 1st Cir. website, "Attorney & Litigants" tab, "Attorney Admissions" link, Application and Oath for Admission to Practice; *id.* R. 46.0(a)(1).

16 2d Cir. website, "Attorneys" tab, "Attorney Admissions and Renewals" link, "Attorney admissions application" link, Attorney Admission Instructions (8).

17 3d Cir. website, "Forms, Fees & Info Sheets" tab, "Fees" link, "Current Fees" link, Attorney Admission.

18 4th Cir. website, "Forms & Fees" tab, "Fee Schedule" link, Attorney admission fee; *id.* R. 46(b).

19 5th Cir. website, "Forms, Fees, & Guides" tab, "Fees" link, "Fee Schedule" link, Attorney Admission-Related Fees.

20 6th Cir. website, "Attorneys" tab, "Attorney Admission Instructions" link, Fee.

21 7th Cir. website, "Forms, Fees, Guides" tab, "Application for Admission to Practice in the Seventh Circuit" link.

22 8th Cir. website, "Appeal Information" tab, "Fee Schedules" link.

23 9th Cir. website, "Forms, FAQs, and Other Instructions" link, "Fee Schedule" link.

24 10th Cir. website, "Forms/Fees" tab, "Fee Schedule" link.

25 11th Cir. website, "Fees & Filing Instructions" tab, "Fee Schedules" link.

26 D.C. Cir. website, "Attorney, Pro Se, and Media" tab, "Attorney Admissions Information" link, "Application for Admission to Practice" link.

27 Fed. Cir. website, "Case Information" tab, "Fee Schedules" link, "Federal Circuit Fee Schedule" link.

28 2d Cir. R. 46.1(d).

a United States court.[29] The Tenth Circuit exempts an attorney appointed by the court to represent a party on appeal.[30]

The Second, Fifth, and Eleventh Circuits require renewal of a lawyer's bar membership every five years with a renewal fee of $25 in the Second Circuit,[31] $50 in the Fifth Circuit,[32] and $20 in the Eleventh Circuit.[33]

16.3 CERTIFICATE OF INTERESTED PERSONS

The Federal Rules of Appellate Procedure contemplate a "disclosure statement" to be made by certain organizations or individuals who have a financial interest in the case. Specifically, FRAP 26.1 requires nongovernmental corporate parties to file a statement disclosing any publicly held corporation that owns 10 percent or more of its stock.[34] Some circuits have additional requirements for identifying "interested persons" – parties or entities not a party to the appeal whose interests might be affected by the disposition of the appeal.

The Fifth Circuit requires a "certificate of interested persons" that is specifically "broader in scope" than the disclosure statement required under FRAP 26.1.[35] The certificate of interested persons "provides the court with additional information concerning parties whose participation in a case may raise a recusal issue" (and a separate disclosure statement is not required).[36] Specifically, counsel and unrepresented parties must submit a certificate for all private parties, which must be incorporated on the first page of each brief, and which certifies a complete list of "all persons, associations of persons, firms, partnerships, corporations, guarantors, insurers, affiliates, parent corporations, or other legal entities who or which are financially interested in the outcome of the ligation."[37]

The Ninth Circuit has its own rule concerning a "certificate of interested parties": "[p]etitions for writs of mandamus or prohibition, and for other

29 6th Cir. R. 46(a)(2); *id.* website, "Attorneys" tab, "Attorney Admission Instructions" link.
30 10th Cir. R. 46.2(B).
31 2d Cir. website, "Attorneys" tab, "Attorney Admissions and Renewals" link, "Attorney Renewal Instructions" link.
32 5th Cir. R. 46.1; *id.* website, "Forms, Fees, & Guides" tab, "Fees" link, "Fee Schedule" link.
33 11th Cir. website, "Attorney Information" tab, "Attorney Admissions" link, "Renewal of Bar Membership" link.
34 5th Cir. R. 28.2.1.
35 Fed. R. App. P. 26.1.
36 *Id.*
37 *Id.*

extraordinary writs, shall include the corporate disclosure statement required by FRAP 26.1" along with a statement of related cases required by Ninth Circuit Rule 28-2.6.[38]

In the Tenth Circuit, each entry of appearance must be accompanied by a certificate listing all interested parties not in the caption so that judges may evaluate possible recusal.[39] The certificate must list all persons, associations, firms, partnerships, corporations, guarantors, insurers, affiliates, and other legal entities that are financially interested in the outcome of the litigation.[40]

In the Eleventh Circuit, every party and amicus curiae must file a "Certificate of Interested Persons" with every brief and motion,[41] containing a list of all trial judges, attorneys, persons, and entities that have an interest in the outcome of the appeal,[42] and, in a criminal case, the identity of any victims.[43]

In the D.C. Circuit, briefs for an appellant/petitioner and an appellee/respondent, as well as briefs for an intervenor and an amicus curiae, must contain a certificate titled "Certificate as to Parties, Rulings, and Related Cases."[44] It should contain all parties, intervenors, and amici who have appeared before the district court, and all persons who are parties, intervenors, or amici in the court of appeals.[45]

In the Federal Circuit, all parties (with limited exception for U.S. Government parties), intervenors, amicus curiae, and movants must file a "certificate of interest" to allow the court to "determine whether recusal by a judge is necessary or appropriate."[46]

As a related matter, some circuits have created their own local rules to supplement the disclosure statement requirements of FRAP 26.1, often concerning who must file the statement and when the statement should be filed. Specifically, the Third,[47] Fourth,[48] Sixth,[49] Seventh,[50] Eighth,[51] Tenth,[52]

38 9th Cir. R. 21-3.
39 10th Cir. R. 46.1(D)(1).
40 *Id.* 46.1(D)(2).
41 11th Cir. R. 26.1-1(a)(1).
42 *Id.* 26.1-2(a).
43 *Id.*
44 D.C. Cir. R. 28(a)(1).
45 *Id.* R. 28(a)(1)(A).
46 Fed. Cir. R. 47.4(a).
47 3d Cir. L.A.R. 26.1.1.
48 4th Cir. R. 26.1.
49 6th Cir. R. 26.1.
50 7th Cir. R. 26.1.
51 8th Cir. R. 26.1A.
52 10th Cir. R. 26.1.

Eleventh,[53] D.C.,[54] and Federal Circuits[55] have local rules on this subject. The Third Circuit, in addition to having a local rule on "Disclosure of Corporate Affiliations and Financial Interest," has a rule on "Notice of Possible Judicial Disqualification" that states "[i]f any judge of this court participated at any stage of the case, in the trial court or in related state court proceedings, appellant, promptly after filing the notice of appeal, must separately file with the clerk a notice of the name of the judge and the other action, and must send a copy of such notice to appellee's counsel."[56]

16.4 CERTIFICATION OF A STATE LAW QUESTION

All states except North Carolina permit a court of appeals to ask their state supreme court to answer a question of state law that arises in a federal appeal, usually in a case between parties from different states. A few courts of appeals have local rules concerning certification of a state law question. Specifically, the Second, Third, Seventh, and Tenth Circuits note that the court may certify a question of state law to that state's highest court *sua sponte* or on motion of a party.[57]

In the Second Circuit, if a party moves to certify a question of state law, it may do so by filing a separate motion or including a request for certification in its brief.[58] By custom, the Second Circuit gives the state supreme court authority "to expand upon or vary the terms of" the question,[59] and, if the case requires a prompt answer, asks the state supreme court to accept the certification only if that court can answer the question within a stated time.[60]

In the Third Circuit, if a party makes a motion for certification, the motion must be included in the moving party's brief.[61] The Third Circuit also provides that whenever a panel certifies a question of state law to the relevant state's highest court, the panel presider sends a copy of the certified question to all the judges of the court, and also circulates the response.[62]

53 11th Cir. R. 26.1-1; *id.* R. 26.1-2; *id.* R. 26.1-3; *id.* R. 26.1-4; *id.* R. 26.1-5.

54 D.C. Cir. R. 26.1.

55 Fed. Cir. R. 26.1.

56 3d Cir. L.A.R. 26.1.2. Appellee has a corresponding responsibility to notify the clerk if appellant fails to comply with the rule fully and accurately. *Id.*

57 2d Cir. R. 27.2.; 3d L.A.R. Misc. 110.0 Certification of Questions of State Law; 7th Cir. R. 52; 10th Cir. R. 27.4.

58 2d Cir. R. 27.2.

59 *See, e.g.*, *Kirschner v. KPMG LLP*, 590 F.3d 186, 195 (2d Cir. 2009).

60 *See Friends of Van Cortland Park v. City of New York*, 232 F.3d 324, 327 (2d Cir. 2000).

61 3d L.A.R. Misc. 11.0 Certification of Questions of State Law.

62 *Id.* IOP 10.9.

In the Seventh Circuit, like the Third, if a party moves for certification, the motion should be included in the party's brief.[63] The Seventh Circuit provides that if the state court issues an opinion deciding the certified issue, then within 21 days the parties must file statements about what actions the court should take to complete the resolution of the appeal.[64]

In the Tenth Circuit, a motion to certify, if one is filed, should be filed at the same time as, but separately from, the moving party's brief on the merits.[65]

16.5 CIVIC EDUCATION

The First, Second, Fourth, Fifth, Sixth, Eighth, Ninth, Tenth, Eleventh, and Federal Circuits' websites have links to various resources that provide some form of public education about their courts, such as court tours, or, more broadly, about federal courts in general.[66] The most extensive is the Second Circuit's program, "Justice for All – Courts and the Community Initiative," developed by the late former Chief Judge Robert A. Katzmann. This program has spurred similar programs in many circuits.

16.6 CONFIDENTIALITY

The Ninth Circuit has written policies governing employees' divulging confidential information.[67]

16.7 CRIMINAL JUSTICE ACT PLANS

Federal law requires federal courts to adopt plans to implement the Criminal Justice Act of 1964,[68] which provides for court-appointed counsel

63 7th Cir. R. 52.

64 *Id.*

65 10th Cir. R. 27.4.

66 1st Cir. website, "Civics Outreach" tab; 2d Cir. website, "Justice for All" photo, https://justiceforall.ca2.uscourts.gov; 4th Cir. website, "Courts4Civics" tab; 5th Cir. website, "Other Resources" heading, "Civics Education" link; 6th Cir. website, "Quick Links" heading, "Sixth Circuit Civics Outreach" link; 8th Cir. website, "About the Court" tab, "Public Education" link; 9th Cir. website, "Civics" in search box, www.ca9.uscourts.gov/assets/civicscontest/2023/2023-Civics-Contest-Rules.pdf; 10th Cir. website, "About the Court" tab, "Public Education" link; 11th Cir. website, "Distance Learning Resources" link; Fed. Cir. website, "Information For…" tab, "Civic Education and Outreach" link.

67 9th Cir. Gen. Ord. 12.12.

68 Pub. L No. 88-455 (codified at 18 U.S.C. § 3006A). The statute explicitly requires district courts to adopt plans for appointing counsel for indigent defendants, *id.*, § 2, and implicitly requires courts of appeals to do so by providing that "Each district court and court of appeals shall place its approved plan in operation within one year from the date of this enactment," *id.* § 3.

for indigent defendants. All 12 circuits with criminal jurisdiction have adopted such plans.[69]

16.8 DISPOSITION OF JUDGES' PERSONAL PAPERS

The Ninth Circuit has a provision concerning disposition of judges' personal papers.[70] Judges are urged to make provision for disposition of confidential court documents, personal papers, and archival material such as judges' commissions, photographs, and public speeches.[71]

16.9 FORMER COURT EMPLOYEES

Some circuits have rules concerning former employees. In the First Circuit, staff attorneys and law clerks may not sit at counsel table or sign a brief in connection with any case heard before the court for one year after their employment, nor practice as an attorney in connection with any case pending in the court during their term of service.[72] In the Ninth Circuit, a former court employee may not participate or assist in any case that was pending in the court during the period of employment, but a former employee who is an attorney may apply for an exemption.[73] A request for an exemption by an attorney who was employed in a judge's chambers must show that the judge did not have any involvement in the case.[74] In the Eleventh Circuit, former employees may not participate in any matter which was pending in the court

[69] 1st Cir. R. 46.5, Appointment of Counsel in Criminal Cases; 2d Cir. App'x to the Local Rules, Part A, United States Court of Appeals for the Second Circuit Criminal Justice Act Plan; 3d Cir. website, "Criminal Justice Act" tab, "Criminal Justice Act Plan" link; 4th Cir. website, "Rules & Procedures" tab, "CJA & Assigned Counsel" link, "CJA Policies & Resources" link, "Fourth Circuit CJA Plan" link; 5th Cir. website, "Attorney Information" tab, "CJA" link, "CJA Plan" link; 6th Cir. website, "Criminal Justice Act" tab, "CJA Plan" link; 7th Cir. website, "Rules and Procedures" tab, "Operating Procedures" link, Seventh Circuit Criminal Justice Act Plan (following OPs); 8th Cir. website, "Rules & Procedures" tab, "Plan to Implement The Criminal Justice Act of 1964" link; 9th Cir. website, "Attorneys" tab, "Appellate CJA Practice and Resources" link, "CJA Policies and Procedures" link, "Ninth Circuit Criminal Justice Act Plan" link; 10th Cir. Rules, Addendum I, Criminal Justice Act Plan; 11th Cir. website, Addenda to Eleventh Circuit Rules, Addendum Four, Eleventh Circuit Plan under the Criminal Justice Act and Guidelines for Counsel Supplementing the Eleventh Circuit Plan under the Criminal Justice Act; D.C. Cir. website, "Attorney, Pro Se, and Media" tab, "Criminal Justice Act Information and CJA eVoucher" link, "Circuit CJA Plan."

[70] 9th Cir. Gen. Ord. 12.13.

[71] *See id.*

[72] 1st Cir. R. 46.0(e).

[73] 9th Cir. R. 46-5.

[74] *Id.* R. 46-5, Cir. Adv. Comm. N.

during their term of employment.[75] In the D.C. Circuit, no former employee is permitted to practice as an attorney in any case that was pending in the court during his or her term of service, and for the purpose of the rule, a case is "pending" in the court upon the docketing of a notice of appeal or the filing of a petition.[76] Additionally, effective September 1, 2016, no former employee may appear at counsel table or on pleadings in any case in the D.C. Circuit for a period of one year after leaving court employment.[77] The Federal Circuit also prohibits former employees from participating in cases pending during their employment and adds that they may not participate in the case if it is subsequently before the court again or if it is before the Supreme Court of the United States.[78]

16.10 IMMIGRATION CASES

Some circuits have special procedures for handling immigration cases, which are mainly petitions to review decisions of the Board of Immigration Appeals (BIA).

In the First Circuit, if the government has scheduled the removal of a petitioner, then the government must file a notice with the court identifying the earliest date upon which removal may occur.[79] When a first motion for stay of removal is timely filed and notification is transmitted to the government, the clerk will enter an administrative order staying removal for ten business days.[80]

In the Second Circuit, the government has agreed to a forbearance policy, whereby the petitioner will not be removed until the petition is adjudicated, but the government retains the right to request prompt removal in specific cases. Also in the Second Circuit, most immigration cases are placed on the court's non-argument calendar (NAC). NAC was instituted in 2005 to handle the court's burgeoning number of petitions challenging a denial of asylum.[81] Any judge on a NAC panel may require oral argument. Cases that are not argued orally are decided on the briefs, using a system of sequential voting.

[75] 11th Cir. R. 47-6.
[76] D.C. Cir. R. 1(c).
[77] *Id.*
[78] Fed. Cir. R. 50 & Prac. N. to R. 50.
[79] 1st Cir. R. 18.0(1).
[80] *Id.* R. 18.0(2).
[81] *See* Jon O. Newman, *The Second Circuit's Expedited Adjudication of Asylum Cases: A Case Study of a Judicial Response to an Unprecedented Problem of Caseload Management*, 74 BROOK. L. REV. 429 (2009).

In the Third Circuit, when a petition for review of a removal order is filed, the clerk issues a stay until a motions panel can consider the motion, provided the petition is timely, venue is proper, the order if arguably final, and the court has authority to review the order.[82] The motion must include a copy of the opinions of the immigration judge,[83] and the BIA.[84]

In the Fourth Circuit, upon the filing of an initial motion for stay in an immigration case, the clerk enters a 14-day administrative stay to enable the government to respond and the court to rule on the motion.[85]

In the Fifth Circuit, emergency consideration is given to a motion to stay removal only where the petitioner has a scheduled removal date and is in custody.[86]

In the Sixth Circuit, in a case where the BIA issued the final order of exclusion, deportation, or removal, the Executive Office of Immigration Review must file four text-searchable, paginated copies of the certified administrative record on CD-ROM.[87] In a case where U.S. Immigration and Custom Enforcement issued the final order of exclusion, deportation, or removal – where the Department of Homeland Security maintains the administrative record – the Attorney General must file the certified administrative record by filing one text-searchable, paginated copy on CD-ROM or filing it using the electronic case filing system.[88]

In the Eighth Circuit, when an immigration case is docketed, petitioner's counsel is notified that a motion for stay of removal should be filed as promptly as possible.

In the Ninth Circuit, upon the filing of a motion to stay removal, the removal is stayed until further order of the court.[89] A petition for review of a BIA decision shall state whether the petitioner is detained in the custody of the Department of Homeland Security or at liberty, and/or has moved the BIA to reopen or applied to the district director for an adjustment of status.[90] The petition shall be accompanied by a copy of the BIA order being challenged.[91]

82 3d Cir. Standing Orders, Stays in Immigration Cases (August 5, 2015).
83 *Id.* L.A.R. 18.1.
84 *Id.* Standing Orders, Motions Practice (May 2021).
85 4th Cir. General Orders, Standing Order 19-01, Temporary Administrative Stay Pending Review of Initial Motion for Stay of Removal in Immigration Cases.
86 5th Cir. R. 27.3.1.
87 6th Cir. R. 30(f)(2)(A).
88 *Id.* R. 30(f)(2)(B).
89 9th Cir. Gen. Ord. 6.4(c)(1).
90 *Id.* R. 15-4; *id.* R. 28-2.4(b).
91 *Id.* R. 15-4.

In the Tenth Circuit, in immigration cases seeking a stay of removal or other emergency relief, the petitioner must attach to the motion a copy of the transcript from the immigration judge's ruling, if relevant, plus copies of the written rulings of the immigration judge and BIA.[92]

In the Eleventh Circuit, the petitioner shall attach to the petition a copy of the immigration judge's order and the Notice to Appear.[93]

In the D.C. Circuit, on petition for review in immigration matters, the Executive Office for Immigration Review must transmit the record to the court within 40 days after the filing of the petition for review.[94]

16.11 *IN FORMA PAUPERIS*

Federal law permits the commencement, prosecution, or defense of any suit or proceeding, civil or criminal, without prepayment of filing fees if a person submits an affidavit of inability to pay such fees.[95] FRAP 24 prescribes how to seek leave to proceed *in forma pauperis*,[96] though there is still some variation on the subject across the circuits.

In the Second Circuit, if the court determines, upon consideration of a motion to proceed *in forma pauperis* (to waive prepayment of filing fees), for a free transcript, or for appointed counsel, that the appeal is frivolous, the court denies the motion and also dismisses the appeal.

In the Third Circuit, the clerk is authorized to appoint counsel for an indigent defendant,[97] and the clerk and the senior staff attorney are authorized to grant, but not deny, an unopposed motion to proceed *in forma pauperis*.[98]

In the Fifth Circuit, the clerk has the discretion to act on a motion to proceed *in forma pauperis*.[99]

In the Seventh Circuit, by circuit rule whenever a district court denies leave to proceed *in forma pauperis* (with or without prejudice), the judge shall give reasons, either orally on the record or by written statement.[100] Additionally, at least two (appellate) judges act on denials of leave to proceed on appeal *in forma pauperis*.[101]

[92] 10th Cir. R. 8.2(5); *id.* R. 15.1; *id.* R. 28.2(A)(4).

[93] 11th Cir. R. 15-2.

[94] D.C. Cir. R. 17.

[95] 28 U.S.C. § 1915(a). Prisoners are required to pay filing fees, *id.*, § 1915(b)(1), but may do so in installments out of their prison accounts, *id.* An appeal may not be pursued *in forma pauperis* if the trial judge certifies that it is not taken in good faith. *Id.* § 1915(a)(3).

[96] Fed. R. App. P. 24.

[97] 3d Cir. Standing Orders, Delegation to the Clerk (February 15, 2001).

[98] *Id.* Standing Orders, Granting In Forma Pauperis Motions (January 22, 1987).

[99] 5th Cir. R. 27.1.17.

[100] 7th Cir. R. 50.

[101] *Id.* O.P. 1(a)(1).

In the Ninth Circuit, the appointment of counsel in a district court creates a rebuttable presumption that the party has pauper status for purposes of dispensing with the appellate docket fee.[102] Also in the Ninth Circuit, the court has authorized the chief judge to delegate to an appellate commissioner authority to issue for the court non-dispositive orders with exceptions – as one of those exceptions, if the appellate commissioner is inclined to recommend that leave to proceed *in forma pauperis* be denied, the matter should be presented to a regularly scheduled motions panel.[103]

In the Eleventh Circuit, one judge is authorized to act, subject to review by the court, on motions to appeal *in forma pauperis*.[104]

In the Federal Circuit, the clerk has the authority to act on a motion for leave to proceed *in forma pauperis* or to refer the motion to a judge or a panel.[105]

16.12 JUDGES' DUTIES TO EACH OTHER

Unique among the circuits, the Seventh Circuit includes in its operating procedures the following section titled "Judges' Duties to Each Other":[106]

1. We will be courteous, respectful, and civil in opinions, ever mindful that a position articulated by another judge is the result of that judge's earnest effort to interpret the law and the facts correctly.
2. In all written and oral communications, we will abstain from disparaging personal remarks or criticisms, or sarcastic or demeaning comments about another judge.
3. We will endeavor to work with other judges in an effort to foster a spirit of cooperation in our mutual goal of enhancing the administration of justice.

16.13 JUDGES ENTERING THE COURTROOM FOR ORAL ARGUMENT

In the Third Circuit, an internal operating procedure (IOP) provides that judges enter the courtroom for oral argument in reverse order of precedence.[107] In most circuits, by custom, the presiding judge enters first.

[102] 9th Cir. Gen. Ord. 2.2.
[103] *Id.* Gen. Ord. 6.3(e).
[104] 11th Cir. R. 27-1(d).
[105] Fed. Cir. Prac. N. to R. 27.
[106] 7th Cir., Standards for Professional Conduct Within the Seventh Federal Judicial Circuit, Judges' Duties to Each Other.
[107] 3d Cir. IOP 3.3.

16.14 LAW CLERKS

The Third Circuit authorizes senior judges to volunteer the use of their law clerks to assist active judges and staff attorneys, especially for tasks that can be carried out in the senior judge's chambers.[108] Senior judges usually do so when taking an extended absence (unless the law clerks will be occupied with work during that time).[109]

16.15 MANDATES

After a court of appeals decides an appeal, it issues what is called a "mandate" – a formal communication to the district court or the administrative agency from which the case came. The mandate is the paperwork that formally transfers jurisdiction from the court of appeals back to the district court or the administrative agency. For a court of appeals to resume acting on an appeal after issuing a mandate, it must recall the mandate to reacquire jurisdiction.

FRAP 41(a) provides that the mandate consists of a certified copy of the court's judgment, a copy of the court's opinion, and any direction as to costs (the printing and a few other expenses that the losing party must pay to the winning party).[110]

In the First Circuit, local rules note that "an increasingly large percentage of unsuccessful petitions for certiorari have been filed in this circuit in recent years" and so "in the interest of minimizing unnecessary delay in the administration of justice," the mandate will not be stayed in criminal cases following the affirmance of a conviction simply upon request.[111] Instead, the mandate will issue and bail will be revoked at such time as the court orders except upon a showing, or an independent finding by the court, of probable cause to believe that the petition would not be frivolous or filed merely for delay.[112]

In the Second Circuit, a judge may place a "hold" on the issuance of a mandate, that is delay its issuance, while considering making a request for an en banc poll, but must notify the court of the hold and the reasons for it. The hold may not last more than 45 days, unless extended with the consent of the opinion writer or presider if the opinion is per curiam. If a panel wishes to have a mandate issue promptly, it must give the judges of the court at least one day's notice.

108 *Id.* IOP ch. 15 (Senior Judge Law Clerk Volunteers).
109 *Id.*
110 Fed. R. App. P. 41(a).
111 1st Cir. R. 41.0.
112 *Id.*

In the Fourth Circuit, a motion for stay of the issuance of the mandate will not be granted simply upon request.[113] The motion will usually be denied unless there is a specific showing that it is not frivolous or being filed for delay.[114] A motion to stay the mandate pending the filing of a petition for certiorari must show that the certiorari petition would present a substantial question and set forth good cause for a stay.[115]

In the Fifth Circuit, any active judge may request that the court withhold issuance of its mandate.[116] The court notes that "[t]his is often done to resolve differences between the judge who requests that the mandate be withheld and the panel or to request that the court be polled on whether rehearing en banc should be granted whether or not a petition for rehearing en banc has been filed by a party."[117] When withholding the mandate, a judge will notify the clerk to withhold the mandate, and the clerk will enter an order withholding the mandate.[118] The court notes that the identity of the judge will not be disclosed in the order.[119]

Also in the Fifth Circuit, a motion to stay or recall a mandate pending action on a petition for a writ of certiorari may be decided by the clerk or one judge.[120] A motion for a stay of the issuance of a mandate in a direct criminal appeal will not be granted simply upon request.[121] Unless the petition sets forth good cause for the stay or clearly demonstrates that a substantial question will be presented to the Supreme Court, the motion will be denied and the mandate issued forthwith.[122]

In the Sixth Circuit, "[i]n the interest of minimizing unnecessary delay in the administration of justice," the issuance of the mandate will not be stayed simply upon request beyond the time necessary for disposition of a motion seeking a stay.[123] The mandate ordinarily will issue unless there is a showing, or an independent determination by the court, that a petition for writ of certiorari would present a substantial question and that there is a good cause for a stay.[124] A motion to stay the mandate must be filed within seven days after the

113 4th Cir. R. 41.
114 *Id.*
115 *Id.*
116 5th Cir. IOP following R. 41.
117 *Id.*
118 *Id.*
119 *Id.*
120 *Id.* IOP Post-Decision Motions (Stay or Recall of Mandate).
121 *Id.* R. 41.1.
122 *Id.*
123 6th Cir. R. 41(a).
124 *Id.*

time to file a petition for rehearing expires or seven days from entry of an order on a petition for rehearing.[125]

The Seventh Circuit states that the mandate will issue immediately when an appeal is dismissed (1) voluntarily, (2) for failure to pay the docket fee, (3) for failure to file the docketing statement, or (4) for failure by the appellant to file a brief.[126]

The Ninth Circuit has a policy against issuing a mandate forthwith,[127] but excepts from this policy cases where a petition for rehearing en banc or for certiorari would be frivolous, where the losing litigant is interposing delaying tactics, or, because of emergency, a prompt mandate is necessary to effectuate a just result.[128] As a general matter, the mandate will not be stayed automatically upon the filing of a petition to the Supreme Court for writ of certiorari, though a stay may be granted upon motion.[129] Such a motion will not be routinely granted, though, and will be denied if the court determines that the application for certiorari would be frivolous or is made merely for delay.[130]

In the Tenth Circuit, in criminal cases, "[t]o minimize delay in the administration of justice," after the affirmance of a conviction the mandate will issue and bail will be revoked.[131] A motion to stay the mandate will not be granted unless the court finds that it is not frivolous or filed merely for delay.[132] In civil cases, a motion to stay the mandate will not be granted unless the court finds that there is a substantial possibility that a petition for writ of certiorari would be granted[133]

In the Eleventh Circuit, a motion for a stay of the issuance of a mandate in a direct criminal appeal is not granted simply upon request.[134] Ordinarily the motion will be denied unless it is not frivolous, not filed for delay, and a substantial question is to be presented to the Supreme Court or otherwise sets forth good cause for a stay.[135] A motion for stay of mandate is disposed of by one judge.[136] Also in the Eleventh Circuit, in any appeal in which a published opinion has issued, the time for issuance of the mandate may be shortened only after all active judges have had notice and an opportunity to notify the clerk to withhold issuance of the mandate.[137]

[125] *Id.* R. 41(b).
[126] 7th Cir. R. 41.
[127] 9th Cir. Gen. Ord. 4.6(a).
[128] *Id.* Gen. Ord. 4.6(b).
[129] *Id.* R. 41-1, Cir. Adv. Comm. N.
[130] *Id.*
[131] 10th Cir. R. 41.1(A).
[132] *Id.*
[133] *Id.* R. 41.1(B).
[134] 11th Cir. R. 41-1(a).
[135] *Id.*
[136] *Id.* R. 41, IOP(1).
[137] *Id.* R. 41-2.

In the D.C. Circuit, the court ordinarily will include as part of its disposition an instruction that the clerk withhold issuance of the mandate until seven days after the expiration of the time for filing a petition for rehearing or a petition for rehearing en banc and, if such a petition is timely filed, until seven days after its disposition.[138] But such an instruction is without prejudice to the right of any party at any time to move for the expedited issuance of the mandate for "good cause shown."[139] A motion for a stay of the issuance of the mandate will not be granted unless the motion sets forth facts showing good cause for the relief sought.[140] If the motion is granted, the stay ordinarily will not extend beyond 90 days from the date that the mandate otherwise would have issued.[141] If a timely motion to stay issuance of the mandate has been filed, the mandate will not issue while the motion is pending.[142] The clerk of court may grant an unopposed motion to stay issuance of the mandate for a period not longer than 90 days from the date that the mandate otherwise would have issued.[143] No motion to stay issuance of the mandate will be granted by the clerk until after the response time has passed, unless the moving party represents in the motion that all other parties consent to the stay or do not object to it.[144] The clerk may also submit the motion to the panel that decided the case.[145]

In the Federal Circuit, an order granting an unopposed motion to dismiss or remand a case will constitute the mandate.[146] Also in the Federal Circuit, a motion to stay the mandate should advance reasons for the stay beyond the intention to apply for certiorari (e.g., to forestall action in the trial court or agency that would necessitate a remedial order of the Supreme Court if the writ of certiorari were granted).[147]

16.16 MEDIATION PROGRAMS

FRAP 33 authorizes every court of appeals to direct attorneys to participate in settlement conferences.[148] All the circuits, except the Eighth Circuit, have

[138] D.C. Cir. R. 41(a)(1).
[139] *Id.*
[140] *Id.* R. 41(a)(2).
[141] *Id.*
[142] *Id.*
[143] *Id.*
[144] *Id.*
[145] *Id.*
[146] Fed. Cir. R. 41.
[147] *Id.* Prac. N. to R. 41.
[148] Fed. R. App. P. 33.

implemented FRAP 33 by creating mediation programs, with slight variations in their details.[149]

Many of the circuits note that although their mediation program is designed for civil cases (and review of administrative orders), there are exceptions – and those exceptions differ slightly from circuit to circuit. Specifically, exceptions to mediation are explicitly made for (1) original proceedings and prisoner petitions in the First and Third Circuits; (2) habeas corpus petitions in the First, Second, Third, Fourth, Fifth, Seventh, Ninth, Tenth, and Eleventh Circuits; (3) summary enforcement of National Labor Relations Board (NLRB) orders in the First Circuit; (4) social security cases in the First, Third, and Tenth Circuits; (5) review of BIA decisions in the First, Second, and Eleventh Circuits; (6) petitions for writs of mandamus or prohibition in the Second, and Seventh Circuits; and (7) *pro se* cases in the First, Second, Third, Fourth, Fifth, Seventh, Tenth, Eleventh, and Federal Circuits.[150] (In the Ninth Circuit, "[o]nly in extraordinary circumstances and with permission of the chief circuit mediator will the mediators participate in negotiations involving pro se litigants."[151] In the D.C. Circuit, though uncounseled cases are not categorically excluded, they are rarely referred to mediation.)[152]

The circuits vary slightly as to who selects cases for mediation, if the program does not include all civil appeals and review of administrative orders (with the exceptions noted above). It is the chief circuit mediator in the Third

[149] 1st Cir. R. 33.0; 2d Cir. R. 33.1; 3d Cir. L.A.R. 33.0; 4th Cir. R. 33; 5th Cir. General Order Governing the Circuit Mediation Program; 6th Cir. R. 33; 7th Cir. website, "Circuit Mediation Office" link, 9th Cir. R. 33-1; *id.* Gen. Order 7.3 "Cases Subject to Mediation"; 10th Cir. R. 33; 11th Cir. R. 33-1; D.C. Cir. App'x III to the Circuit Rules, Appellate Mediation Program; Fed. Cir. website, "Case Information" tab, "Mediation" tab, "Guidelines" link. (The Eighth Circuit formerly had a mediation program, as set out in prior Eighth Circuit Rules 3B and 33A, but no longer does.)

[150] 1st Cir. R. 33.0(f); 2d Cir. R. 33.1(a); 3d Cir. L.A.R. 33.2; 4th Cir. R. 33; *id.* website, "Mediation" tab, "About Mediations" link; 5th Cir. website, "About the Court" heading, "Court Offices" tab, "Circuit Mediation Program (formerly "Appellate Conference Program") link; 7th Cir. website, "Circuit Mediation Office" link; 9th Cir. Gen. Order 7.3 "Cases Subject to Mediation"; 10th Cir. website, "Circuit Mediation Office" link, "Mediation FAQ" link; 11th Cir. website, "Forms and Information" heading, "Mediation Forms and Information" link, "Mediation in the Eleventh Circuit Court of Appeals" link; Fed. Cir. website, "Case Information" tab, "Mediation" tab, "Guidelines" link.

By local rule the Third Circuit states that *pro se* cases are not eligible for referral to the Appellate Mediation Program, 3d Cir. L.A.R. 33.2, though by standing order the court notes that the director of mediation may decide whether to appoint counsel for purposes of mediation (in a *pro se* case), *id.* Standing Order, Delegation to Director of Mediation (January 9, 2001).

[151] 9th Cir. Gen. Order 7.3 "Cases Subject to Mediation."

[152] D.C. Cir. App'x III to the Circuit Rules, Appellate Mediation Program.

Circuit.[153] In the Fourth Circuit, cases are selected by referral by the clerk of court, request of a party, and referral by a panel of the court.[154] In the Fifth Circuit, most cases are selected by the chief circuit mediator, but additionally, either party can request that a case be assigned to the program and the court itself occasionally refers specific cases to the program.[155] Similarly, in the Sixth Circuit, most cases that are selected for mediation are selected by the mediation office, though mediation may also be scheduled at the request of a party or based on a referral by the court.[156] In the Eleventh Circuit, the mediation center, a judge, or a panel of judges may direct counsel and parties in an appeal to participate in mediation.[157] In the D.C. Circuit, though a party may request mediation, and though the Director of the Legal Division can recommend that a case be considered for mediation, the Office of the Circuit Mediator ultimately determines which cases are appropriate for mediation. The circuit mediator and his staff screen all civil appeals where both sides are represented by counsel to determine whether mediation might be appropriate.

The circuits also vary slightly as to who performs the mediation. In addition to mediators on the staff of several courts of appeals, mediations are conducted by the chief circuit mediator, circuit mediator, or a senior judge of the court of appeals or a district court in the Third Circuit.[158] In the D.C. Circuit, mediations are conducted by senior members of the bar, academics, and attorneys with broad experience in complex cases who volunteer their services.[159] In the Federal Circuit, the court maintains a roster of outside mediators, including magistrate judges and volunteer mediators (who are experienced attorneys and others with expertise in the substantive areas of the court's jurisdiction).[160]

16.17 SABBATICALS

Unique among the circuits, the Ninth Circuit has a sabbatical program. An active judge after seven years of service may request a one-year reduction to five monthly calendars with three consecutive months without calendar

[153] 3d Cir. L.A.R. 33.3.
[154] 4th Cir. website, "Mediation" tab, "FAQs" link.
[155] 5th Cir. website, "About the Court" heading, "Court Offices" tab, "Circuit Mediation Program" (formerly "Appellate Conference Program") link.
[156] 6th Cir. R. 33(b)(1); *id.* website, "Mediation" link.
[157] 11th Cir. website, "Forms and Information" heading, "Mediation Forms and Information" link, "Mediation in the Eleventh Circuit Court of Appeals" link.
[158] 3d Cir. L.A.R. 33.1; *id.* website, "Mediation" tab.
[159] D.C. Cir. App'x III to the Circuit Rules, Appellate Mediation Program.
[160] Fed. Cir. website, "Case Information" tab, "Mediation" tab, "Guidelines" link.

duties.[161] The chief judge may grant the request if the judge's disposition backlog is "reasonably current" with the additional proviso that no more than three active judges may take such a reduction in a given year.[162]

The Fifth Circuit has what might be considered a mini-sabbatical program. A judge on that court may elect to take up to two weeks of "respite" each year in which that judge will not be assigned any new matters. The respite period does not have to be taken all at the same time.

16.18 SEALED DOCUMENTS

Several of the courts of appeals have rules for handling sealed documents.[163] The First and Fourth Circuits expect motions to seal all or part of a district court or administrative agency record to be presented to, and resolved by, the district court or the agency.[164] The First and Eighth Circuits require motions to seal and sealed documents to be filed in paper format.[165] The Fourth Circuit provides that a motion to seal filed with the court of appeals will be placed on the public docket for at least five days before the court rules on the motion (though the materials subject to a motion to seal will be held under seal pending the court's disposition of the motion).[166]

The Second Circuit requires that a sealed document be filed in a manner prescribed by the clerk and a redacted version of the sealed document be placed on the docket within seven days of filing the sealed document.[167]

The Ninth Circuit has a particularly detailed rule on sealed documents, including a provision that the court will not seal a case or a document solely on the stipulation of the parties.[168]

The Sixth Circuit specifies that a person seeking to *unseal* a document sealed by the district court must first make a motion to unseal in the district court.[169] In the D.C. Circuit, in any case in which the record is under seal (in whole or in part) and a motion of appeal or petition for review has been filed, each party is expected to review the record to determine whether

[161] 9th Cir. Gen. Ord. 3.2(k).
[162] *Id.*
[163] *See, e.g.*, 1st Cir. R. 11.0(c); 3d Cir. L.A.R. 113.7; 4th Cir. R. 25(c)(2); 5th Cir. R. 25.2.8; 6th Cir. R. 11(c)(2); *id.* R. 25(h); 7th Cir. O.P. 10; 8th Cir. R. 25A(h); *id.* Standing Order 21-01; 9th Cir. R. 27-13; 10th Cir. R. 11.3; 11th Cir. R. 25-3(h); D.C. Cir. R. 47.1; Fed. Cir. R. 25.1, 45(b).
[164] 1st Cir. R. 11.0(c)(1); 4th Cir. R. 25(c)(2).
[165] 1st Cir. R. (c)(2); 8th Cir. R. 25A(h).
[166] 4th Cir. R. 25(c)(2)(C).
[167] 2d Cir. R. 25.1(j).
[168] 9th Cir. R. 27-13(a).
[169] 6th Cir. R. 11(c)(2).

any portions of the record need to remain under seal on appeal; if a party determines that some portions should be unsealed, that party must seek an agreement on the unsealing, which should be presented promptly to the district court or agency.[170] But at any time a party or other interested person may move to unseal any portion of the record in the court of appeals; on appeals from the district court, the motion will ordinarily be referred to the district court, though the court of appeals may, "when the interests of justice require," decide the motion and if unsealing is ordered, remand the record for unsealing.[171]

16.19 TERMS OF COURT

Some courts of appeals, like the Supreme Court,[172] have a formal term, while others do not. Among those that do, the start and end dates vary. What follows is a reporting of the terms of court for the various circuits.

First Circuit: The court states that it does not have a formal term.[173]

Second Circuit: The court "holds a continuous annual term commencing in August or September as the court may designate, and ending the day before the first day of the next term."[174]

Third Circuit: The court does not have a term.

Fourth Circuit: The court has a term that runs from September to May.

Fifth Circuit: The court has a term that runs from July 1 to June 30.

Sixth Circuit: The court has no formal term, but what is generally considered an unofficial term begins in the fall, after the August and September break from oral arguments. However, the court's annual sitting schedule runs from January to December.[175]

Seventh Circuit: The court has a term that runs from Labor Day until mid-June.

Eighth Circuit: The court conducts oral arguments from September to June, and that has historically been considered the court's term.

Ninth Circuit: The court does not have a formal term. The court sits 12 months a year, with a sitting schedule that runs from January to December.[176]

170 D.C. Cir. R. 47.1(b).

171 *Id.* R. 47.1(c).

172 28 U.S.C. § 2.

173 1st Cir. R. 34.1(a).

174 2d Cir. IOP D.

175 *See* 6th Cir. website, "Opinions and Oral Arguments" tab, "Oral Argument Calendar" link, "2024 Master Sitting Schedule" link.

176 9th Cir. website, "Calendar" link, "Court Sessions" link, "2024 Court Sessions – Dates and Locations" link.

Tenth Circuit: The court hears oral arguments on a regularly scheduled basis for a total of five weeks per year (one week in January, March, May, September, and November). Those weeks are considered sessions of court.[177]

Eleventh Circuit: The court has no formal term; however, the circuit's "Court Year" runs from October 1 to September 30.

D.C. Circuit: The court has a term that runs from September through August. (Arguments are scheduled from September through mid-May, although emergency arguments may be scheduled over the summer.)

Federal Circuit: The court has no formal term, though the circuit's court sessions calendar runs from October to September.[178]

16.20 THREE-JUDGE DISTRICT COURTS

Federal law requires three-judge district courts in cases challenging "the constitutionality of the apportionment of congressional districts or the apportionment of any statewide legislative body" or when required by an Act of Congress.[179] The district judge to whom the case is assigned becomes a member of the three-judge district court,[180] and notifies the chief circuit judge, who "shall designate" two other judges, one of whom must be a circuit judge.[181] "Designate" does not always mean "select," and a few circuits have distinctive provisions concerning how names of the other two judges are furnished to the chief judge for designation.

In the Fourth Circuit, the chief judge selects an additional district judge and a circuit judge, both generally from the same state where the case is filed, after considering workload and prior assignments.

In the Ninth Circuit, an active circuit judge is drawn at random, and the chief district judge of the district where the case is filed draws a second district judge.

In the D.C. Circuit, the chief judge selects the circuit judge and the second district judge based on rotation.

[177] 10th Cir. website, "Decisions/Oral Argument" tab, "Oral Argument Calendar" link, "2024 Court Argument Calendar Sessions" link.

[178] Fed. Cir. website, "Oral Argument" tab, "Court Sessions Calendars" link.

[179] 28 U.S.C. § 2284(a). In an earlier time, a three-judge district court was required in any case where the constitutionality of a state statute was challenged.

[180] *Id.* § 2284(b)(1).

[181] *Id.*

Conclusion

As our book shows, the courts of appeals vary in the way they perform their common task of deciding cases on appeal. Some differences are to be expected because they reflect the differences among the circuits themselves, regarding, say, size and docket. And yet some differences are surprising and may simply reflect different values or interests in approaching the same task.

Perhaps even more interesting are the many topics on which only one court of appeals has a written or unwritten procedure or custom. The courts of appeals do not vary just in their practices on common topics; they even vary as to which topics deserve a specific practice (written or not).

As we said at the outset, we have not reported court of appeals differences or distinctive practices to urge any circuit to follow what one or more other circuits do. We simply think it useful for every court of appeals to know what other courts do.

More broadly, we hope the information we have reported will enlighten not only judges of the courts of appeals but also everyone interested in court administration – those working within the federal appellate system, academics, lawyers, and curious members of the public.

Index

For EU product safety concerns, contact us at Calle de José Abascal, 56–1°, 28003 Madrid, Spain or eugpsr@cambridge.org.

www.ingramcontent.com/pod-product-compliance
Lightning Source LLC
LaVergne TN
LVHW011814200926
848484LV00005B/1187

* 9 7 8 1 0 0 9 4 2 6 1 8 3 *